T0162639

CRYING
IN THE EARS OF
JERUSALEM

CRYING
IN THE EARS OF
JERUSALEM

THE WORLD AGAINST
THE WORD OF GOD

DAN EZE

iUniverse books may be ordered through booksellers or by contacting:

iUniverse
1663 Liberty Drive
Bloomington, IN 47403
www.iuniverse.com
1-800-Authors (1-800-288-4677)

Because of the dynamic nature of the Internet, any web addresses or links contained in this book may have changed since publication and may no longer be valid. The views expressed in this work are solely those of the author and do not necessarily reflect the views of the publisher, and the publisher hereby disclaims any responsibility for them.

Any people depicted in stock imagery provided by Thinkstock are models, and such images are being used for illustrative purposes only.
Certain stock imagery © Thinkstock.

ISBN: 978-1-4917-8967-4 (sc)
ISBN: 978-1-4917-8968-1 (e)

Library of Congress Control Number: 2016905981

Print information available on the last page.

iUniverse rev. date: 4/20/2016

CONTENTS

TO ALL PEACE LOVERS OF THE WORLD

I wrote this message based on the things I know are true regarding the conflict situations around us, and particularly, the spiritual implication of waging the war that is intended to end the country of Israel. I ascertained that the true meaning of waging war on the holy land is the search for personal truth that constitutes humanity's long history of unfaithfulness to God. People suffer as a result of the endless search, and the explanation from the Bible concerning the downfall of peace identifies the deep circumstances that made us have a world of war without end.

Living well and dying well is the concern of people who believe in the eternity of life. But there are other concerns about the aftermath of this life in spite of religious faith. Everybody is worried because death is not the ultimate obstacle that stands against the living but is what the living could die for. According to Cynthia Arduin, how this life might end matters more to people that live in it than that everybody understands the things that go on around them. Without the divine aspect of humanity, living in this life alone satisfies nothing. We live, and at the same time we position ourselves for the life of eternity either by following or by ignoring the ethical principles that God set before us.

Every judgment that we make is crucial. It might lead us to the happy moment of the afterlife, or it might beckon an eternity of suffering. Humanity broke into the coalition of evil forces that inflicts suffering upon righteousness. The inclination to sin motivated humanity to join the evil forces in the fight against the righteousness of God. Suffering multiplied, and the will of righteousness dwindles among the suffering humanity. But the human faith in God must stand up and challenge the suffering of righteousness with conviction that every evil plan that comes up will receive the judgment of God.

God placed His tabernacle on the sacred land of Israel, and so He brought His peace to spread among the peoples of the earth throughout all subsequent times of life. The general response to His plan should be to realize His goal. But the history of humanity's response has been interrupted countless times with evil-minded work. I examined both the political and the religious suffering that exist in parts of the world, and I provided means that should help readers to understand the decisions that hurt people, such as the decisions people make without making reference to righteousness.

Living the righteous life is to a majority of people a naive way to seek happiness and prosperity. Unrighteousness manifests from people choosing to live from the wrong outlook. People show determined disloyalty to the will of God and refuse to follow the principles according to which God required everyone to live this life. It is sad that few people appreciate that the loving truth of God should lead the way of life.

I offer this book to you to support your hope that real peace shall come and exist within you and in everything that exists in your life. The Psalmist said, "Pray for the peace of Jerusalem; may those who love you be secure. May there be peace within your walls and prosperity within your palaces."[1] It is my hope that this book will help you to determine for yourself the change of heart that must be employed to stimulate the lasting peace that the earth desperately wants.

Peace is not a cheap achievement for any people, and the philosophy

---

[1] Psalm 122: 6-7.

that could stabilize the peace of the earth must have an extended view of the Creator's intent. Whatever the philosophy is, the mindset for peace must begin with the absolute truth, as it promotes the oneness of love. Truth is the boldness to promote the legitimate right of everyone through works of righteousness. Our planet is arranged in a way that allows nations to exist according to cultural attributes, and thereby citizens of the earth are born differently but with one blood.

People that claim things in the Bible are not necessarily so also claim that God has no absolute right over the land of Canaan and that His goal in establishing the nation of Israel on the land is therefore subject to disapproval. The anti-Semitic spirit is the result of widespread prejudice against the true benefit of God. God is forever God, and if Jews live by their true meaning and tell the Bible story as it concerns the origin of Israel, then people that oppose Israel will realize the work of the covenant of grace. It is a moral obligation for the people of Israel to teach both the spiritual and the historical relevance of the Jewish nation in every generations of the earth. The understanding of the salvation of God is relevant to peace, especially on the land that He marked as holy ground.

We read in the Bible that no act of man can prevent any plan of God. So deep is the sovereignty of God that He is able to transform the wrath of men into praise for Him. His enemies end up serving Him in spite of themselves. Jews and Gentiles are the two peoples of the earth. By rational and irrational judgments, both the Jews and the Gentiles advance God's plan and His blessing.

CHAPTER 1

GOD REDEEMS AND MAN DESTROYS

The earth is shattered with both hate and corruption. The complimentary co-existence of hate and corruption is working according to the perspective that twisted human thinking. Humanity is engaged in a long history of racial and personal discrimination, which dishonors good reasoning with both violent and criminal acts. Hate-motivated violence is quickly supported through the action of people instead of through the love and peace that God inspires people to adopt.

The modern generation is a product of fear; hate and corruption are held in every culture. Violent behavior grows in every side of our society, and people feel as if they live in houses that are engulfed by fire. The bitterness that the hate-motivated violence brings out of people is being engraved in the corrupt politics that plunge our society into deep chaos. The situation reflects true love like the tale of misguided trust. Hate gave people the tendency to believe that taking revenge on other people's offenses rather than forgiving them is the good way to gain justice. They intend to feel secured by destroying their enemy. People that kill their enemy may temporally gain relief through the killing, but they do not necessarily have the peace and security that they wanted. One killed enemy is equal to the creation of a generation of enemies.

God alone can decide the true way to avenge any wrongdoing. His judgment is just, even though His patience can endure a long while. The Lord said,

> "It is mine to avenge; I will repay."[2]
> "Do not say, "I'll do to them as they have done to me;
> I'll pay them back for what they did.""[3]

In all the history of humanity, the opposite of the Lord's command is the case. The truth is not a temporal measure to maneuver, and people should not deny its rights. Corruption, along with its bad influences, is the only relationship that exists between people and politics. Where righteousness is found guilty is where corruption is perceived as living like a king. People sow hate and act wickedly when they exercise the wrong mind. The inclination that moves people to do things the wrong way is mingled with hate. This is the struggle that exists in people; it stands against accepting the sovereignty of God.

Through the corrupt politics entangled with hate, the inclination of our world is not the mind-set of peace that God wanted. Hate and corruption are the two sides of people's indecent behavior. Hate is engaged to every good thing that people hope for, and so it destroys both the present and the future of humanity. The fighting in the holy land of Israel served bitterness to many past generations, and now it is frustrating the very peace that should serve in our time. The current level of the conflict is like pouring old wine in new wineskin. The conflict has the mark of children playing in a marketplace. The children said to their various friends,

> "We played the flute for you, and you did not dance.
> We sang a dirge, and you did not mourn."[4]

---

[2] Deuteronomy 32:35.
[3] Proverbs 24:29.
[4] Matthew 11:17.

Jesus Christ gave the metaphor to a stubborn generation such as ours, and He indicates through metaphor that the earth as we know it is bearing fruits of defiance. By adopting hate as a way of life, people treat righteousness with great suffering. We might not realize the full response of righteousness to the slanderous rebellion of hate and corruption, but we know it, as the Bible teaches us that every action that opposes the way of righteousness is like chasing the wind. God prefers to have us reformed to better humanity rather than allow us to exist with wickedness in us. Every instance of suffering that we endure exists because we are defiant to the help that God offers to us. The Lord said, "A person who walks by day will not stumble, for he sees the light of this world. But if he walks in the night, he stumbles because the light is not in him."[5]

The crisis of conflict that we suffer should not define humanity in the same way it has deeply divided us. The book of Hosea suggests that we return to God and pursue His knowledge. The Lord knows, and He will heal us and bind us up.[6] The loving relationship of God is real and enduring even when it is not clearly seen in the relationships of individuals. The earth is corrupted, and human life is broken by the sin of the corruption. But the universe is loveable to God. Jesus Christ is the standpoint of the love of God to the world. He is both the love of God and the love that unites the humankind in God. All people should follow His teaching of love and fully bring the will of God into their lives. The principle is to love your neighbor as you love yourself. The Gospel is focused on fulfilling this principle.

If all peoples and nations would have the care that the Son of God wants in us, allowing the principle of love to exist in us would bring two things into effect: Every wicked ways of this life would be retouched. The evil mindset that makes people hate other people would in time be reversed, and the future would not be too late for anyone to have the true happiness. Personal conviction may never die out in the minds of people, and therefore the ways people might choose to live will always form a big circle around the public norm. But if everybody adopts the righteousness

---

[5] John 11:9-10.
[6] See Hosea 6:1-3.

of God, we will have less trouble in dealing with the times in which we feel distressed about the right thing to do. The distressed times of life are when we mostly exercise our minds with doing negative things. But the principle of love, which God wants us to adopt, can necessarily guide our mind not to bring every thought into action. The wilderness of the mind is vast, but according to the Gospel, the action of people must demonstrate the wisdom from God.

From the beginning, the Bible explains that the racial conflict that started in the family of Abraham is the result of the illusive mindset of Sarah. Abraham's wife, Sarah, adopted a fantasy in which she developed the desire to have a son through Hagar, her Egyptian maidservant. She went to her husband Abraham with the idea and convinced him to have the child with Hagar. The fantasy was biologically more sensible to Sarah than the pledge God gave to her and her husband. Abraham believed his wife, Sarah, and took in her maidservant Hagar. Hagar conceived with Abraham and bore the son that the family named Ishmael.[7]

The plan to accept Ishmael into the family of Abraham was made out of ignorance of the future. Sarah did not foresee the real outcome of her plan to receive a child through Hagar, and Abraham would not have donated his seed to Hagar if he had known that in the genes of Hagar lived the worm that would feed violence to the peace of his covenant descendants.

The boy Ishmael represented the curse that Sarah brought to her own blood. Her fault was in her inclination that she had to disbelieve the Word of God. Ishmael came into the family of Abraham and brought with him the jealousy and hatred that boiled over between Hagar and Sarah. From then on, the descendants of Ishmael and the descendants of Isaac hated each other.

Abraham caught himself in the middle of his own family trouble. He was father to both Ishmael and Isaac, but according to the decree of God, only Isaac was destined to inherit the covenant blessing of Abraham.

---

[7] "The angel of the Lord said to Hagar: 'You are now with child and you will have a son. You shall name him Ishmael for the Lord has heard of your misery'" (Genesis 16:11).

The grace of God was not hindered by the lack of trust. God sheltered all people from Abraham according to His plan.

But the war of hate persistently expanded through the families from Abraham, so much so that everybody is connected to the war because of the covenant of Abraham. We hardly taste the love of peace that God planned for all peoples and nations that worship Him.

What Caused the Situation We Live In:

God spoke His covenant to Abraham, and Abraham accepted to fulfill the process. Abraham took his wife, Sarah, and they left the household of his father, Terah, in Ur of the Chaldean.[8] Abraham and Sarah traveled as far as Haran and Egypt and came to the land of Canaan. They settled in Canaan among the Canaanites. God wanted Abraham to have His blessing. He offered to Abraham the covenant of worship and fully separated the family of Abraham from the rest of his generation. The Lord told Abraham that he would be the father of many nations and that all peoples of the earth would be blessed through him and his covenant descendants. Abraham had no child at the time, and he most cherished his beautiful wife, Sarah. The promise of God meant that Abraham and his wife, Sarah must live by faith in order to reach the goal. Abraham must do the work of righteousness and hope that things would work well, both for him and for the rest of the world.

God appeared to Abraham in a vision and said to him, "I will make you a great nation, and I will bless you; I will make your name great; and you will be a blessing. I will bless those who bless you, and whoever curses you I will curse; and all the peoples of the earth will be blessed through you."[9] Abraham and his wife, Sarah, had concern over their aging. They felt old age would hinder the chance they had to produce the children God had promised to their family. Then Abraham turned to the Lord and said to Him, "O sovereign Lord, what can you give me since I remain childless and the one who will inherit my estate is Eliezer of Damascus?

---

[8] Ur is in modern-day Iraq.
[9] Genesis 12:2-3.

You have given me no children; so a servant in my household will be my heir."[10]

Abraham had many servants who worked for him on his estate in Canaan. According to the practice of the time, the chief of the servants, Eliezer[11] was the heir of Abraham's fortune if Abraham should die without having any children. Abraham's fear was part of his human nature. But God had the solution to his fear, and that solution was far beyond the human characteristic.

Sarah distrusted the Word of God because of her age. The Lord visited the family again and comforted them with His promise of an appointed time. "So the word of the Lord came to Abram, 'This man will not be your heir, but a son coming from your own body will be your heir.'"[12]

Abraham was quick to acquire wealth and fame in Canaan according to the promise the Lord gave to him. But Abraham did not receive the children that he desperately wanted to be part of his family. Only by the divine appointed time would Abraham and his wife Sarah receive the son of their life's time. God assured Abraham on occasions that his wife, Sarah, would bear him a child upon whom the covenant blessing would be established. God made Abraham understand the future of the relationship, which He prepared for his descendants. The Lord said to Abraham, "Know for certain that your descendants will be strangers in a country not their own, and they will be enslaved and mistreated for four hundred years. But I will punish the nation they serve as slaves, and afterward they will come out with great possession. You, however, will go to your fathers in peace and be buried at a good old age. In the fourth generation your descendants will come back here; for the sins of the Amorites has not yet reached its full measure."[13]

But Sarah, even on hearing the promise of God, failed to honor the Lord by being impatient with her situation. She did not caution herself to stop her race against time. From the hour when Sarah gave to Abraham

---

[10] Genesis 15:2-3.
[11] Genesis 24:1-2.
[12] Genesis 15:4-5.
[13] Genesis 15:13-16.

her maidservant Hagar and he slept with her, God said nothing more about the promise that He had made until the appointed time arrived. The action of the family represents a serious obstruction to the flow of true goodness, such as the model of self-betrayal that was exposed in humankind at the beginning of time, when Adam and Eve disobeyed God. At the expense of every good thing that humanity hopes for, we fail both God and ourselves on each day's account through exercising lack of faith. The human factor of self-centeredness is holding this world captive in the capacity of unfaithfulness. God gave His assurance to Abraham and his wife, Sarah, and He watched the couple as they took the matter into their own hands.

God is the upright judge and the standard of justice. From conception to the time of birth, humans have the freedom to pledge a good conscience to God. We are not compelled by the rule of God's law to obey and worship God. God knows that every inclination of a human heart is rebellious from the first beat. Yet He is faithful to His promise, and He patiently loves us to wholly rescue us from the spirit of rebellion. God uses His power according to His moral perfection. Whatever God decides and does is good, even when we do not understand the purpose. The best response to any moment of difficulty is to appeal directly to God and patiently discern His mind about any situation.

People often add the approval of God, like a rubber stamp, to something they already decided. But ultimately they end up creating a bigger problem than the problem they solved. People may question the circumstances that bring pain and frustration, and they have the right to say to God that the experience of pain and frustration hurts. But people must have faith in the power of God and believe that He loves us. Everybody must work together and with faith in both pleasant and difficult times. We ought to seek God's face in order to know what the purpose of God is in every situation, and we should place His need above our need.

Abraham and his wife, Sarah, were not compelled to obey any of the guidelines from God. God wanted them to respond to His command by trusting Him. Both the promise of God and the instruction that goes according to the promise are made of love. The opportunity that the couple had was set upon them for reckoning. It is likewise true about everybody else; we should hear the Word of God and learn to keep it. Abraham was responsible for his action to Hagar. God explained to him the implication of his action, and part of the implication was the trouble that he brought on the future of his covenant children. The error Abraham made was that he wanted to have children sooner than the time God had arranged for him to have the children. Abraham was from then onward cautiously bold in showing to God his personal trust and his faith in whatever the plan of God was, especially when he was asked to sacrifice his son Isaac on the altar.[14]

Abraham developed strong faith in God through doing the work of righteousness. He enjoyed a better relationship with God, and he was elevated with honors in the community of saints. God's provision comes with affordable risk. No people may enjoy the special blessing of God without increased effort. God intended us to follow the pathway of obeying His ordinance. We keep ourselves prepared to enjoy His blessing while we are being faithful to His word. The action of every man and every woman is accordingly rewarded.

The Apostle Paul wrote in the epistle to the Romans that Abraham was a friend of God both by his faith and by his righteous work. Paul said, "If in fact Abraham was justified by works, he had something to boast about – but not before God. What does the scripture say? Abraham believed God and it was credited to him for righteousness."[15]

Some Bible readers suggest that the attitude of Sarah, by which she allowed Abraham to sexually engage her maidservant Hagar, is humanly sympathetic. They say that the concern Sarah had should be seen as a case of aging family trying to cope with the ambiguous promise of almighty God. Those who show sympathy to Sarah argue that the Word of God should not be literally believed in all human situations. The people who suggest these things are against those of us who are totally faithful to God. In the case of Sarah, the opinion is poorly determined, but it

---

[14] Genesis 22.
[15] Romans 4:1-3.

explains other secular opinions that people hold against the sovereignty of God. Even in some congregations of believers where the Word of God is duly served, the instruction of God is often placed second to whatever the believers feel. The result is always bad news, as it is wrong to exchange the Word of God with imperfect wisdom. Divine instruction is not second to any value.

We live through religious trouble, and we suffer because of the corruption in politics. We should determine by the results if bearing God's instruction with personal attribute is any gain to our means of survival. It is common knowledge that the violent acts that persist in the name of religious faith have nothing to do with religion. Hate is spread through rebellion, and rebellion is activated through corrupted minds. This is the case in all situations where people exercise the wrong opinion about God. People often invoke their own opinions about the will of God to bypass fulfilling the demand of His ethical law. The Word of God is self-explanatory in all the circumstances where His word engages humankind to love and to uphold justice. The Word of God is direct and to the point, especially from the point where His word compels us to love.

We should not disrespect the leadership of God when He takes a turn that we cannot immediately discern, and we should not amend God's purpose to create a purpose that suits personal ambition. God is conscious of whatever He does. There is no fairness that is higher and more absolute than God Himself. Whatever God says and does is fair, even when we appreciate neither Him nor His plan. The serious errors of humanity are revealed by their effect on humanity's suffering well-being. The failure to uphold the goodness of God is the inclination that bears the fruit of hate. It brings forth in people the corruption that is the experience of politics.

People cling to false conviction as though it is the right thing to do. We demonstrate hardness of heart by giving our concern to the consequences that we suffer, rather than retreat from deviating. We cry out for comfort and ask for security and relief. Yet we fail to take the first step first, which is to turn away from rebellion and hate and open the channel toward loving both God and our neighbor. It is easy to presume that there is no God and act out of secular free will rather than love our neighbors.

Living only the life of personal preference is the difficulty that brings about chaos in every family. Individuals, societies, and institutions make themselves the final authority in decision making. No one verifies his or her conviction in the Word of God, and nearly all decisions people make are set outside the will of God. People adore wickedness and celebrate the harsh conditions that other people endure as though such things do not contribute to the crisis going on everywhere. God should be ours, and He should be invited to join us in all we say and do. He helped our forebears at the beginning of time, and He helps us now. God does not make personal decisions for us. We should hold on to His way even when we go through distressed circumstances in which God acts in strange ways. When things are far from clear, we should hold on to what is clear, which is that our God is faithful to His word. We must trust in God to work things out for us. Otherwise, we create the choice to end our lives by means of our unrighteousness.

The world exists by the coalition of both good and bad actions. People who act and pray know that an act of goodness can reach the heart of God quicker than any voice of prayer can reach His ears. We should help our neighbors to have godly lives. In doing so every day, everybody helps each other to reach new heights of loving God. Nothing feels good in life like the moments when you realize that the Spirit of God is actively working through you.

A society that lacks moral judgment cannot prosper peace and justice. People are aware that they are at war with the things that they should and should not do, but sometimes they seem powerless to follow the ethical light they have. The violence of hate is self-defeating, and corruption can be eradicated both in the politics of our society and in our personal religious beliefs. People that are violently opposed to universal goodness are presumptively in possession of a heritage that does not belong to them.

Our problem is as the Apostle Paul prefigured regarding the system of this world. We live in a system that is worked by those who gather around them great number of teachers to say what their itching ears want them to hear.[16] These are people who desire truth that makes sense according to what they feel, what works for them, and what seems compelling, to which they claim an absolute right. They gather viewpoints that suit their selfish desire and profess objectivity that defends their viewpoints.

Paul said in his letter to the Galatians that humankind is responsible for the consequences that cause pain to them. We can begin the counting with the loss of immortality in the Garden of Eden, the confusion of tongues in Babel,[17] and the birth of Ishmael in Canaan. God can easily forgive us of any sin, and when He does, the punishment for the offense is averted, but this does not necessarily mean we must not suffer the consequence of the done damage. God can forgive you for killing your son, but you will never again see your son alive. We are spiritual beings, and every human action fills in a vacuum. We have the rule of God's law within our reach, and every nation and people should not suffer because of lawlessness. We read in Romans chapter 13 that people in authority and the society they rule should communicate love to each other on behalf of the common good. Together, we should encourage the better angels of our nature and oppose the attitude that uses political conflict and religious hatred to heighten division.

---

[16] 2 Timothy 4:3.

[17] "But the Lord came down to see the city and the tower which the sons of men had built. And the Lord said, "Indeed the people are one and they all have one language, and this is what they began to do; now nothing that they propose to do will be withheld from them. Come let us go down and there confuse their language, that they may not understand one another's speech." So the Lord scattered them abroad, from there over the face of all the earth, and they ceased building the city" (Genesis11:5-8).

CHAPTER 2

THE PARAMETER OF THE HOLY LAND

The Bible uses the Lord's Prayer essentially on two levels to demonstrate desire in the coming of the kingdom of God. The prayer asks that the will of God be done on earth as it is in heaven. Jesus Christ taught the prayer to His disciples. He allows the prayer to work for all people in the same way that John the Baptist proposed the work of righteousness, which began on earth the process to the End Time. The age of the End Time comes upon us as the hour of the Holy Spirit. During this time, the Holy Spirit prepares the faithful for the coming of the kingdom of God and will make clear the seriousness of the negative attitudes held by many people who abuse the life on earth. John the Baptist said, "Prepare the way of the Lord and make straight His path for Him."[18]

Both the message of John the Baptist and the Lord's Prayer connect humanity to the work of the Holy Spirit. He renews the everyday hope in God's salvation and helps us to repair our damaged integrity. It is the will of God to return creation to what it was in the beginning. The book of Genesis and the book of Revelation speak about the influence of the corrupt angels who were chased out of heaven and out of the righteousness of God. We feel the presence of the corrupt angels, and we know their wickedness.

---

[18] Matthew 3:2-3.

God helps us to overcome the fake angels, and graciously God offered the world His forgiveness through the death of His Son, Jesus Christ. The death of His Son brought the salvation of God nearer to every soul. The kingdom of God is not fully realized, and it won't be until the evil on earth is judged and destroyed. The Holy Spirit is at work preparing the way on which the kingdom of God will spread. We expect the Lord Jesus Christ to return soon, and hopefully He will harvest the fruits of humanity's response to the salvation of God. For the meantime, we should move forward in the struggle to overtake the evil on earth. We should realize the righteousness of God that is in us and use the experience to be better prepared for the coming kingdom of God.

Nonetheless, the earth is full of suffering because in reality people do not prepare for the coming of God. The attitude that should allow people to follow the good examples of righteousness is not popular among the children of men. As in the days of John the Baptist,[19] people lack the desire to move on achieving righteousness. Humankind works against the very goodness that God intended when He appointed Abraham to receive His blessing. Humanity ought to demonstrate the purpose of God in every way that He extends the blessing of Abraham to nations of the earth. God is good to us, and by giving His blessing to Abraham, He made it known that we should occupy the earth as He meant it to be – one big family temple where He is duly loved. Our lives will be better if we seriously consider the motivation from God and find the path to recover the faithfulness of peace that we lost.

Imagine the joy of an everlasting time, which the unity of love and peace will bring about in people if people abandon the rebellion and hate that rule in their decisions. Humanity continues to seek the meaning of life with personal attitude and neglects the grand purpose of living life with harmony. God puts us here to live in harmony and to take good

---

[19] "For John the Baptist came neither eating bread nor drinking wine and you say, 'He has a demon.' The Son of Man came eating and drinking and you say, 'Here is a glutton and a drunkard; a friend of tax collectors and sinners.' But wisdom is proved right by all her children" (Luke 7:33-35).

charge of the earth, but people struggle to make names for themselves, as if the names God gave them were no names at all.

The lives people choose to live are full of lust. It was lust that derailed the happiness of our earliest parents. Nothing changed in people in spite of mental and social civilization, which the human generation claimed to have undergone. People question the Word of God with unqualified imagination, and every day we disappoint both God and ourselves by living the false imagination in our actions. The Word of God proposed that no curse of the evil one would befall humanity if humanity lived according to the wisdom from God.

You have the opportunity to work for your salvation with the true knowledge of goodness that you have. The opportunity is here, and it is here for us to use it and amend our vision of life. You must not lose hope yet, in spite of the problem you endure. Know that humanity failed the test of faithfulness from the beginning. Yet the fullness of God's mercy remains and it demonstrates the beckoning of His love.

God blessed humanity with a strength of character that should help everyone pull everyone else out from the failed state. People who failed either once, twice, or more times must not remain on the downside of the failed state. The worst part of any unfaithfulness to God is being unable to try to receive Him again. The bounty of God's love represents the mission of His plan. He called all people to be the children of Abraham so that everyone might receive His blessing. The infinite love of God for the things He created and for the people He made in His image is the asset that humanity should care for.

Both the state of Israel and the community of nations failed the arrangement by which God prepared peace and prosperity to exist in the Middle East. Israel should be a light to all peoples and nations of the earth, as God told Abraham that his descendants from Isaac would bring blessings upon the nations of the earth. In laying down His love, God meant with the blessing of Abraham that the rest of His purpose would come to pass through the very means by which He provided for the children of Israel. The feeling of all nations, to be loved and to be given peace, should correspond to loving the place of Israel.

The city of Jerusalem is the worship center of the God's kingdom on earth. The place shall be the throne of the everlasting King of Peace for a thousand years. The redemptive plan is ready, and it should motivate people to love peace and pursue the pattern. But even as the grace of God exists to bring every person back to safety, the forces that oppose the peace of Israel are fighting to prevent the fullness of God's love from prevailing. The true sense of humanity is frustrated by the attitudes of leaders who redefine both the meaning and the purpose of living in this life. We are doomed if we follow whichever course they decide.

The Hebrews root is settled in sacred land, and it should be given the privilege to stay undisturbed. The nation of Israel deserved to be wholly preserved for the Lord's purpose, as He saved the place with the covenant of Abraham. The Lord said to Abraham, "The whole land of Canaan, where you now reside as a foreigner, I will give as an everlasting possession to you and your descendants after you; and I will be their God."[20] The Kingdom of Israel should be restored, and it should be allowed to function theologically as it is meant to be by God. We are bound by the law of God to commit ourselves to safeguard the principle of the territorial integrity, which God decreed with the blueprint He gave to Moses. The divine blueprint was provided so all people should know it, both as evidence of the truth and as law that must guide everybody into being part of the holiness of God. The document is, by the rule of God's law, binding to all peoples and nations.

Partitioning the holy land is against the command of God. This habit is a political process that has no righteous definition to show for the effort. Creating Islamic states all over the Promised Land is an aspiration that confuses the pledge Moses handed over to the world. Trespassing into the private property of God denies peace to the Middle East and fully gets every nation of the earth into the trouble.

Two factors motivated me when I wrote this book. The first factor is a desire to explain the complex mindset of native Arabs who claim to be the owners of the Promised Land. The second factor is a questioning of

---

[20] Genesis 17:8.

the attitude of disregard that people show to the sovereignty of God. Both physical and mental rejection exist in people concerning the care-taker status God gave to the children of Israel on the holy land. O Jerusalem, you are the thought that bothers me so much so that I feel the return of your King. "Glorious things are said of you O city of God. God has set His foundation on the city mountain and the Lord loves the gates of Zion than all the dwellings of Jacob."[21]

The nations and the institutions that made it their business to resettle native Arabs on the Promised Land are responsible for the unrest that happens on the private territory of God. The political road map to peace is a hypothesis with no means to match the spiritual mandate that provided natural boundaries to both the Jews and the Arabs of the region. The plan to set aside the spiritual mandate of Israel is ironic. Deadly mistakes of history are constantly repeated via charters that redefine the private territory of God.

The political process to peace is staged, and the process easily reveals the political elites involved in the exercise as spiritually dangerous people. If the reason for the political process is to create a new concept of the holiness of God, the process is unnecessary. The idea is too dangerous to live with, and it is rather puzzling that any people or institutions would predicate the outcome of peace on the ambiguous claim of a people (Arabs) in a nonexistent homeland. The claim is consigned to this new generation, who will apparently act upon historical fact with greater disregard than the previous generation.

The truth about the holy land is deliberately made to exist in a context that has no real element as its object. The political parody is growing. The modern generation uses the name of Palestine as an Arab state increasingly often than it is the natural territory of Israel. In the same context, the term "Palestinians" refers to the Arab residents of the holy land as citizens of the state of Palestine. Most likely to the false perception of a people and a homeland, those that are being regarded as the Palestinians are not traditional folks of any part of the historical Palestine. The Arab

---

[21] Psalm 87:1-3.

Palestinians are in towns and villages of the Jewish Kingdom of Israel, and only the Jews can separate any part of the native territory to enable the Arabs have another state. The big challenge to Arabs in the Middle East is to convince the state of Israel to commit political suicide on behalf of peace and thereby abandon the natural border that clearly identifies the property of God.

The Arab Palestinians have the ancient bloodline of Ishmael, and they do not deny to themselves their natural right to belong to the traditional Arabian community. They do not oppose both the cultural and the political sentiments that united them with the other Arab communities in the Middle East. The Arab Palestinians do not admit with public statements that they belonged to the Arab origins that broke into the Jewish Kingdom of Israel from the Arabian Desert.

The international community funded the first Arab Palestinian state on the Transjordan district of the Kingdom of Israel. The international community is funding another autonomous Arab Palestinian society in the West Bank and Gaza. Rather than disrupting the divine order of the land, and without any reasonable caution, the Arab communities in Transjordan, the West Bank, and Gaza should be motivated to settle on the land like any other groups of immigrants that lived on the Jewish Kingdom. Or perhaps the Arab society in Israel should withdraw to the traditional Arab territory in the Arabian Desert.

The monetary and the infrastructural support that the Arab Palestinians receive from the international community are being used to bring about various tones of violence on the peace of the region. From Saudi Arabia onward, there is no difference between the Arabians of the West Bank and the Arabians of Jordan, Egypt, Iraq, Syria and Lebanon. It is only for political and tactical reasons that any institution speaks today about the rising of Arab Palestinian nationalism in Israel. Arab Palestinian nationalism distinctively exists only as a means to continue to disrupt the divinity of the Kingdom of Israel.

The Kingdom of Israel and the Jews who lived on the land were known from the age of the Roman Empire as Palestine and Palestinians, respectively. The political context was slowly redefined to imply the

Arabs' concentration in the West Bank and Gaza. The Oslo Accord of 1993 was a United Nations document that provided for the creation of the Arab Palestinian interim self-government in the West Bank and Gaza. The document, "Declaration of Principles on Interim Self-Government Arrangement" was anticipated to serve a five-year interim period, during which time a permanent solution would be negotiated between the two peoples.

From the beginning of the negotiations at the 1949 Armistice Agreements[22] and at the Madrid Conference of 1991 and then to the Oslo Accord of 1993, there were many failed attempts to get Arabs and Jews to live in peace in the official territory of Israel. What made the Oslo Accord different from the rest of the negotiations was the government of Israel, which decided to hold face-to-face negotiations with members of the Palestine Liberation Organization (PLO) as independent representatives of the Arab community in Israel. The negotiation transformed the PLO into being a strong political faction to fight for Arab autonomy in the West Bank.

The international community gradually moved into the center stage of the political negotiation and dangerously convinced the Jews to transform the state of Israel into a multicultural democracy. Now the democratic system of government, which the political state of Israel adopted, shows that Jews have abandoned the rule of God's law.

Arab Muslims in Israel gained the right to vote in Jewish elections, and perhaps they can influence the results, while the Jews living in Arab nations – such as in Saudi Arabia, Egypt, Syria, Jordan, Iraq, and Lebanon – may never get the right to vote in any election.

The ancient Arab war against the Jewish state of Israel has been cleverly repackaged into a conflict that now shows the Jews as people who occupy the Arab Palestinians' land. The conflict is an Arab public relations stunt against the Jewish nation.

---

[22] The 1949 Armistice Agreements are a set of agreements signed during 1949 between Israel and neighboring Egypt, Lebanon, Jordan and Syria. The agreements ended the hostility of the 1948 Arab–Israeli War and established armistice demarcation lines, known as the Green Line, between Israeli forces and the forces in the Jordan-held West Bank.

The League of Nations created the country of Jordan to be the home of Arabs in Palestine. Israel should be tougher in disrupting any further formations that unite segments of Arab people on any parts of its sacred territory. Except in the most recent years, the confederation of Arab regimes in the Middle East showed no interest in the emerging Arab Palestinian nationalism. The Arab groups' current struggling to create Palestinian nationalism did not exist until after Israel won in the 1967 war. The Arab Palestinians do not have a native dialect. They speak in what is known as the mutual Arabic tongue. There is not an independent culture among Arab Palestinians; theirs is the culture common to all native Arabians. There is neither any ancient community of Canaan nor any people from the outside the Middle East who are uniquely associated with the Arab Palestinians' origin.

The Arab Palestinian movement for an independent state was started by the late Mr. Yasser Arafat. Mr. Arafat was born in Egypt in 1929. Arab settlers in the West Bank and Gaza prudently claim the name "Palestinians" and serve the goal of frontier Islamic groups who are determined to overrun the Promised Land with Islamic control. The Middle East war of Arabs and Jews has been ongoing for about a thousand years. Except for the last few decades, the focus of the war was not chasing Jews out of the homeland of Arabs. Arabs have a well-defined homeland in the Middle East, and Jews are not inheriting any part of it. We read in the Bible that the origin of Arabs is the Arabian Desert.

Arabs in the West Bank were flag-bearers in the long history of the anti-Jewish atrocity. They ignited the massacre in Hebron that happened to the Jews in 1929. But the people were not an important part of the conflict between Arabs and Jews until 1967. The idea of creating an Arab state in the territory of Israel is a new development in the conflict. It is not the solution for peace among the Arab immigrants in the West Bank and Gaza. The partition plan, which created the Kingdom of Jordan in the last few decades, did not foresee the current situation as something that was possible. The people who mediated on behalf of the partition plan did not realize the struggle was spiritually motivated, and therefore they did not discover that it has no political solution. The Jews should realize from Scripture the longstanding struggle to destroy the country of Israel and know that the struggle will continue as it is happening now.

Before 1970, virtually no one considered the conflict to be about the Jews fighting to stop the advance of the Arab Palestinians. On the other hand, the struggle of the Arab Palestinians is not the case of a minority group fighting against ethnic cleansing. Arabs developed serious violent behavior toward the Jewish religious faith since the birth of the Prophet Muhammad, owing partially to the rule of Islamic caliphates in the region. Arabs would stop besieging the Promised Land if the conflict focused on the rights of the Arab Palestinians to settle down. But this is not so. The conflict is, in many ways, the continuation of Islamic jihad, which started centuries ago against the origin of Judaism and Christianity on the holy land. The conflict has now spread to secular civilization, truly spiritual faith, and barbarism.

It is unfortunate that the political leadership in Israel negotiates everything that should not be on the negotiating table. Israel is the kingdom of the biblical faith, and both the national security of the Jewish Kingdom and the dignity of the Jewish people should hold the country together. A new Arab Palestinian state would imply that the state of Israel has been further reduced to advance the course of Islam.

Judaism is not directly targeted by the struggle. The hope to worship Yahweh forever on the territory of Israel is founded in the Gospel. The historical root of the Gospel is directly targeted by the struggle. People who argue against the biblical land, especially against the New Testament view, know that the Gospel is grounded on the historical lives of Jews in showing what God did for humanity. If the historical basis goes, Christianity and all its worth might as well disappear with it.

Islamic scholars and critics of the Jewish nation often claim that the root of Israel is not the Middle East. In the Bible, we learn that Abraham was a native of Ur. His father, Terah, came from a bloodline in the land of modern-day Iraq. If not for the divine call that separated Abraham and his native folks, his descendants from Isaac and Jacob would have been subjects of Iraq. Also, the Koran contains about forty-three references that established the children of Israel in the land of Canaan.

The aspirations of the Arab Palestinians could take longer than they expected. As a matter of fact, the concept of Arabia's Palestine state gives the world's most powerful nations both the political will and the economic ammunition to change the image of the Middle East. Nothing dominates discussions during gatherings of nations like the political and economic conflicts that exist in and around the Middle East. Truth is the real victim in all the situations of conflict the world faces. The moral deficiency in people works against everything true humanity represents.

Truth refers to God's character. His character embodies His dealings with people and defines the way people should deal with themselves. Those that occupy leadership positions in the world rejected this most powerful instrument of peace and pretended to assume that the world is firmly under their control. The concept of peace, which the leaders exercise by means of war, is the madness of abused technology. It allows powerful nations to flex their muscles anywhere they want. The current situation of war in the Middle East is very much in support of sales of ammunition. The opportunity is there for leaders to maximize the chance of economic exploitation. Even the nations that support the state of Israel provide support for political gain. Almost no nation appreciates the divine worth of Israel.

The Bible concludes that the Jewish nation in the land of the Canaanites is a test of righteousness. The children of Israel inherited with the land the character of God's friendliness. As part of the blessing of God, the Jews should portray the power to do the work of righteousness. The ideal nation of Israel is intended by God to be a nation of high moral character. Jews were given both the duty and the ability to lead the rest of humanity to the true worship of the living God. But Israel supports nations who defy the righteousness of God.

Just as the rest of humanity does not live within the original creation, which was very good, but in a restored one (the existence that is guaranteed by God's grace), so does Israel. The Jews do not live within the covenant of Abraham but in the reestablished covenant that is guaranteed by grace. The rest of humanity and the nation of Israel are both sinful and have remained sinful. Yet God keeps the nation of Israel out of the ordinary nations. There is a divine scheme to reckon with in the case of Israel. The political peace envoys to the region should realize that the divine plan should come first. Peace in both Israel and the rest of the Middle East has a sensibility that is dependent on the plan of God.

Some member states of the United Nations developed an alternative plan to the problem of the Arab Palestinian state, and the plan is to make no reference to the Word of God. The plan is as though the nations are bringing into the conflict the nonspiritual sympathy that causes the peace talks to be based largely on natural sensation. In other to give sympathy the chance to succeed, the Jews are being asked to set aside both the history of the Promised Land and the divine mandate that brought about the Kingdom of Israel on the land. The United Nations knew that if both the historical fact of the Promised Land and the spiritual mandate to Israel should continue to prevail as justice, the Arab Palestinians might as well remain on the land – but as strangers or, rather, with irrevocable resident permits.

Perhaps the state of Israel is realizing that the alternative solution to the conflict resembles the Gibeonites' deception.[23] Or is it that the current political leadership in Israel is on the pathway to conclude the struggle in an error similar to its judgment of the future? Strangers lived on the biblical land for thousands of years – but not as sovereign people. The call of Abraham and the apparent risks in developing the children of Jacob from Egypt to the present nation of Israel indicates that whatever the purpose is captivates God, who started the process.

Jews faced extermination in different phases of their past history. The attempts happened through wars that ended with foreigners occupying the Jewish land. The history of Israel is characterized by fierce battles. During each point of the conflict, the saving hand of God took the Jews out of trouble. The people endured 430 years of brutality in the Egyptians' bondage, and God saved them. They spent 70 years of suffering in the

---

[23] Out of fear of the Israelites, the Gibeonites resorted to use deception to save their lives. The leaders disguised themselves and came to the Israelites camp as a people in need. They claimed to have come from a distance land while in fact they lived nearby. Without consulting the Lord, Joshua made peace treaty with the Gibeonites. The treaty eventually prolonged the Gibeonites' stay on the land (See Joshua 9).

Babylonian exile, and God rescued them. The Roman Empire's soldiers destroyed many parts of Jewish national pride. Next was the 460 years of occupation of Israel by both the association of caliphate rulers and the Ottoman Empire. There was then the Holocaust by the Nazis, and now there is the crisis being brought to the Jews by both the Arabs in the West Bank and the United Nations.

God's plan is unchanged, and the nation of Israel survives. But Israel will be at the center of conflict for a longer period of time to come, unless the people redirect their focus toward doing the work of righteousness, which is according to the covenant of grace. The nation of Israel will not survive the plot of its enemies with the nonspiritual foreign and domestic influences that redraw the map of the holy land. Peace will not return to the Middle East through people who deny the existence of God in Israel – which, by the way, is the reason they want to redefine the Jewish national identity. The Lord said to the people of Israel, "If you should return I will restore you so you can continue to serve me. If you speak good words rather than worthless ones you will be my spokesperson again. They shall fight against you but they shall not prevail against you for I am with you to save you and to deliver you."[24]

The reason this book presumes that a future Arab Palestinian state is temporally viable comes from the Bible. There could be an Arab Palestine state in the homeland of Israel, but the arrangement would not last long. The claim by the Arab Palestinians is not historically legitimate, and the claim will never be spiritually reconcilable with the pattern God started in the Kingdom of Israel. The Bible does not view the rising of gentile influence on His private territory as a tribute to faithfulness. The political alliance for peace, which exists in the union of nations for the region, is determined by humanity's disapproval of loyalty to God.

There will ultimately be, by way of political effort, a peace treaty that will involve the state of Israel on the land. The treaty will be cleverly adopted by the union of nations, according to the prophecy in the book of Daniel. In Matthew chapter 24, Jesus Christ confirmed both the effect

---

[24] Jeremiah 15:19-20.

that the vision of the gentile nations will create and how the implication of the vision will unfold into serious world conflict. The national Israel will finally enter into a remarkable peace agreement with the influence of the Antichrist.

The book of Daniel says, "He will confirm a covenant with many for one 'seven'. In the middle of the 'seven' he will put an end to sacrifice and offering. And on a wing of the temple he will set up an abomination that causes desolation, until the end that is declared is poured out on him."[25] And Matthew chapter 24 says, "So when you see standing in the Holy Places 'the abomination that causes desolation, spoken of through the Prophet, Daniel – let the reader understand then, let those who are in Judea flee to the mountains. Let no one on the roof of his house go down to take anything out of the house. Let no one in the field go back to get his cloak. How dreadful it will be in those days for pregnant women and nursing mothers! Pray that your flight will not take place in winter or on the Sabbath. For then there will be a great distress, unequaled from the beginning of the world until now – and never to be equaled again. If those days had not been cut short, no one would survive, but for the sake of the elect those days will be shortened. At that time if anyone says to you, 'look, here is the Christ!' or 'there he is!' Do not believe it. For, false Christs and false prophets will appear and perform great signs and miracles to deceive even the elect – if it were possible. See, I have told you ahead of time."[26]

The prophecy in the book of Daniel suggests an arrangement that could further undermine the spiritual survival of Israel. But the Lord will intervene in the situation, and He will restore the glory of His people of Israel. The book of Daniel predicates that the Antichrist will at some future date bring a peace treaty to the state of Israel. The Antichrist will stand by the peace treaty for seven years, and he will have the support of many nations. The Antichrist will then start war on the land by breaking the peace treaty and by desecrating the Jewish holy places. The nations that favor the end of Israel will organize a multinational action force to

---

[25] Daniel 9:27.
[26] Matthew 24:15-25.

fight and to destroy the Jewish nation. The act of war will set the anger of God upon the union of nations.

What the "abomination that causes desolation" implies in this context might not depend on one specific event, object, or person, but it could refer to all the deliberate attempts to mock and deny the reality of God's presence in and around Jerusalem. The prophecy in the book of Daniel does not suggest that any person, authority, or institution that encourages Israel to sign a peace treaty with its neighbors is the Antichrist. Possibly the events referred to in the book of Daniel, and confirmed in Saint Matthew's Gospel may not occur anytime soon. The Bible does not predict the time for the prophecy to come true. But be assured that everything in the Word of God will come to pass.

A number of statements by Jesus Christ connect the problem in Israel to His second coming. The statements that Jesus Christ made about securing the national Kingdom of Israel tells people how they must understand the things He said about His own death on the cross. Jesus Christ explained that the struggle against the future glory of Israel is the fight of the evil forces. Israel will realize the glory when it attains its final spiritual importance at the end of time. Fighting the Jewish nation means preventing the salvation of God from getting to all His creation. But it is better not to cloud the hope of Jesus' return with theories that seek to determine what could happen when He comes. Perhaps people would be disappointed if Jesus Christ failed to follow the schedule they mapped out for Him.

The Kingdom of Israel and the state of Israel are two different structures. A big difference exists in the geography and in the citizenship of both the state of Israel and the Kingdom of Israel. The Kingdom of Israel and its citizens will be glorified, but the state of Israel will soon be gone. The state of Israel exits in a small part of the Kingdom of Israel, and it consists of Jews and Gentile citizens of the state having equal political rights. The Kingdom of Israel has temporarily gone underground, and according to the book of the prophecy, it will rise up again with the final glory of Israel. The prayer of the Jews for the restoration of the Kingdom of Israel is rewarded.

At the moment, the state of Israel is useful only as a structure that keeps alive the memory of the heritage of the Kingdom of Israel. Jesus Christ was unambiguous in saying that the historical Israel was neglected, and the people that besieged it do not fully understand the worth of its spiritual legacy. The error that will trigger the anger of God comes with the plan to pluralize the right of the holiest site in the Kingdom of Israel. The plan technically allows the position of the temple of Jerusalem to be in a foreign land. God did not approve the existence of the site of His millennial temple in any foreign land. The leadership of Israel could allow Zion to be the new Islamic capital of the state of Arab Palestinians and also adopt the state of Israel fully as a secular state. But the rising anger of God is the element that the Jews should fear most.

Perhaps the regrouping of the gentiles' aggression against the Jewish state is the tool that must make the people of Israel rethink who they are. The proposed Arab Palestinian state will particularly help in any major attack against the state of Israel, especially when the aim of the enemy is wholly to destroy the divinity of the land. The struggle to create an Arab Palestine state will perhaps complete the process of destruction that God predicted for the region. The great threat that Israel faces in the conflict is the new warfare technology that is bred in the Western world.

The people of Israel live under intolerable risk. The Jewish political defense mechanism might result in a nightmare when the associated nations of the Islamic jihad fully process advanced military know-how. Israel's right to exist is being discussed, as some conclude that creating the state of Israel was a mistake. The discussion brings about opinionated foreign and domestic attacks on Jewish heritage. The Bible foresees these dangerous political factors, which emanate from human deviation. It predicts the battle of Armageddon will happen in the region. The battle will evidently bring the region to a halt.[27] Israel continues to undermine its national integrity both on the land and in the gathering of nations.

---

[27] The battle of Armageddon is the last war that will take place between the forces of good and evil. Armageddon is the prophesied battlefield; it is a land mass near the city of Megiddo in northern Israel. Sinful people will unite and fight to destroy God's people in a final display of rebellion against God. The war will be against Jesus Christ and His people (See Revelation 16:16).

Israel was misguided when the people allowed the Emirate of Jordan to exist. Israel is being deluded again to honor the demands of Arabs in the West Bank and Gaza with statehood. It is easily forgotten in the current situation of the conflict that the country of Jordan was the state of all Arabs who came to live in the Kingdom of Israel.

For seven hundred years after Jesus Christ ascended to heaven, the birth of Islam gave room to the Islamic caliphates, which produced the Islamic groups that fight to maintain the caliphates' legacy in the current age of the Middle East. The Lord said, "I will return to Zion, and dwell in the midst of Jerusalem. Then Jerusalem shall be called the City of Truth, and the mountain of the Lord of hosts will be called the Holy Mountain"[28] The prophecy by Zechariah refers to the time when the joyous aftermath of Zion's freedom will vastly increase the spiritual beauty of the land. Destruction will likely come to the land of Israel by way of the multinational war force. But the people of God will be delivered from the attack, and with them will come the new earth, of which Jerusalem will be the capital. When the time of the peace arrives, "Every pot in Jerusalem and in Judah will be holy to the Lord Almighty and all who come to sacrifice in the temple will take some of the pots and cook in them. On that day, there will no longer be a Canaanite in the house of the Lord Almighty."[29] The coming of the Messiah's Kingdom is the hope of the believers rallying to support Jerusalem the faithful and the blessed city.

The prophecy of a single, undivided Jerusalem is grounded in the Word of God and proclaimed by faithful servants of the Lord. Even when the city is forcefully taken and be divided, the truth of the prophecy will finally prevail. Habakkuk said that the revelation of the Lord's mission must wait for the appointed time to come, and it will not prove false. It speaks of the end and will not fail. If it linger, wait. It will certainly come to pass and will not delay any longer than it is necessary.[30] The Lord said, "I am very jealous for Jerusalem and Zion, but I am angry with the

---

[28] Zechariah 8:3.
[29] Zechariah 14:21.
[30] Habakkuk 2:3.

nations that feel secure. I was only a little angry but they added to the calamity. Therefore, this is what the Lord says, 'I will return to Jerusalem with mercy and there my house will be rebuilt. And the measuring line will be stretched out over Jerusalem. My town will again overflow with prosperity and the Lord will again comfort Zion and choose Jerusalem.'"[31]

---

[31] Zechariah 1:14-17.

CHAPTER 3

THE LAND OF CANAAN AND
THE CANAANITE TRIBES

The name of Canaan is derived from a Semitic root. "Canaan" means "subdued." In a sense, the name could be taken to mean "humbled." The Bible connects the name and its meaning to Canaan, son of Ham, grandson of Noah. Canaan was the father of the eleven children who brought forth the eleven tribes of the Canaanites. The descendants of Canaan were the earliest ethnic groups that lived in the Promised Land. The eleven sons of Canaan were the founding fathers of the tribes of the Sidonites, the Hittites, the Jebusites, the Amorites, the Girgashites, the Hivites, the Arkites, the Sinites, the Arvadites, the Zemarites, and the Hamathites. All the eleven tribes of Canaan are listed in Genesis chapter 10, where the Bible gives the Table of Nations. Sidon was the eldest son of Canaan, and his tribe was the Sidonites. Each of the Canaanite tribes inherited the name of its founding parent. Also, the Perizzites lived in the Promised Land in the days of the Canaanites.

The tribes of the Canaanites grew large in number and were gradually scattered in all over the place. "Their borders extended across the Mediterranean coast from Sidon to Gerar and Gaza, and around the Jordan valley toward Sodom, Gomorrah, Admah and Zeboiim and as far as Lasha."[32] "Canaanite" was a general name used for the pagan tribes. They inhabited the Canaan peninsula when God freed the children of Israel from the Egyptians' bondage. The Amorites dwelled on the eastern side of the Dead Sea, the Perizzites and the Jebusites occupied the mountainous areas of the southern region, and the Hivites and the Hittites were in the region near Lebanon. The Girgashites were on the eastern part of the Sea of Galilee.

The land of the Canaanites, which is described in the Bible as including the tribal groups, was suitable for conquest on moral ground. God called the land of Canaan the Promised Land and guided the children of Israel in all the years during which they traveled from Egypt to enter the land. The Israelites fought their way into the land with the support of God. The Canaanites engaged the children of Israel on several battlefields, and most of the fighting happened at the border fortress of Canaan. The people came out of their cities and took war to the Israelites, who were coming across the desert. They wanted to prevent the Hebrew folks from reaching the mainland of Canaan.

But God was with the Hebrew folks in the fight against their enemy. He helped the people of Israel solve other political troubles, which bothered them while they were on their way to secure the land. The Lord maintained His presence with the Israelites even after the people entered the land. Before they occupied the land, God said to the leaders of the Israelites, "In the cities of the nations the Lord is giving you as an inheritance do not leave alive anything that breathes. Completely destroy them; the Hittites, Amorites, Perizzites, Hivites, and Jebusites – as the Lord your God has commanded you. Otherwise, they will teach you to follow all the detestable things they do in worshipping their gods and you will sin against the Lord your God."[33] God often repeated this warning to Moses in many of the cases where the voice of the Lord came to Moses. It was important to the Lord then, as it is still important to Him now, that holiness was preserved on the land. The Lord said to Moses, "Tell the people of Israel, 'Do not defile yourselves in any of these ways, because

---

[32] Genesis10:19.
[33] Deuteronomy 20:16-18.

this is how the nation that I am going to drive out before you became defiled. Even the land was defiled; so I punished it for its sin, and the land vomited out its inhabitants. But you must keep my decrees and my laws. The native-born and the aliens living among you must not do any of these detestable things.'"[34]

God is completely holy. He does not allow sin in His presence. Until Jesus Christ came to the earth, humans were separated from the presence of God because of sin. Jesus christ died for sins of humanity and through Him we can again approach the presence of God.

The Origin of the Promised Land:

The Bible calls the Promised Land the inheritance of Canaan. The father of Canaan was Ham, and Ham was one of the three sons of Noah that survived the flood when God destroyed the earth and saved only Noah and his family. According to the account of the flood in Genesis chapter 9, "The sons of Noah that came out of the ark were Shem, Ham, and Japheth. (Ham was the father of Canaan). These were the three sons of Noah and from them came the people who scattered over the earth."[35]

The problem Canaan faced regarding his inheritance started with his father, Ham. Ham was the only son of Noah who did not receive his father's blessing. Noah cursed his son Ham because Ham disrespected him. The curse to Ham brought bad luck to him and destroyed the future of his generation. The Bible tells the story of Ham and his son Canaan in this way:

> "Noah, a man of the soil proceeded to plant a vineyard.
> When he drank some of its wine, he became drunk and
> lay uncovered inside his tent. Ham, the father of Canaan
> saw his father's nakedness and told his two brothers
> outside. But, Shem and Japheth took a garment and laid
> it across their shoulder; then they walked in backward
> and covered their father's nakedness. Their faces were

---

[34] Leviticus 18:24-26.
[35] Genesis 9:19.

turned the other way so that they would not see their father's nakedness. When Noah woke up from his wine sleep and knew what his younger son had done to him, he said,
"Cursed be Canaan!
The lowest of servants he will be to his brothers."
Noah also said, "Blessed be the Lord, the God of Shem! May Canaan be the servant of Shem; may God extend the territory of Japheth, and may Canaan be his servant.""[36]

The blessing from Noah followed Shem for generations and prospered his descendants. Abraham, son of Terah, was a direct descendant of Shem.[37] The covenant children of Abraham received from God the grace to take over the land of Canaan. God recognized the curse to Ham through serious sinful conducts of the children of Canaan. At His own appointed time God ordered Abraham to go and dwell on the land. "Abram traveled through the land as far as the site of the great tree of Moreh at Shechem. At the time the Canaanites were on the land. The Lord appeared to Abram and said, 'To your offspring I will give this land. So Abram built an altar there to the Lord, who had appeared to him.'"[38]

Abraham first settled in Canaan as a stranger. His earliest sons, Ishmael and Isaac, were born in that land. Isaac had twin sons, Esau and Jacob, and the sons were born to him in the land of Canaan. An angel of the Lord gave Jacob the name Israel in that land, in a place Jacob called Peniel. Jacob wrestled an angel across the ford of Jabbok, and then the angel said to him, "Your name will no longer be Jacob but Israel, because you have struggled with God and with men and have overcome."[39] God appeared to Jacob in a dream in Bethel, which is also in Canaan. In that place, the Lord confirmed to him that his new name was Israel. The Lord said to Jacob, "'Your name is Jacob, but you will no longer be called Jacob;

---

[36] Genesis 9:20-27.
[37] Genesis 11:10-31.
[38] Genesis 12:6-7.
[39] Genesis 32:28.

your name will be Israel.' So He named him Israel. Again the Lord said to him, "'I am God Almighty, be fruitful and increase in number. A nation and a community of nations will come from you, and kings will come from your body. The land I gave to Abraham and Isaac I also give to you, and I will give this land to your descendants after you.'"[40]

Jacob had twelve sons with four wives. The wives of Jacob were Leah, Rachel, Zilpah, and Bilhah. The descendants of the twelve sons of Jacob were the people God used to create the twelve tribes of the Kingdom of Israel. Jacob and his family lived in Canaan alongside the Canaanites. Then the family went out of Canaan and lived in Egypt, where four generations of the descendants of Jacob spent a long, hard time serving the Egyptians. The task of developing the family of Jacob occurred in Egypt because of Joseph, son of Jacob.[41] It was because of Joseph that Jacob and the rest of his family members came to live in Egypt. Joseph was the favorite son of Jacob and the firstborn son of his second wife, Rachel.

Joseph was sold into slavery by his ten brothers. He was first sold as a slave boy to a caravan of Ishmaelite merchants who were traveling to Egypt. On reaching Egypt, the merchant that bought Joseph sold him to Potiphar, the captain of the Egyptian guards. The brothers of Joseph were jealous of him. They hated Joseph and alleged against him that their father Jacob loved him more than he loved them. The brothers of Joseph conspired to kill Joseph. They seized Joseph in a field to kill him. But Reuben, the eldest son of Jacob, convinced both himself and his other brothers to sell the boy into slavery rather than kill him.

Joseph grew up in Egypt being a slave. He spent some time in prison owing to the wife of Potiphar. Joseph survived the slavery ordeal with direct help from God. Joseph was made a prince in Egypt because of the dreams that only he interpreted correctly for the pharaoh.[42] In all the years since Joseph's brothers sold him, their father, Jacob, was made to believe by his other sons that wild animals had killed Joseph.

---

[40] Genesis 35:10-12.

[41] The story of the life of Joseph (See Genesis 37-50).

[42] Genesis 41.

Then drought came on the land of Canaan, and with the drought came severe famine. There was a huge food reserve in Egypt, and Jacob sent ten of his sons to Egypt to buy some of the food for the family. Joseph recognized his brothers when they arrived in Egypt to buy some food. Joseph was well established in Egypt, and his brothers did not recognize him, because of the royal prestige Joseph had. Joseph finally revealed himself to the family of his father, Jacob, and forgave his brothers for selling him into slavery. It was through Joseph that the pharaoh of Egypt invited all the members of the family of Jacob to stay in Egypt. The people multiplied in Egypt and grew to a population, the size of a nation, in just over four hundred years.

Joseph lived 110 years, and he died in the land of the Egyptians. The Hebrew folks were forced to live lives of severe suffering after the last of the pharaohs who knew about the story of Joseph died. The Israelites stayed in bondage 430 years. Then the hand of almighty God paved a path of freedom for the people.

Beginning with the time that He spoke to Moses in the burning bush, God reached out His hands and saved the people. Moses was forty years old when he fled into the desert to escape the wrath of the pharaoh and he came to the land of Midian. In Midian, Moses was attendant to the flock of Jethro, and he married Zipporah, the eldest daughter of Jethro. One day, Moses led out the flock to the far end of the desert, and he came near with the flock to the mountain of Horeb. In Horeb the Lord made Moses witness a strange sight. The Lord let flames of fire burn a nearby bush, but the bush was not consumed. Moses went closer to observe the strange sight, and the Lord spoke to him there.[43]

> The Lord said to Moses,
> "I have indeed seen the misery of my people in Egypt.
> I have heard them crying out because of their slave
> drivers, and I am concerned about their suffering. So I
> have come down to rescue them from the hand of the

---

[43] Exodus 3:1-2.

Egyptians and to bring them up out of that land into a good and spacious land, a land flowing with milk and honey – the home of the Canaanites; Hittites, Amorites, Perizzites, Hivites and Jebusites. And now the cry of the Israelites has reached me, and I have seen the way the Egyptians are oppressing them. So, now go. I am sending you to pharaoh to bring my people the Israelites out of Egypt."[44]

From Moses to the National Phase of the Israelites:

Moses was born in Egypt to enslaved Hebrew parents, Amram and Jochebed. Both the father and the mother of Moses were from the tribe of Levi. The date of the birth of Moses is presumed to be around 1393 BC. The parents of Moses feared the decree of pharaoh according to which every newborn male child of the Hebrews was to be killed at birth. The parents of Moses hid the baby Moses in a waterproof basket and placed the basket on the Nile River to flow downstream.

The daughter of pharaoh discovered Moses inside the floating basket when she came down to bathe on the Nile River. She took the baby Moses to her home and adopted him as if he were her own son. The daughter of pharaoh presumed that the baby boy was a gift to her from the god of the Nile. She gave him the name Moses and trained him with pharaoh's honor.

Moses fled from the Egyptians when he came to be forty years of age. The Egyptian authorities wanted to kill Moses because Moses had killed an Egyptian over a dispute. Moses was eighty years old when the Lord spoke to him through the burning bush. His word commanded Moses to go back to Egypt and get His people out of Egypt. Aaron and Joshua helped Moses organize the people according to the command of the Lord. Moses led the people across the Red Sea and into the deserts of Sin and Sinai. From Sinai he set them on the path to the Promised Land. The Lord called Moses to his resting place on Mount Nebo, near the plain of Moab.

---

[44] Exodus 3:7-10.

There, in the land of Moab, the Lord appointed Joshua Moses' assistant to lead the people.

> "So, Moses the servant of the Lord died there in the land of Moab, according to the word of the Lord. And He buried him in a valley in the land of Moab, opposite Beth Peor; but no one knows his grave to this day. Moses was one hundred and twenty years old when he died. His eyes were not dim nor his natural vigor diminished. And the children of Israel wept for Moses in the plains of Moab thirty days. So the days of weeping and mourning for Moses ended. Now Joshua, the son of Nun was full of the spirit of wisdom, for Moses had laid his hands on him; so the children of Israel obeyed him, and did to him as the Lord had commanded Moses."[45]

The Lord commanded Joshua to lead the people of Israel into the Promised Land, and He stood him on the battlefield to defeat the Canaanites. By His order, Joshua fought and destroyed the Canaanites on the land. The Canaanites were serious idol worshippers. They had temples of the god Baal and the goddess Ashtoreth scattered all over the land. The Canaanite system of idol worship contained the most extravagant evil celebrations. Both the temples of the idols and the people's lifestyles were centers of serious evil practices. The people lived by performing deadly rituals and by practicing divination at high levels. They were known for using newborn babies as sacrifices to their gods. God predicted the evil the Canaanites would do when He told Abraham that his generations from Isaac would rescue the land and end the evil hands of the Amorites on the land. God said to Abraham before Abraham died, "In the fourth generation, your descendants will come back here; for the sins of the Amorites has not yet reached its full measure."[46]

Also, the Kingdom of Edom was located on the Wadi Tumilat, which

---

[45] Deuteronomy 34:5-9.
[46] Genesis 15:16.

from the edge of Sinai reached as far as Kadesh Barnea. On the north of Edom was the territory of Moab. The Moabites were descendants of Lot. The boundary between the territory of Moab and the kingdom of Edom was the Wadi Zered in western Jordan. The Edomites were direct descendants of Esau, the twin brother of Jacob. Edom was the son of Esau, and his descendants lived next to the Canaanites when the Israelites were arriving in the region from Egypt. The Edomites formed bitterness against the Israelites. Perhaps the Edomites' animosity toward the Israelites was formed by the betrayal of trust that happened between Esau and Jacob.

From Kadesh, Moses sent a personal appeal to the King of Edom and asked from him that the people of Israel be allowed to pass through the territory to the Promised Land. But the King of Edom was adamantly against the appeal. Moses sent messengers from Kadesh to the King of Edom, saying, "This is what your brother Israel says, you know about all the hardships that have come upon us. Our forefathers went down to Egypt, and we lived there many years. The Egyptians mistreated us and our fathers, but we cried out to the Lord, He heard our cry and sent an angel and brought us out of Egypt. Now we are here at Kadesh, a town on the edge of your territory. Please let us pass through your country. We will not go through any field or vineyard, or drink water from your well. We will travel along the king's highway and not turn to the right or to the left until we have passed through your territory." But the King of Edom replied to Moses, "You may not pass through here; if you try, we will march out and attack you with sword."[47]

In 586 BC, the Prophet Obadiah predicted that the Lord would cut off the Edomites as though the people did not exist on the land.[48] The Edomites were removed from the land, according to the word of the prophecy. The first defeat of the Edomites was in 582 BC, four years before the Babylonians burned down the temple of Jerusalem. The Babylonian army raided and desolated the cities of the Edomites. The Jewish family of Mattathias Ben Johanan (the Maccabees) was responsible for rooting out

[47] Numbers 20:14-18.
[48] Obadiah 18-19.

the remnant of the Edomites in 126 BC. A few of the Edomite survivors were perhaps absorbed into the Jewish community.

The Canaanites and the Edomites were the most important tribes of the Canaan peninsula before the Israelites conquered the land. The tribes of the Canaanites were rooted out of their natural environment by the children of Israel. Thus, the Canaanites' history was sunk into silence. The Hebrew language is similar to the language of the Canaanites. The Jews maintained the ancient language, and now the language is one of the most recognizable connections to their origin in the land. The Arabic language evolved much later. The Arabic language got its origin from the ancient language of Syria and belonged to the sixth century AD Semitic family of languages. Some aspect of the Arabic vocabulary was adopted from the Babylonians' Aramaic language. There were no historical or cultural associations between the Canaanites and the Arabs.

In the three hundred years since the Israelites entered the land of Canaan, the Hebrews were ruled by the Judges until the period when the Kingdom of Israel had kings. The family of the Maccabees[49] ruled the Israelites after they led the people to revolt against the Greek King Antiochus Epiphanes of the Seleucid Empire. The Maccabees lost control of the land to the Roman Empire in 63 BC. The Roman army, under General Pompey, captured the Jewish Kingdom of Israel. Rome held the land until the time the Ottoman Empire rose to power. The Ottoman Empire defeated the last stronghold of the Roman Empire. They took control of the entire Middle East and forced the Romans' command post in Constantinople to collapse.

The Herodian dynasty was the first family of Rome to rule the Kingdom of Israel. Rome divided the Kingdom of Israel into the districts of Judea, Galilee, Peraea, and Transjordan after King Herod the Great

---

[49] The Maccabees were the Jewish family of Mattathias Ben Johanan that led the Israelites' revolt against the Greek Syrian King, Antiochus Epiphanes IV. The aged priest and his five sons served the people both as high priests and as rulers after the revolt was won. The name "Maccabee" means "hammer" in Hebrew. This refers to the hammer-like attack of Mattathias and his sons against the Greek Seleucid Empire. The book of Maccabees covers the whole story of the revolt from 175 BC to 134 BC. In 168 BC, the temple was recaptured by the Jews, and sacrifices were resumed in the temple in 165 BC. The books of Maccabees first and second are in the Apocrypha.

died in the fourth century BC. The four districts of Israel were governed by the four sons of King Herod the Great. Jerusalem was part of the central area of Judea. The Bible relates the account of the Roman occupation to the time when Jesus Christ was born in Bethlehem of Judea.

The Roman military command and the administration left behind in Canaan serious signs of their authority, as was the case in all parts of the Mediterranean. Rome and Babylon were the great symbols of organized paganism. Rome was the master of secular economic and political principles. Many Jews and Christians saw the tyranny of the Roman civilization as a serious threat to true spirituality. The principles of Roman tyranny were deeply engraved in all the places where the Romans had command.

In Israel the Jews created serious resistance groups that attacked the Roman institutions and the army through guerrilla warfare. The people took up arms against the Romans not merely in the interest of their national independent but rather to achieve the kingdom of God, that God rather than Rome might rule over His people. The Jewish men Bar Kokhba and Judas the Galilean led the bands of people that revolted against the Romans. The Bar Kokhba revolt was barely helpful to the Jews, and it ended in a decisive defeat. Rome deeply disliked the Jews because of the revolts, and the administration tried to end Jewish national pride by way of strong military siege.

Rome was particularly suspicious of the Christians because of the presence and the growing influence of the Lord Jesus Christ, whom the Christians – or rather Christ's followers – held as King. Rome would not tolerate any king except the Caesar. The Roman governors of the districts of Galilee and Judea monitored the ministry of Jesus Christ with great interest, and finally His life was delivered into their hands.

King Herod Antipas was one of the four sons of King Herod the Great. Antipas ruled over the districts of Galilee and Perea from the fourth century BC to AD 39. King Antipas was particularly baffled when he heard about the miracles the Lord Jesus Christ was performing, and he sought to see the Lord. Saint Luke's Gospel describes the concern of King Antipas over who the Lord Jesus Christ was. Luke wrote, "Herod, the tetrarch[50] heard about all that was going on. And he was perplexed because some were saying that John the Baptist had been raised from the dead, others that Elijah had appeared, and still others that one of the prophets of long ago had come back to life. But Herod said, 'I beheaded John. Who, then, is this I hear such things about? And he tried to see him.'"[51]

In AD 135, the Kingdom of Israel was renamed Palestine by the Roman Emperor Hadrian after the Roman soldiers finally crushed the stronghold of the Jewish rebellion. Hadrian was determined to wipe out the identity of Israel from human memory for the damages caused by the Bar Kokhba revolt. Renaming Israel to Palestine was the final twist of the knife by the Emperor Hadrian after massacres and exiles that largely extinguished the presence of many Jews in Judea.

From the time of the Roman Emperor Hadrian to recent history, the Kingdom of Israel has been widely called Palestine with reference to Jews and the Jewish nation. The name of Palestine in the Roman political context refers to the defeat of the Israelites and describes the geographical area of the Kingdom of Israel according to the concept of the defeat. The Kingdom of Israel was renamed as Palestine to establish forever the symbol of the Romans' military power, which suppressed both the religious and political wills of the Jewish people. Many Jews were forced out of their homeland and into exile. The mass exodus of the Jews from the land was the second Diaspora, taking place after the Babylonian exile.

Arabs from the neighboring Arabian Peninsula gradually became the lords of the land, especially during the four hundred years of rule by the Ottoman Empire. Between the years of 1830 and 1838, the population of Jewish families was about three thousand in Jerusalem and eleven thousand in all of Palestine. The history of the place shows that Arab Muslims struggled to own Jerusalem's temple site since the Muhammadans' jihad movement was launched to capture all nations of the world.

The struggle over Jerusalem has been extended into the present age

---

[50] A tetrarch was a Roman ruler of one fourth of a region.
[51] Luke 9:7-9.

because of the long time during which the caliphate regimes consolidated the Islamic power of control throughout the Middle East. After the caliphate ended came the four hundred years of rule by the Ottoman Empire. The word "Filastin," which Arabs use to refer to Palestine, is not Arabic. The name of Palestine evolved from the Greek word "Plesheth." "Palestine," or "Plesheth," is pronounced as "Filastin" in a natural Arabic accent. "Plesheth" is derived from the ancient Greek word "Pelesh," or simply "Palah," and it was used as general term to describe the Greek invaders that lived on the southeastern coast of the Kingdom of Israel.

Major Foreign Empires that Occupied the Holy Land:

- The Babylonian army destroyed the first temple of Jerusalem in 586 BC and forced the Jews into the Babylonian captivity, which lasted seventy years. Life in captivity was lived as the Prophets Jeremiah, Ezekiel, and Daniel describe in the holy book of prophecy. In all the years that the Jews were kept in Babylon, they held in them the compassion for Jerusalem. They wept and hoped for the salvation of God. During the captivity, the Jews were sad because they were not able to love and sing again in the place of God in Jerusalem. The people lamented, "By the rivers of Babylon, there we sat down, and yes we wept when we remembered Zion."[52]

- The exiled Jews were permitted to return home by the order of King Cyrus the Great. Reconstruction work on the temple site in Jerusalem was later authorized by King Darius. Work on the temple site lasted from 538 BC and 333 BC. The lengthy stages of the reconstruction work were caused by physical and spiritual changes regarding the development of the city. The results of the changes were the main theme of the books of Ezra, Nehemiah, and Haggai. The book of Esther contains the ordeal of the Jewish families that stayed in Babylon after the exilic period ended. Nehemiah returned home from Persia at

---

[52] Psalm 137:1.

that time and became the governor of Judea, while Esther and Mordecai led the Jews in Babylon.

- The Hellenistic period started with the death of Alexander the great in 323 BC. This period witnessed the spread of Greek philosophy throughout the eastern and western regions of Europe. The Macedonian King Alexander the Great conquered both the Kingdom of Israel and the Persian Empire. He allowed Jews the right to have self-rule in matters of their religious rites. The opportunity was not long served, and the Greeks desecrated the temple of the Lord during the reign of King Antiochus IV. Jews revolted against the Greek authority and followed the headship of the family of Maccabees in reestablishing independent Jewish rule in Judea. Victory over the dominion of the Seleucid Greek Empire is the main theme of the rededication festival that the Jewish holiday Hanukkah reflects. The Festival of Lights is observed over eight days and nights.

- The Roman army General Gnaeus Pompeius Magnus (Pompey the Great) led the Roman army to capture Jerusalem in 63 BC. The Roman Empire ruled the Kingdom of Israel from 63 BC to AD 313. During this period, the Roman emperors appointed Roman political elites, such as Pilate and Herod Agrippa, as prefects of the holy land. In AD 70, the Roman army General Titus (son of Vespasian) waged the final siege of Jerusalem. Flavius Josephus referred to the siege as the wars of the Jews in one of his books. He stated the attack was one of the most horrific sieges in history. In writing about the siege in his fifth book, Josephus described in detail the serious destruction that happened in Jerusalem. General Titus and his army surrounded Jerusalem during the season of the Passover festival. More people than usual visited Jerusalem during the feast of Passover. At the time of the attack, the number of people in the city was double the norm. The Roman army then broke into the Jerusalem defenses and began an assault on the city. The account of the attack suggests that General Titus ordered his soldiers not to harm the temple itself and that it was not clear who set fire to the temple structures. Some historians suggest it was the overzealous Roman soldiers that started the fire, and others say it was the Jews themselves that set the fire in a final act of defiance. However, after the fire ran its course, the Roman soldiers tore down the stone structures of the temple to recover the vast quantities of gold that the fire had melted. To collect the gold, the Roman soldiers left no stone on top of another stone. In Matthew chapter 24, Jesus Christ predicts the part the Roman soldiers played in destroying the temple of Jerusalem.

- Bar Kokhba was killed in the battle of Bethar on the hillside of Judea. His men and the revolt that he led them to stage against the Roman forces were defeated in AD 132. Rome renamed the Jewish Kingdom of Israel as Palestine and called Jerusalem the city of Aelia Capitolina.

- Emperor Constantine converted to Christianity in AD 313. He was the first Christian emperor of the Roman Empire. In the same year in Milan, the Emperor signed the edict that made Christianity the official religion of Rome. The Edict of Milan was particularly helpful in repealing the state's sponsored persecution, which injured both the Jewish identity and the Christian institutions around the Roman Empire. Jerusalem was restored to its name. Many citizens of Rome joined the Christian Church because of the influence of Emperor Constantine, and they contributed the secular influence that helped divide the Church of Rome.

- The Byzantine Empire emerged as a world power in the late AD 313 through the fall of the Western Roman Empire. The Geek-speaking Byzantine Empire had its capital in Constantinople (now Istanbul). The Empire existed until 636, and it was often called the Eastern Roman Empire. The term "Byzantine" is derived from "Byzantium," which is the original Greek name for Constantinople. The territory of the Greek Byzantine Empire was the entire eastern half of the Western Roman Empire around the Mediterranean Sea. The Byzantines controlled the territory until

1453, when the Ottoman Empire arose to power. The Byzantine army finally fell to the forces of the Ottoman Empire.

- The years of 636 to 1099 were marked by both the Muhammadan invasion and the rising of caliphates in the Middle East.

- By the end of 1099, different groups of Christian men from Europe were fighting to save both the holy land and the continent of Europe from falling deeper into the hands of the caliphates' jihad movement. These men were known as Christian Crusaders. They were formed into the Christians' defensive army alliance, which restricted the spread of Islam on both the European and the African continents. Serious human rights abuses occurred between the Christian fighting men and the Islamic jihadists during the years of 1099 to 1291. The Christian Crusaders are most remembered for providing peace during the tenure of Pope Urban II in Jerusalem.

- From Cairo, the Islamic group of Mamluks reigned over the Middle East and North Africa from 1291 to 1516. The word "Mamluk" is derived from classical Egyptian letters, and can be translated as "slave" in the English language. The Mamluks were slave boys that Abbasid caliphs brought into the Islamic Empire of nineteen-century Baghdad. The caliphs chose to preserve Islamic orthodoxy in the Abbasid Empire. They trained the slave army that became a force of Sunni Muslim soldiers. Armenians, Turks, and Sudanese boys formed the bulk of the slave soldiers and the administration. After the breakup of the Abbasid Empire, the base of the military slaves (Ghilman) in Cairo became the center of military power throughout the Islamic world. The Mamluks inherited the last Ayyubid stronghold in the Eastern Mediterranean and created the great Islamic Empire of the late middle ages. The Mamluks controlled the Jewish holy land, Mecca, and Medina from their base in Cairo and made Egypt the center of the Islamic civilization. The army of the Ottoman Empire defeated the Mamluks in a final battle. The Mamluk survivors of the war were integrated into the forces of the Ottoman Empire.

The Mamluks are best remembered for driving out the Christian Crusaders in Jerusalem.

- The Ottoman Empire originated in the region now called Turkey. The empire existed from the years of 1516 to 1918 and was the longest-lasting Islamic occupier on the holy land. The Ottoman Empire sealed the East Gate of Jerusalem and recreated the wall of the old city.

- The British Army entered Jerusalem in 1917 and occupied the holy land until 1948. The British military regiment took Palestine after the European allied forces defeated the army of the Islamic Ottoman Empire during the First World War. The British administrators were the first group to manage the problem of Arabs and Jews with a two-state solution. The League of Nations provided the draft mandate that allowed Arabs to own the Jordan province of Israel.

The power of God and His goodness to the people of Israel are strong supports for faith. Children of God often choose to pray for the present condition. Jews must continue engaging in open conversation about God's help to His people, especially in praying for the restoration of the Kingdom of Israel. David openly took the conversation to the Lord in Psalm 44. He used the experience to ask God to fight the enemies that accused His people of illegally acquiring the land of the Canaanites. David acknowledged the victory of Israel came about not by any human strength and merit, but by the free grace of God. The Lord fought for Israel; if He had not, Israel would have fought in vain. David said, "We have heard with our ears, O God. Our fathers have told us what you did in their days, in days long ago. With your hand, you drove out the nations and planted our fathers. You crushed the people and made our father flourish. It was not by their sword that they won over the land, nor did their arm bring them victory. It was your right hand; your arm, and the light of your face, for you love them for a purpose."[53]

---

[53] Psalm 44:1-3.

CHAPTER 4

THE PHILISTINES OF A TIME AGO

The Greek word "Plesheth" is translated to "Philistine" in English and refers to the people that are known in the Bible as the Philistines. These people were the Mycenaeans – early proto-Greeks that lived on the southeastern coast of the Kingdom of Israel. Their associations with the Philistines are mentioned almost three hundred times in the Old Testament. The Philistines are mentioned nowhere in the New Testament, except when it refers to the events of older times.

The Roman Empire occupied the Mediterranean before Jesus Christ was born, and the Roman occupation lasted beyond the period of the apostles. There is no evidence that the Roman administration was associated with the Philistine community. The Philistines were eliminated from the region of Israel before the Roman conquerors conquered the Mediterranean. The Philistines and the community they lived in were wiped out in the region a long time before Jesus Christ was born. More evidence to support that the Philistine community did not exist in the region during the earliest time of the New Testament is based on fact. None of the visits by Jesus Christ in and around the Philistine-occupied area happened among the Philistine people. Both the ministry of Jesus Christ and the ministry of John the Baptist happened in the region where the Philistines lived, but the associations were built on the Jews and the Samaritans of the territory. The twelve disciples of Jesus Christ, including the Apostle Paul, carried the Gospel beyond the province of Judea and Samaria. None of the disciples wrote any record that associated their visits with the Philistine community.

The Bible first recognized the origin of the Philistines in the book of Genesis, where the people were listed as descendants of Ham, son of Noah. We read in the book of Genesis, "Mizraim was the father of the Ludim, Anamim, Lehabim, Naphtuhim, Pathrusim, and Casluhim; (from whom came the Philistines and Caphtorim.)"[54] The Philistines and the Canaanites were related people. The Bible explains that both communities shared the same ancestor who came from Ham, son of Noah. The book of Deuteronomy identifies the island of Crete as the home of Caphtor, son of Casluhim, grandson of Ham, son of Noah. Caphtor formed the origin of the Philistines on the island of Crete. The book of Deuteronomy says, "And as for the Avim, who lived in villages as far as Gaza, the Caphtorim who came from Caphtor."[55] The book of the Prophet Amos qualifies the Philistines as people that immigrated to the territory of Israel from ancient Greece. Amos quoted the Lord when the Lord said to the people of Israel, "Are you not like the people of Ethiopia to me, O children of Israel, says the Lord. Did I not bring up Israel from the land of Egypt, the Philistines from Caphtor and the Syrians from Kir?"[56]

The Prophet Jeremiah predicted the time the Lord wiped out the Philistines from the Kingdom of Israel. Jeremiah wrote about the origin of the Philistines and the coming of the invading army of King Nebuchadnezzar that destroyed the people. Jeremiah said, "For the day has come to destroy all the Philistines and to remove all survivors who could help Tyre and Sidon. The Lord is about to destroy the Philistines, the remnant of the coasts of Caphtor. Gaza shall shave her head in mourning; Ashkelon will be silenced."[57]

---

[54] Genesis 10:13-14.
[55] Deuteronomy 2:23.
[56] Amos 9:7.
[57] Jeremiah 47:4-5.

The Bible is not alone in associating the origin of the Philistines with Caphtor. Archeological studies about the life of the Philistines have provided strong evidence suggesting that the Mycenaean sea people of Greece are the earliest cultural link of the Philistines. The Mycenaean people were presumed to have emigrated from northwest of the island of Crete and to have reached the southeastern coast of Canaan in several waves. The people started arriving in the region as early as the prepatriarchal period and settled in the south of Beersheba. The area of Beersheba included Gaza, Negev, and Gerar. The Philistines occupied the territory until 830 BC. The area where the Philistines lived was known as Philistia. More foreign immigrants, chiefly from the Mediterranean islands, overran the Canaan district during the Greco-Persian wars of the years 499 to 449 BC. They settled among the families of the sons of Jacob. Herodotus wrote some part of the history of the period.[58] His history refers to the eastern coast of the Mediterranean Sea as Syrian Palestine. The Kingdom of Israel, or rather Palestine, was described in the book according to the vision of the decree by the Roman Emperor Hadrian. Herodotus adopted the political opinion of the decree when he wrote the history. The Philistines were not Arabs, and they were not Semitic in origin. They lived several aspects of their lives by adopting Canaanite culture and language.

The Bible describes the Philistines as uncircumcised. They were ruled by lords in each of their five cities. Major cities of the Philistines were Ashdod, Ashkelon, Gath, Gaza, and Ekron.[59] The book of Samuel discusses the events of war that happened between the Israelites and the Philistines. The writer of the second book of Samuel described David's emotional state of mind when David mourned the death of King Saul and his son Jonathan. The two commanders of the Israelite army died on Mount Gilboa, in the battle in which they led the Israelite men to fight against the Philistines. David grieved openly for the loss of the leaders

---

[58] Herodotus was a famous Greek historian.

[59] "These are the golden tumors which the Philistines returned as a trespass offering to the Lord; one for Ashdod, one for Gaza, one for Ashkelon, one for Gath, one for Ekron, and the golden rats according to the number of all the cities of the Philistines belonging to the five lords, both fortified cities and country villages" (1Samuel 6:17-18).

and said, "Thy glory, O Israel is slain upon thy high places. How are the mighty fallen! Tell it not in Gath and proclaim it not in the streets of Ashkelon – least the daughters of the Philistines rejoice; the daughters of uncircumcised triumph."[60]

The most dramatic political phase of the Philistines' history in the Bible is the period of the Judges. The Philistines and the Amorites were at the time the chief enemies of the Israelites, and both peoples formed major political threats to the existence of the Kingdom of Israel. The Philistine soldiers were forceful on the battlefield. The soldiers were skilled in combat, which gave them significant influence in the region.

During the time of the Philistines, Samson was Judge of the Israelites, and he was married to a Philistine woman, Delilah.[61] Samson was an exceptionally brave man and was highly vigorous in defending Israel against its enemies. The Spirit of the Lord empowered Samson to fight, and he defeated the Philistines. He halted the Philistines' military advance into the mainland of Israel by killing many of the fighting men with his bare hands. Samson significantly reduced the number of the Philistine fighting men by personally taking the fight into their occupied territory.

The Philistines' military threat to Israel dangerously escalated after Samson died. The fighting men of Philistine encroached further into the northwest region of Israel and threatened to overrun the territory of Dan. The Amorites ultimately forced the tribe of Dan to move further north.[62] The Israelites defeated the Philistines on many battlefronts, especially in the period during which the Prophet Samuel was Judge of the Israelites. But the Philistines kept regrouping their war advances, and they got themselves to a point where the army almost destroyed all of the fighting men of Israel.

The Philistine threat to destroy the Israelites reached a crisis point at the Battle of Ebenezer. Thousands of the Israelite foot soldiers were

---

[60] 2 Samuel 1:19-20.
[61] Judges 13-16; "Again the children of Israel did what was evil in the sight of the Lord and the Lord delivered them into the hand of the Philistines for forty years" (Judges 13:1).
[62] Judges 1:34-35.

brutally defeated on the battlefield, and the ark of the Lord's covenant was captured. This was not an ordinary victory to the Philistines but was the result of sin that the people of Israel committed against God in His temple. Eli was the high priest of the Lord's house in Shiloh. He was aged, and his two sons, Hophni and Phinehas, were required to help him attend to the offering of the people. The two sons of Eli desecrated the sacrifice to the Lord by misbehaving with the people that visited the house of God. This conduct displeased the Lord, and He turned against the Israelites on the battlefield. The Lord led the fighting men of Israel into the hands of the Philistines. "So, the Philistines fought and Israel was defeated, and every man fled to his tent. There was a very great slaughter, and there fell of Israel thirty thousand foot soldiers. Also, the ark of God was captured and the two sons of Eli, Hophni and Phinehas died in the battle."[63]

King David finally checked the intrusion of the Philistines in the Battle of Rephaim. "The Philistines went up once again and deployed themselves in the valley of Rephaim. Therefore, David inquired of the Lord, and He said, "You shall not go up; circle around behind them and come upon them in front of the mulberry trees. And it shall be, when you hear the sound of marching on the tops of mulberry trees, and then you shall advance quickly. For then the Lord will go out before you to strike the camp of the Philistines." And David did so, as the Lord commanded him; and he drove back the Philistines from Geba as far as Gezer."[64]

The Bible attributes any defeat of the Israelites in conflict to their sin against God. This is the case in all the circumstances where the Kings of Israel engaged the people to fight in unauthorized warfare and when idol worship, injustice, and allegiance to both pagan nations and gods ruled the lives of the people. The land of Israel is not a place where sin can be deliberately harbored. Any harbored sin will in time develop to have more serious repercussions on the people. National humiliation being inflicted upon the Israelites by any gentile nation is not about the failure of God's power to protect His people. The defeat of Israel on the battlefield is a

---

[63] 1 Samuel 4:10-11.
[64] 2 Samuel 5:22-25.

repercussion from God as a result of the sins of the Israelites and their guests.

Several unique features of Philistine culture are reflected in the Bible. The people had skill in metal processing, and they were well advanced in the skill of designing new tools. The Philistines' military commanders had their soldiers trained to win in both land and sea battles. There was no blacksmith in Israel at the time of the Philistines. The Israelites relied on Philistine craftsmen to make and repair domestic tools. The Bible says, "All the Israelites would go down to the Philistines to sharpen each man's plowshare, his mattock, his ax and his sickle. And the charge for a sharpening was a pim for the plowshares, the mattocks, the folks, and the axes, and to set the points on the goads."[65]

The Philistine warriors used horses and chariots to engage their enemies on the battlefield. Their foot soldiers were most effective when they fought along with archers.[66] The armor of the Philistine soldiers included bronze helmets, iron coats of mail, iron leg protectors, and iron breastplates. These armors of war evolved during the following century's combat. This form of armor was the standard equipment of the army of Rome, the army of the Ottoman Empire, and the Christian Crusaders. The fight of David and Goliath indicates that the Philistines sometimes used single combat to engage their enemies. "Goliath had a bronze helmet on his head, and he was armed with a coat of mail, and the weight of the coat was five thousand shekels of bronze. And he had bronze armor on his legs and a bronze javelin between his shoulders. Now the staff of his spear was like a weaver's beam, and his iron spearhead weighed six hundred shekels; and a shield-bearer went before him."[67]

The Bible states that the Philistines were pagans. Three Philistine gods that the Bible talks about are Dagon, Ashtoreth, and Baal-zebub. Dagon was the chief among the gods, and temples of Dagon were located both in Gaza and in Ashdod.[68] It could be that the Philistines

---

[65] 1 Samuel 13:19-21.
[66] 1 Samuel 13:5; 1Samuel 31:3.
[67] 1 Samuel 17:5-7.
[68] See Judges 16:21-23 and 1Samuel 5:1-7.

adopted Ashtoreth, the popular fertility goddess of the Canaanites. The Philistines had male prostitutes in temples of Baal. They had also female prostitutes whose services in the temples of both Baal and Ashtoreth were equivalent to the services the Canaanite priestesses performed for their gods. The Philistines worshipped Baal in the city of Ekron as both the sun and the storm god. They called on Baal to save them from these three situations:

- To protect them against pestilence.

- To fight for them against their enemies.

- To provide rainwater for their crops.

Many Israelites performed evil practices against the worship of the living God by imitating the Philistines' atrocious worship. The Prophet Elijah was particularly keen in the fight that destroyed Baal worship in Israel. The Lord used the Prophet Elijah to fight the passion that the Israelites developed for the worship of foreign gods. In His anger, the Lord destroyed the household of King Ahaziah of Samaria because the king put his trust in the prophets of Baal.

> "King Ahaziah fell down through a lattice in his upper chamber that was in Samaria, and was sick; and he sent messengers, and said to them 'Go, consult Baal-zebub, the god of Ekron, to see if I will recover from this injury.' But the angel of the Lord said to Elijah, the Tishbite, "Go up and meet the messengers of the king of Samaria and ask them, 'Is it because there is no God in Israel that you are going off to consult Baal-zebub, the god of Ekron?' Therefore this is what the Lord says, 'You will not leave the bed you are lying on. You will certainly die.'"[69]

---

[69] 2 Kings 1:2-4.

The messengers of the king returned to Samaria with the message of the Prophet Elijah. King Ahaziah died on his sickbed from his injury, according to the Word of God.

The second account of Baal worship in Israel involved King Ahab and his wife, Queen Jezebel. Queen Jezebel did the most to popularize the worship of Baal in Israel. Jezebel adopted Baal worship into her marriage to King Ahab. She made thousands of the King's servants become prophets of Baal. The father of Queen Jezebel was Ethbaal, the king of Sidon, and he was the chief attendant to Baal. Ethbaal gave the gift of gods and goddesses of his fatherland to his daughter Jezebel. As chief priest to Baal, Ethbaal wanted to advance the legacy of Baal worship chiefly to Israel. He wanted the gods to protect the marriage of his daughter Jezebel according to his beliefs.

King Ahab agreed to have the gods of Jezebel for worship in Israel in spite of the sovereign presence of the almighty God. God predicted beforehand the abominable practices the people of Israel would do if they were to serve foreign gods. The Lord warned the children of Israel not to marry foreign women (pagans). According to God, they must not have any association with foreigners or nations whose lifestyles and beliefs could dishonor the holiness of the land. God gave the people of Israel a code of conduct – the Ten Commandments. The Lord said to the people, "I am the Lord your God who brought you out of Egypt, out of the land of slavery. You shall have no other gods beside me. You shall not make for yourself an idol in the form of anything in heaven above or on earth beneath or in the waters below. You shall not bow down to them or worship them"[70]

In 843 BC, the Prophet Elisha appointed Jehu, son of Jehoshaphat and grandson of Nimshi, king over the people of Israel in Samaria. Jehu received two special tasks from the Lord: "Cut off among the people of Israel all remnants of the house of King Ahab and eradicate the worship of Baal from the land of Israel."[71] Baal worship brought unspeakable evil to the people of Israel. The prophets of Baal were the official murderers

---

[70] Exodus 20:1-5.
[71] 2 Kings 9-10.

of little children. The prophets of Baal offered children's body parts to Baal in ritual sacrifices. The Prophet Elisha engaged the prophets of Baal in a contest through which he destroyed most of the temples of Baal. Thousands of Baal's prophets and their supporters were killed in Israel when Baal failed to consume the sacrifice of its worshippers with a miracle of fire.[72]

God gave His power to Elisha, and Elisha closed the heavens for three and a half years. No drop of rainwater fell on the land of Israel in the three and half years of trouble, and the brooks dried up. The Lord showed the people of Israel that He alone can control both the rainfall and the harvest. He severely punished King Ahab and cut off his families from Israel for the atrocities they had led the Israelites to commit with the worship of Baal.

British archeologists did some excavation in the area of Megiddo and revealed evidence from the time of King Ahab. Clustered infants graves were found in the area. The archeologists concluded from the evidence that the cemetery is located in the area where the temple of Baal once stood. The skeletal remains of the infants were deemed to be the children sacrificed to Baal.

Jesus Christ calls Satan Baal-zebub in Matthew chapter 12. He implied with that statement that the Baalism of the Old Testament era was demon worship. Even today demons masquerade as gods and people worship them. The Apostle Paul wrote to the Corinthians and warned them about the harm in worshipping idols. In 1 Corinthians 10:20, Paul describes all idolatry as demon worship. According to Psalm 135, "Those who make them shall be like them and likewise shall be every one that heeded their counsel and trusted in them."[73]

King Nebuchadnezzar and his Neo-Babylonian army destroyed Ashkelon and the other four major cities of the Philistines in a raid that happened during 604 BC. The Babylonians kept records of the attack in the Babylonian chronicle for 604 BC. The chronicle states, "Nebuchadnezzar marched against Ashkelon, took its King captive,

---

[72] 1 Kings 18: 40.
[73] Psalm 135:18.

carried off booty and prisoners, turning the city into ruins and a heap of rubbles."[74]

The last Philistines king of Ashkelon was King Aga. The Neo-Babylonian army marched King Aga, his sons, and the nobles of Philistine to exile in Babylon. Less than twenty years later, in 586 BC, King Nebuchadnezzar captured Jerusalem and destroyed the temple that King Solomon built on Mount Zion. The Neo-Babylonian army led the Israelites out of their natural environment and into the exile that lasted seventy years.

The events that happened in Israel before and immediately after the exilic period were narrated in the Bible mostly by Jeremiah, Ezekiel, Daniel, Esther, Nehemiah, Ezra, Haggai, and Malachi. Nehemiah and his associate priest Ezra led the Israelites to rebuild both the ruined temple of Jerusalem and the fallen wall of Jerusalem. The second temple era in Israel was ended in AD 70 when the Roman soldiers destroyed many parts of Jerusalem and the rebuilt temple.

There was nothing that remained of the Philistine community after the Babylonian exile. The exiled Philistines were not returned by the Babylonians and the cultural communities where they lived ceased to exist on the coastal area of the Promised Land. Except for the historic record that remains, the ethnic identity of the Philistines was gradually stifled in Babylon. The territory of the tribes of Judah was the area where the Philistines once settled and culturally dominated. Evidence in the Bible is showing that the Prophet Jeremiah was not the only prophet of God who prophesied the end of Philistine. The books of Isaiah, Zephaniah, Ezekiel, and Amos contain perfectly fulfilled predictions about the end of the Philistines.

Zephaniah said, "For Gaza will be abandoned and Ashkelon left in ruins. At midnight Ashdod will be emptied and Ekron uprooted. Woe to the inhabitants of the seacoast, you the people of the Kerethites! The word of the Lord is against you O Canaan, land of the Philistines. And I will destroy you so that there will be no inhabitant. So the seacoast will

---

[74] G.D.C. Howley, F.F. Bruce, and H.L Ellison, eds., *The New Layman's Bible Commentary* (Grand Rapids, Michigan: Zondervan 1979), 845.

be pastures and having wells for shepherds and pens for flocks. The coast will be for the remnant of the house of Judah. They will pasture on it. In the evening they will lie down in the houses of Ashkelon. For the Lord their God will care for them; He will restore their fortune."[75]

Today the Arab natives in the state of Israel call themselves Palestinians and echo the Philistines of the ancient past, which have nothing to do with their Arabian ethnicity. The land of the Canaanites predates both the Jewish kingdom on it and the state of Israel that survives within the kingdom. But Arabs have no genuine business claiming any part of the land.

---

[75] Zephaniah 2:4-7.

CHAPTER 5

THE HISTORICAL PRESENT

It is by natural instinct that everybody aspires to spend his or her lifetime in a peaceful environment. All of us want to have the finest of things the living conditions on earth can offer. But peace as any people can possibly have it on earth is not entirely arrived at by the absence of war. Even riches are not supplements to peace. The huge amount of material wealth that many people and nations acquire does not guarantee their existence on earth can be completed peacefully. Peace creates the atmosphere that makes a human life worth living. Peace can be found in the absence of both the finest riches and the best military security. The prospect of peace expresses the true moral nature of humanity in all circumstances where humanity demonstrates decent behavior.

We live in the absence of peace. Peace hardly reaches us because of the complex situations of conflict that exist in our midst. Neither the origins of nor the remedies to the conflicts are the things people want the truth to explain. Because of humans' lack of integrity, the truth is the first casualty of people who experience conflict. People neglect to engage the truth in any business of our society. The inclination to stand against the truth is the influence that decreases the peace of our time. It frustrates the capability we have to love each other. This is the case in the situation of conflict between Arabs and the state of Israel.

Attacks on truth bring serious setbacks to any peace that is an outcome of conflict. Political conflict is articulated with the deceit of hate, and the aim is to disrupt the good living conditions of any unwanted people of the region. For the sake of Islam, the Middle East is a zone of no mercy to any minority group. The religion of Islam has no second chance to offer people of the region if those people cannot defend themselves in the event of war. Fighting the jihad is one major way the religion of Islam suggests its followers should settle disputes with foreign beliefs. Fighting the jihad is not necessarily in line with righteousness of mind.

The war of Islam is called the holy war, and Muslims who fight in it believe that dying in the war should lead people to paradise. Regarding jihad, the Koran states that those who died while defending righteousness shall be rewarded by God in heaven.[76] In speaking of jihad, the Arab Palestinians hope that the state of Israel will have to withdraw to the border the six allied Arab nations created on the mainland of Israel with the 1948 Palestine war. The Arab Palestinians keep hope alive by making it a key condition for any peaceful settlement of the conflict. The state of Israel dismantled part of the border after the Israeli army won the Arabs' allied nations in the Six-Day War of 1967.

Brief Overview of the 1967 Six-Day War Situation:

In 1923, the Kingdom of Israel was divided between the Jews and the Arabs by the British Army commissioners that controlled the region when the First World War ended in 1918. On the course of fighting to end the First World War, both British and French army regiments took control of the Middle East and held it until 1948. Arabs living in the Kingdom of Israel often rioted to engage the Jewish inhabitants in fighting. The vast Transjordan province of Israel was allotted to the Arabs through the partition plan that was drafted by the League of Nations. The Islamic emirate of Transjordan was the first country established for the Arabs in Palestine. The rest of the Jewish territory was therefore declared the independent state of Israel in 1948.

---

[76] See Matthew 5:10.

There was almost immediately a dramatic reversal of approach to the signed peace agreement. The leaderships of Egypt, Lebanon, Jordan, Iraq, Syria, and Saudi Arabia formed a military alliance and invaded the young state of Israel a few days after Israel declared its political independence. The attack on Israel happened in the first critical week after the British armed forces and the army contingents left the region. The combined armies of Egypt, Syria, Lebanon, Iraq, Jordan, and the army contingents from Yemen and Saudi Arabia aimed at destroying the state of Israel with both military tanks and artillery fire.

The Jewish state of Israel had no air defense force at the time, but it managed to fight the enemy forces with a small Jewish militia. The young state of Israel practically relied on nothing but the militia for defense until arms were rushed into the country from abroad. The state of Israel had a national population of about sixty thousand Jews in 1948. More than six thousand of them were killed and over fifteen thousand were wounded in the attack. The aim of the invasion was to eradicate the young Jewish state and sever the people of Israel from rebuilding the civil society of the homeland.

The governments of Syria, Jordan, and Egypt annexed to their countries parts of the territory of Israel that each nation captured during the invasion. Jordan controlled both East Jerusalem and the West Bank, Egypt took control of Gaza, and Syria occupied the Golan Heights. The Arab allied countries were emboldened both by their success in invading Israel in 1948 and by the administration that they created in the occupied Jewish territory.

In 1967, the Arab nations engaged the state of Israel in another joint military attack, this time with more military determination to overrun the Jewish nation. The 1967 joint attack was intended to destroy the state of Israel. The attack is known as the Six-Day War because the military confrontation lasted only six days. The Six-Day War was an offensive military campaign fought by the Arab countries that signed a mutual defense pact in May 1967 to abolish the Jewish state of Israel.

Egypt provided the air power during the attack. On the ground were the foot soldiers and military tanks of the Arab allied nations. The outcome of the war was unexpected by the enthusiastic Arab warmongers that planned the attack. The military command of Israel was brave in its defense. The Israeli Defense Forces were able to hold back the enemy's forces both on the air and on the ground. The 1967 plan to destroy the state of Israel was sufficiently frustrated by the result of the war. Israel regained control of some of its territory that the Arab countries had occupied since the war of 1948. However, the outcome of the Six-Day War came nowhere near to recovering all the territory of Israel, which is in the hands of its Arab neighbors. Still, the dramatic outcome of the war is an occasion that all the parties of the conflict should remember. The Arabs in the West Bank, East Jerusalem and Gaza changed the dimension of the war to political conflict after the state of Israel recovered the territory in the 1967 war. The Arab residents of the West Bank and East Jerusalem were mainly the Jordanian diasporas. They united themselves under the single name of Arab Palestinians and started the struggle to independently regain control of the territory.

Except for the Oslo Accord, the Arab population in the state of Israel is not a formal community but a number of clustered immigrant families of common Arab origin. The alleged border that existed before the 1967 war has never represented the true and natural border of the country of Israel.

The Arab residents of the West Bank, East Jerusalem, and Gaza had settlement rights and home building permits issued by the Jordanian and Egyptian municipal councils, which controlled the area. On reclaiming the area, the state of Israel forced out the foreign municipal councils. Israel dismantled the Arab made border, which had run into its mainland since the war of 1948. The Jewish state also overturned the land ownership rights of the Arab population. The Arab Palestinians cleverly called the occupied Jewish land their homeland because the charters created by the United Nations supported the plan with a guarantee that they would own the land.

Neither the declaration by the Arabs nor the United Nations charters over the disputed territory are integrated with any real truth about the Promised Land. The only purpose of the claim is to regain control of the land from which the allied Arab countries chased out the Jews from 1920 to 1948. The fact that the Jews recovered part of their homeland during the war of 1967 did not make them illegal occupiers of their own property.

The United Nations engaged the political land conflict in Israel in the wrong way. The organization has reshaped the Promised Land since the end of the Second World War, but ultimately, God will return on the ground. The organization of the United Nations does not have the power to influence the politics of the place for good, even if it wants to continue doing so. The position of the United Nations concerning the conflict in Palestine is viewed in this book as the Bible predicted; the insurgence against the Kingdom of Israel was deliberately started to harm the divinity of the nation. The United Nations' guarantee to the Arabs is the influence that confuses the Arabs to make confiscating the Jewish heritage the subject of their ultimate goal.

Both the Arabs and the United Nations deny the outstanding history of the Promised Land, and both proclaim as nonsense the divine mandate that established the Jewish Kingdom of Israel on the land. The concept of the occupied West Bank and East Jerusalem, which the Arab Palestinians proclaim, was invented after the Israeli Defense Forces recovered the territory by defeating the Arabs allied countries. The West Bank is the area of the Promised Land known to the Jews as Judea and Samaria. The area contains the coastline on the western bank of the Dead Sea. When the Arab Jordanians annexed the territory in year of 1948, they meant to maintain the coastline and to use it as the extended border of the country of Jordan. But the plan was lost on the battlefield.

In view of the divine mandate that established the covenant of Israel on the land of Canaan, the whole world has been put at risk by the passion of a political experiment in which the United Nations and its agencies have resettled Arab Muslims on the holy ground. The thought that the Jews must abandon any of their homelands dangerously places the political authority of the United Nations against the sovereignty of God.

The Lord gave the entire land of Canaan to the generations of Israel. The land of Canaan is wholly represented as the Promised Land. God laid the boundary of the land at the south of Lebanon and across Gaza to the Brook of Egypt and eastward beyond the valley of the Jordan River. God defined the border and constituted the area, which He described as a land with overlapping boundaries. The name of Israel is established by the decree of God. Israel as the name of a country is derived from the standpoint of the inheritance of Isaac and Jacob, and Israel marks the origin of the concept of a holy land. Naming the land of Canaan after Israel was done by divine approval, and it happened when the children of Israel entered the land of the Canaanites as a free nation born in the Egyptians' bondage. Emperor Hadrian of the Roman Empire called the Kingdom of Israel Palestine in accord with the political rudeness of his age. He left in the generations of the Middle East the legacy to live life under the consequences of his action.

The name "Zion" refers to Jerusalem, and for thousands of years the city of Zion represented the capital of the inherited Promised Land. Mount Zion is the Temple Mount. The Hebrew prophets used the name of Zion in contexts that symbolized Judaism. "Zion" in the Bible refers to both the future prophecy of the holy land and the lasting Jewish identity. Modern Zionism is a concept with the associated meaning of Israel, especially as a movement for improving the established independence of the Jewish state or rather with concern to developing national unity in Israel.

The border of the Promised Land is intended to stand as the Lord decreed when He commanded the whole land of Canaan into the hands of Moses. The Lord said to Moses, "Command the Israelites and say to them, 'when you enter Canaan, the land that will be allotted to you as an inheritance will have these boundaries: your southern side will include some of the Desert of Zin along the border of Edom. On the east, your southern boundary will start from the end of the Salt Sea, across south of Scorpion Pass continue on to Zin and go south of Kadesh Barnea. Then it will go to Hazar Addar and over to Azmon where it will turn to join the Wadi of Egypt, and end at the Sea. Your western boundary will be the coast of the Great Sea. This will be your boundary on the west. For the northern boundary, run a line from the Great Sea to Mount Hor and from Mount Hor to Lebo Hamath. Then, the boundary will go to Zedad, continue to Ziphron and end at Hazar Enan. This will be your boundary on the north. For your eastern boundary, run a line from Hazar Enan to Shepham. The boundary will go down from Shepham to Ribiah on the east of Ain and continue along the slopes east of the Sea of Kinnereth. Then the boundary will go down along the Jordan and end at the Salt Sea. This will be your land, with its boundary on every side.'"[77]

According to modern geography, the state of Israel exists in a small part of the holy land. The Jews are confined to less than 30 percent of the God's constituted Promised Land.

The fourth generation of the children of Jacob was in 14 BC the freed nation of Israel. Moses, Joshua, and Aaron served the people in the desert as mentors. They guided the people in the rule of God's law. The Israelites lived under theocracy and worked according to the ordinance of the Lord's covenant of grace.[78] The quote, "I am your God and you are my people" contains the words of the covenant, which brought every Israelite from the Egyptian bondage face-to-face with the rule of God's law.[79] The people promised by the covenant to be on the Lord's side. They followed the Lord by living in His ordinance of worship. The Lord made Israel a great nation and stood up the people with the covenant of their father Abraham.[80] The divine system of leadership was led into the time of the Judges. God used the Judges to govern both the religious and the political lives of the people. He made the rules and appointed the Judges.

Then the Lord approved Saul, son of Kish[81] the Benjamite, and he ruled over the Israelites as king. Since then, the nation of Israel was ruled by kings until the modern political era, during which the people made themselves into a political state.

---

[77] Numbers 34:1-12.

[78] See Exodus 7:4, Numbers 21:14 and Deuteronomy 33:5. Theocracy is a governing system in which God is the supreme leader of the people. The nation of Israel had the terms of the rule of God's law in its early history. The people were His army, and every war that came upon the nation was Yahweh's war. He defended the people.

[79] Leviticus 26:12; "You have declared this day that the Lord is your God and that you will walk in His way, that you will keep His decrees, commands and laws; and that you will obey Him. And the Lord has declared this day that you are His people, His treasured possession as He promised, and that you are to keep all His commands" (Deuteronomy 26:17-18).

[80] Exodus 19-24.

[81] 1 Samuel 8-9.

In 1946, the United Nations formally returned to the Jews the portion of the land that formed the political state of Israel. More Jewish Diasporas returned home when the Second World War ended, and they rebuilt the homeland. The Jewish nation has been openly called both Israel and Palestine since the time of the Roman Emperor Hadrian. The political independence of the Jewish nation was officially upheld in 1948 when the United Nations terminated the mandate that deployed both the British and the French armies in the region.

Arabs have lived in the Kingdom of Israel since the Muhammadans' invasion, and they enjoyed the strength of the Islamic rulers (the caliphates and the Ottoman Empire) that extended control over the Promised Land.

The world inherited twisted facts of history with the growing population of Arabs in the West Bank and Gaza. Every known historical fact about the Jewish territory is being confused owing to the problem of population increase. The right of the Jews to return home after the Second World War was their birthright. Many Jews left the homeland of Israel for long periods of time because of the terrors of foreign occupying powers. The Arab allied countries did not lose practically any Arab land during the war of 1967. The war forced them to surrender to the Jews a fraction of the Jewish land in their possession.

Both the Arab Palestinians and the Arab Jordanians are foreign members of the Jewish Kingdom of Israel. By the rule of God's law, the Islamic country of Jordan is an illegal settlement. God's law settled the right that Jews have to forever own the land of Canaan. This is stronger than the passion by which the United Nations and its agencies declare that Arabs deserve to exist in as many false nations as is sufficient for them to destroy the future of humanity.

Both the Arab Palestinians and the United Nations are nervous in looking at any divine circumstance that could determine the final outcome of the conflict. Popular opinion regarding the conflict is that the solution should not be a matter of the divine truth. The Arabs know as well as the United Nations that the Promised Land belonged to the Israelites. The organization of the United Nations drafts charters that counter the divine mandate of the Promised Land and helps the Arabs to publicly suppress evidence that shows the land dispute as being motivated by humanity's disloyalty to God.

The government of Israel understands the importance of the legitimate position of Jews not as occupiers but as the rightful owners of the land. It is a political fact that the state of Israel asked the Arabs in the West Bank and Gaza to recognize both the legality of the Jewish state and the right Jews have to exist on the land. The demand by the state of Israel is a huge political weight on the real motive of the conflict. But it is not yet clear to me, and perhaps to other people, if the Jewish state of Israel should stand by the demand.

The impression of the demand is that the Arab Palestinians should have a say in deciding the fate of Israel. The fate of Israel is in the hands of God. Israel is more meaningful in being the nation of God than it is in being reprimanded about peace by its unwavering enemy.

The Arab Jordanians significantly lost the authority to control both East Jerusalem and the West Bank in 1967 by losing the Six-Day War. The Arab Palestinians are by no means surrendering to the reality that exists according to the defeat.

On the other hand, the demand by Israel is adequate if the confederation of the Arab regimes in the Middle East, and particularly the Arab Palestinians, understand that the state of Israel wants them to always remember that all Arabs on the Promised Land are strangers.

The Arab Palestinians that reject the demand of Israel know they have nothing to lose in the struggle. Every negotiation on the political settlement of the conflict provides gain to the Arabs. The Arab Palestinians are proud that they are able to withstand the Jews in every step of the conflict. They have the courage that opens the channel for global hostility toward the state of Israel.

People should pay attention to the political analysis of the conflict, which shows the Western secular movement and the radicalized Islamic groups complementing each other in the fight to destroy the state of Israel. The Arab Palestinians receive the support of both the radicalized Islamic groups and the Western secular government. Israel is a nation with a strong connection to God's business, and the Lord's name is the reason the Jewish nation is hated by secular minds. The secular movement prefers a secular Jewish state to exist in Israel rather than the everyday attitude about the coming of the Lord. The strong sentiment of welcoming the throne of God in Israel is something that the secular movement wants to stop by giving support to the Arab Muslims. There is a systematic move on the part of secular movement to uproot from reality and confused within history everything that made the Christian faith unique. Christianity is the only belief that strongly confronts the conscience of the secular world, using the Word of God, in both historical and the present and future concept. The Word of God is standing out, and is challenging humanity's diversion from the works of righteousness. Therefore, the rising climate of anti-theological opinion is more and more to remove the Christian belief from its foundation in history, and to place Christianity in a supra-temporal and supra-history realm. A good way they believe they could achieve this aim is the twisted and unrealistic perception of the state of Israel among the gathering of nations, by which Arab Palestinians play victims of the land conflict. These people know that Christianity is strong evidence of the historical work of God with humanity, which reveals the present and predicts the future.

Also, the radicalized Islamic groups are frustrated by the length of the conflict with the Jews. Their frustration, however, stems not from the failure of the plan to make Islam the ruler of the Promised Land. The Islamic groups are frustrated by the slow nature of the progress. The expanding housing projects in Israel and the military defense assistance package to the state of Israel by the United States of America are both serious setbacks to the Muslims' plan. Second, the growth of Christianity has returned in many parts of the Middle East. Christianity did not die out in the region as the Caliphates expected. Third, the Messianic Jews have an ongoing plan to rebuild the temple of Jerusalem on its original site. The difficult political obstacles in the way of rebuilding the temple are not the real concern the people of Israel face regarding the site.

The demand for the Arab Palestinians to first and foremost recognize the state of Israel as the legitimate homeland of all Jews is politically a gateway to get temporal peace to exist between the two people. An official and more practical recognition of the state of Israel as the rightful home of the Jews will benefit the political peace process for the time being. The recognition will, in practice, bring back some respect to the right that the Jews have to exist on their home territory. In return, the neighborhood of the Arab Palestinians could become a country created out of political goodwill. The demand is a measure that appeals to the Arab Palestinians to acknowledge that Israel owns the land and that only Israel can offer the humanitarian goodwill that would enable them to call any part of the holy land their home country.

The whole land of Canaan is the Jewish heritage, but the Arab Palestinians exist in the West Bank and Gaza with an increasing population that has no other place to go. The thought that the Arab Palestinian state can exist next door to the state of Israel as a demilitarized friendly state is a humane gesture, but we must not forget that God is not always in our thoughts. The state of Israel has considered the platform of the two-state solution out of willingness to live in peace with its Arab neighbors. If I may clarify, the idea of both the Emirate of Transjordan and a Palestinian state is a three-state solution with Israel.

The people that forget history are those that repeat the mistakes of history. It is not the Arab birthright to inherit any part of the Promised Land. The plan for a three-state solution could be a path to peace, but it is a serious danger to the national security of Israel. The Arab Palestinians have no military threat of any kind and are currently unable to organize a strong and advanced military defense system of their own. Except the Jewish nation of Israel, the rest of the Middle East countries are largely in the confederation of the Arab Muslim Brotherhood. The military defense system of Israel is sufficient to protect the Arab Palestinian state if war is waged on its people. This offer by the state of Israel is politically as good as it should be. But the offer is like a bitter pill to the Islamic extremist groups who fight to end the existence of Israel.

The Arab Palestinians are faced with two difficult political scenarios: to achieve the Arab Palestinian state and, through the state, help to extinguish the nation of Israel. The Arab Palestinians opposed the concept of creating a demilitarized friendly state next to the state of

Israel. Eventually the Arab Palestinians will bring about the reason that the Bible predicted humiliation to Israel on the occasion of the upcoming multinational war that will divide Jerusalem. Sympathetic voices are rising and congregating in favor of the Arab Palestinians' voices that cry out for help. Every piece of the land associated with the Arab Palestinians' struggle is gradually being examined for the international community to decide the range of their support for the war against the Jews. The upcoming war will be justified by hatred, and some nations will follow the lead and repeat the crimes that Adolf Hitler committed against the Jews in the Second World War. Jews will temporally forfeit the part of Jerusalem that has been the consciousness of Israel for over four thousand years and has been settled by Jews for thousands of years.

Demography plays a crucial role in the conflict. The Arab Palestinians use population increase as a war tactic. A high number of Arab Palestinians are in deprived conditions, and this situation strengthens their demand to have more of the Jewish land. The populations of the Arab Palestinians in the West Bank, Gaza, and East Jerusalem have significantly increased in recent years. The general populations in these areas are higher than the populations of some recognized sovereign states. Humanitarian organizations do not necessarily admire the things that the Jews have accomplished in the land, because of their view of the suffering of the Arab Palestinians among the degraded conditions of refugee camps.

The state of Israel has its own problem that is opposed to the Arab Palestinians' suffering. Securing better living conditions for the Arab Palestinians must not cause others to ignore the real cause of their suffering. The Arab Palestinians refuse to compromise for peace as the Jews have repeatedly done in all the years of the conflict. Israel suffers from a fundamental diplomatic failure of its own, beyond misreading the true intention of the PLO. Israel focuses its negotiating power on the abstract goal of peace, whereas the Arab Palestinians' diplomatic energy is centered on the concrete goal of achieving a new Arab state on the homeland of Israel. These positions led the negotiation in the direction of Arab Palestinians' articulated objective and caused the erosion of Israel's legitimate rights.

Jerusalem is the unifying capital of Israel under the exclusive Jewish sovereignty. Israel is considered lucky by any careful study of the historic record. The history of the region vindicates Israel of any wrongdoing in the disputed territory. Israel has a well-defined title in the entire territory of Canaan. The Arab Palestinians failed to realize that they had already gotten what they wanted from the conflict. The Arab Palestinians endured the process of becoming the people that they are not. Like any other foreign people who have lived on the Promised Land, they have only this moment of history to enjoy their gain. It is necessary for their own political survival that the Arab Palestinians adopt politics without bitterness.

CHAPTER 6

ISRAEL AND THE GOSPEL

The kingdom of heaven came to earth when God entered human history as a man. He first came as a suffering servant for the sins of the world and then in the Spirit as a victorious conqueror of sin and death. The kingdom of heaven will not be fully realized until the second coming of the Lord Jesus Christ. Then the devil in our world will be judged and removed. Jesus Christ departed the earth, living behind Him the advocate of the truth who guides and helps people that want to achieve victory over the devil. That advocate is the Holy Spirit. His work of righteousness is done through His influence on people via the willpower of the human conscience.

We do not know the Holy Spirit by His appearance but by what He does and by feeling His presence. The Bible describes the Holy Spirit as a living breath, a redeemer, and a divine force. He does not pay attention to Himself but to the love of God. The Father wants to express Himself in the lives of people through the influence of the Holy Spirit, that people may walk in the righteousness of His truth and lives by His means. The Holy Spirit guided the Jewish scribes to write the Holy Scripture. The holy book of prophecy gave a motive for the coming of the Messiah and provoked the reason He was nailed to the cross.

The Psalmist wrote, "The stone the builders rejected has become the cornerstone."[82] The old man Simeon said when he held the child Jesus Christ in the temple, "Behold this child is destined to cause the falling and rising of many in Israel, and to be a sign that will be spoken against, so that the thoughts of many hearts will be revealed."[83] The stone the builders rejected is the one true Spirit force that affects people differently through the same means. He gives various knowledge and abilities to different people. The Jews were familiar with the prophecy that spoke of the Messiah's blessing to their nation, but they did not give their attention to the prophecy that brought the salvation of God to the entire world. God prepared the nation of Israel to gather people of all nations into the one kingdom of God. The Lord said to the Israelites in the book of Isaiah, "It is too small a thing for you to be my servant to restore the tribes of Jacob and bring back those of Israel I have kept. I will also make you a light for the Gentiles that you may bring my salvation to the end of the earth."[84] The Pharisees missed the point of the message and disrespected the Messiah when He came to the earth. As descendants of Abraham, the Pharisees thought they knew the mind of God better than others.[85]

The Jewish unbelief represented one of the greatest obstacles to general acceptance of the Gospel in all circumstances of persecution, which the Church of Christ suffered for spreading the Gospel. A considerable number of Jews believed the Gospel and became Christians. But the nation of Israel was not only unbelieving but also bitterly hostile to the mission of the Christ. The young Christian Church took upon itself serious persecutions that followed after Jesus Christ ascended to heaven. The persecutions were severe and painful, but the Gospel survives by the guiding influence of the Holy Spirit.

The Jews of the time of the Apostles were keen in persecuting the Church from the point of every opportunity they had. Their unbelief made trouble for the Apostles in almost every place the Apostles went on their mission. Even today many Jews refute the Christian faith and

---

[82] Psalm 118:22.

[83] Luke 2:34-35.

[84] Isaiah 49:6.

[85] "They answered Him, 'We are Abraham's descendants and have never been slaves to anyone. How can you say that we shall be set free?'" (John 8:33).

resent the salvation that Jesus Christ died for. Christians does not impress the Jews by proclaiming the Lord Jesus Christ is the Messiah. The smear campaign that the unbelieving Jews directed against the lordship of Jesus Christ, is the main reason some Christian scholars raised questions about the priesthood of Israel. The Christian scholars concluded that the Church is the spiritual Israel. The point they made for the argument is that Jesus Christ is the High Priest of all worshippers of God "and therefore everyone who receives Him and believes in Him, to those He gave the right to become children of God – children that were not born of natural descent and a husband's will, but people born of God."[86]

There are other reasons the Christian scholars kept themselves arguing the case. Among their thoughts is the notion that the Church should focus on spreading the good news of repentance rather than being distracted by the Jewish unbelief. Another is that the death of Jesus Christ on the Cross of Calvary paid the wages of humanity's sin and ended the atonement of animal sacrifice. Both Jewish and Christian worshippers enjoy the privilege of the freedom from animal sacrifice, and both people celebrate worship with the spiritual freedom that Jesus Christ provided to reach all peoples and nations. Yet Christians are alone in proclaiming to the world the importance of receiving spiritual freedom.

The unbelieving Jews support denying Jesus Christ. There is no other authority that the Jewish Scripture indicates to replace the Lord Jesus Christ. If the Jews are truly expecting another messiah than the Lord Jesus Christ, they should exercise the law of burnt offerings until the Messiah arrives. Or is it that Christians are misreading the Jewish hope? The hope to receive a political messiah has been the national desire in Israel. It has been expressed by the Jewish religious leadership since the time of the Roman Empire. The expectation of a political messiah in Israel is certain to make the Jews welcome the Antichrist before they recognize the Messiah by His second coming.

The Jews say that they expect a messiah who will both unite the world in God the Father and bring peace to the world. They fail to really

---

[86] John 1:12-13.

understand that no one united the world like Jesus Christ and no one unites the world like He is doing. More than two thousand years ago, the Lord Jesus Christ started His message of "love from God's Kingdom"[87] in the tiny village of the ancient Nazareth. His message is alive and reaches worldwide in the salvation of God.

Righteousness is not a religion, and the Lord Jesus Christ is the spirit's faith. The salvation of God is His response to human suffering. The true congregation of God's worshippers is not determined by any particular folk or temple but by the indwelling influence of the Holy Spirit. Jesus Christ is the Messiah of the Jews' own Scripture and prophecy. The Jewish unbelief tells about the work of Satan and his way of depriving people of the love of God. The Holy Spirit is the guide to lead the Jews from the wrong way into the right way to love God. It is not done by power, and it is not done by might – says the Lord.

God said to the people of Israel when they entered the land of the Canaanites, "The Lord will grant that the enemies who rise against you will be defeated before you. They will come at you from one direction, but flee from you in seven. The Lord will send a blessing on your barns and on everything you put your hand to. The Lord will establish you as His holy people, as He promised you on oath. If you keep the commands of the Lord your God and walk in His way; then all the peoples on earth will see that you are called by the name of the Lord, and they will fear you… However, if you do not obey the Lord your God and do not carefully follow all His commands and decrees I am giving you today, all these curses will come upon you and overtake you. You will be cursed in the city and cursed in the country. Your basket and your kneading trough will be cursed. The fruit of your womb will be cursed, and the crops of your land, and the calves of your herds and the lambs of your flocks. You will be cursed when you come in and when you go out."[88]

The nation of Israel is intended to be a holy nation, and the Jews are

---

[87] "As my Father has loved me, so I have loved you. Now remain in my love. If you obey my commands, you will remain in my love, just as I have obeyed my Father's command and remain in His love" (John 15: 9 -10).

[88] . Deuteronomy 28:7-10 and Deuteronomy 28:15-19.

not ordinary people in God's plan. The country of Israel is not a land to be reckoned with the secular things of this world. The people and the administration suffer punishment from God whenever they ride on evil's wing. The open gate stands before the nation of Israel, and the ingathering of the saints is happening now. The Spirit gives evidence that the Gospel is not part of any human agenda. The Apostle Paul said, "I speak the truth in Christ – I am not lying, my conscience confirms it in the Holy Spirit. I have great sorrow and unceasing anguish in my heart. For, I could wish that I myself were cursed and cut off from Christ for the sake of my brothers, those of my own race, the people of Israel. Theirs is the adoption as sons; theirs is the divine glory, the covenant, the receiving of the law, the temple worship, and the promises. Theirs are the patriarchs, and from them is traced the human ancestry of Christ, who is God over all, forever praised! Amen."[89]

Paul lived the experience of religious duplicity. Paul, as Saul, was active in politicizing the worship of God before he repented and believed the Gospel. He opposed the viewpoint of Jews who embraced both God and the attitude of this secular world. His letter to the Romans is part of the debate about Israel ceasing being the vanguard of the way to God. Nonetheless, the New Testament concept of salvation did not in any way set aside the importance of the Jewish nation as a people of God. The basic framework of the New Testament is reconciliation, and none of the Gospel writers dwelled on the sins of any people. The New Testament explains the love of God as it joins all people in God and to the final salvation that will conclude the spiritual history of Israel. God will fully gather the saints and then bring the age to its end.

The debate over how the Church should tackle the problem of non-Christian Jews is the brainchild of the so-called replacement theology. The concept of replacement theology has raised controversy between evangelical Christian scholars and mainstream church theologians. The evangelical Christian scholars favor the presumption that the Church takes the place and the role of Israel in conventional worship. They say

---

[89] Romans 9:1-5.

that Christians dominate evangelizing the world and by all practical standpoints they lead biblical worship. The current nation of Israel lacks the momentum that performs the function of spiritual leadership, especially in reconciling the world to God. Evangelical Christians perceive the modern state of Israel as a spiritually failing state. Moral crimes in Israel and elsewhere are the same. There is no difference in the state's sponsored ethical policy on the chosen people of God and the rest of the world.

I prefer that the state of Israel engage its citizens to do the work of righteousness than that the Lord raise in Israel a new nation of faith to bring His millennial goal to fulfillment. The nation of Israel departs the center stage of true worship and embraces the secular lifestyle of its gentile allies. The Jews that reject the Gospel also persecute the Christians. More Christians defend the covenant of God and Israel than there are Jews who would want to defend the Gospel.

Devoted Christians around the world see the land of Canaan wholly as representing the Jewish national homeland. But there was the holocaust, when the nations of the earth – including the institution of the Church – failed the Jews. The Church leaders failed to speak out in defense of the Jewish populations that were faced with extinction. The holocaust would not have been massive had this been the case. The crimes that were committed during the holocaust are serious crimes, and it should never again happen to any people. The institution of the Church is as guilty as the secular nations are on this matter. But the love of Christ is here to bear the anger that lingers in the minds of new generations of Jews about the holocaust. It is the wrong thing to do when Christians of any nation put national interest above the defense of righteousness. It is our duty as Christians to defend righteousness even if our actions could mean either death to us or disobedience of government rule in order to safe innocent lives.

People who examine the Gospel of Jesus Christ through studying the history of the Church must distinguish between the Gospel itself and the things corrupt and unfaithful Christians did to other people in the name of serving the Lord. We know that without the influence of the Holy

Spirit, the Gospel would vanish in the minds of people. The moments of both the evil rulers of this earth and the evil spiritual kingdom in high places are critical. The consequence of evil's repression of righteousness is felt in every nation by innocent blood. Jews and Gentiles alike bear the suffering of righteousness. The dark powers of this world are not restricted to any boundaries or peoples. The Iraq War is a useful analogy for this subject.

The Iraq War, which began in 2003, was a key factor among recent political problems that helped me to understand some past events. Through the events that led to the actual bombardment of Iraq, I was able to understand how it was possible that nations of the earth, including the Christian Church, did not prevent the holocaust from happening. The Nazis otherwise would have been prevented from carrying out the massive attack, or many Jews and other victims of the war would have been carefully protected from the attack. But the world was silent to the crimes of the war, and people looked aside. The experience of war crimes is alive in current political affairs.

Mass murder is still being committed around the world, and the attitude of people reacting to the crimes is the same today as it was when the holocaust was committed. People would rather talk about what was done wrong than stand up and prevent the wrong that is about to happen. During the years that led to the Iraq War, every nation and institution perceived the reality of an evil slaughter that was about to come upon the people of Iraq, the fluxes of economic and political sanctions on the state of Iraq, the falsification of a cause to fight the war, and the arrogant spirits that laid out the plan of the war. Yet no nation or institution did what should have been done in righteousness to prevent the most brutal bloodshed of our modern history.

As was the case with the holocaust, the Iraqis did not deserve the slaughter that was wrought on them. The political freedom and democracy the Americans and the British brought to Iraq through the 2003 invasion was the jolt that produced the increase in Islamic militia insurgence. Leaders of big countries and heads of big institutions have the great power to do whatever can be done to help secure the earth with peace.

But on the contrary, no court of justice holds them accountable for the occasions when they abuse the power they have. As a matter of fact, chaos and bloodshed in the aftermath of the Iraq invasion are holding strong across the Middle East. The rise of militant Islamic insurgence both in the region and elsewhere in Africa and Europe is a direct result of the war that was started in Iraq. The official reason for starting the bloodshed in Iraq is confusing; no truth has been told in any public statement concerning the real motive for invading Iraq. Any lesson from the invasion of Iraq cannot change the past, and it does not make the warmongers look differently at the current situation.

Other grievances might exist between the leadership of Judaism and the heads of the Christian Church. But speaking generally, the Jews are less eager to defend the Christian faith; otherwise the concern of the Church on the holy land would have been solved. The Jews that persecute the Church inspire heathens and the Muslim community to look upon Christians as separate people.

Some members of the Christian Church do not properly recognize the relationship that exists between the Old Testament and the New Testament. The Jews themselves does not regard the Gospel as a relevant part of the Scripture. They do not believe in Jesus Christ, the son of God. The debate about God's salvation exists on both sides.

So far the Arab Palestinians have benefited from the lukewarm relationship that exists between the Christians and the non-Christian Jews. The political concern that prompted the unbelieving Jews to misunderstand the mission of Jesus Christ is unfortunate. Both the Jews and the Christians should learn to protect each other. The sites and the cities of our common faith should be protected from the Muslims Brotherhood. The Shia and the Sunni Muslims may have bitter differences, and sometimes they engage each other in war. But nothing divides them when they protect Islamic heritage against foreign beliefs.

Jesus Christ suffered at the hands of the Jews, but He neither denied His Jewish identity nor supported anyone that denied His Jewish rights. His people rejected Him, but He did not give any different meaning to His relationship with His people. Nothing can change the fact that Jesus

Christ was Jewish. God appointed His Son from the Kingdom of Israel. Nothing can change the fact that the first Apostles to the gentile nations were Jewish. Abraham, on whom the blessing of God rested to reach all peoples of the earth, was Jewish. Abraham was the father of the Jewish nation and the first biblical person to be called Hebrew. These facts came from a divine source. They are non-amendable, even though the current political situation in Israel does not impress many Christians.

God acts in the history of humanity even when humanity is not aware of His presence or the purpose of His act. The election of Israel is an expression of the mystery of God's ways. We may not be able to explain why the revelation of God came when it did and where it did. The prophets of Israel provided no evidence to show that the Jews are religiously more discerning and better in character than other peoples of the world. The book of Deuteronomy says that God's choice of Israel is not for the worth of Israel but is a free act of grace bestowed for the sake of all humanity. Moses said to the people of Israel, "It is not because of your righteousness or your integrity that you are going to take possession of their land; but on account of the wickedness of these nations. The Lord your God will drive them out before you, to accomplish what He swore to your fathers; to Abraham, Isaac, and Jacob. Understand, then, that it is not because of your righteousness that the Lord your God is giving you this good land to possess, for you are stiff-necked people."[90]

God raised the nation of Israel out of slavery in Egypt as an expression of sovereign freedom and unmerited love. If we can provide another reason as to why God elected the people of Israel, we can also make God's actions conditional and thereby reduce them to something less than an expression of divine freedom and grace.

God manifests His sovereignty over the whole world through the history of the people of Israel. Paul said, "The Scripture foresaw that God would justify the Gentiles by faith and announced the Gospel in advance to Abraham. 'All nations will be blessed through you.' So those who have faith are blessed along with Abraham, the man of faith...' God redeemed

---

[90] Deuteronomy 9:5-6.

the nation of Israel in order that the blessing given to Abraham might come to the Gentiles through Christ Jesus; so that by faith we might receive the promise of the Spirit... If you belong to Christ, then you are Abraham's seed, and heirs according to the promise."[91]

It could be argued that Jesus Christ looked upon His disciples as the spiritual lifeline of Israel. That is to say, that the disciples of Jesus Christ accepted His proclamation of the kingdom of God and therefore formed the true people of God. People that argue using this line of thought forget that neither Jesus Christ nor His disciples formed a separate synagogue or separate temple of worship because of the New Testament approach. Jesus Christ and His disciples did not start any separate movement outside the foundation of worship that is in Israel. Jesus Christ prayed and preached in the temple of Jerusalem, and He asked His followers to copy His example. Jesus Christ paid homage to the temple of Jerusalem in celebration of God, who came and dwelled among His people. He did not set aside His day of return that will bring with Him the heavenly ideal tabernacle.

Severe persecution came upon the Church after Jesus Christ ascended to heaven and His disciples did not in any outward way break away from the traditional temple worship in Israel. Instead, the disciples kept up the externally distinguished practice of spreading the Gospel in the name of the Lord Jesus Christ. The Gospel expands worldwide owing to the effort of the sent Holy Spirit, and today church buildings exist nearly everywhere; more churches exist than Jewish synagogues. The ideological gap that exists between Judaism and Christianity is present because of the unrighteousness in people.

It is arguable, and it is historically correct to say, that the religion of Islam came about because of leadership failures by both the Christians and the Jews. In search of other influences that could form true faith in God, the Prophet Muhammad started the religion of Islam and called his new faith the true way to God.

---

[91] Galatians 3:8-9, Galatians3:14 and Galatians. 3:29.

CHAPTER 7

SNATCHING THE HOLY LAND

The Jewish political leaders have made the national security of Israel more dependent on foreign military alliances than on the promise of God. The Kingdom of Israel is exclusively established in the rule of God's law, and any political classification of the law of God should neither redefine nor redact the basic principles of the law. The United Nations does not have jurisdiction over the Promised Land; it should support the sovereignty of the rule of God's law. What happens is that the United Nations bases its political charter on the holiness of the land, knowing that the organization is not a qualified partner of holiness.

The mixed outlook of Israel formulating national defense policy largely by trusting in foreign political alliance is affecting the public perception of Israel's relationship with God. Israel deals with highly sensitive spiritual subjects in its conflict with the Arab Muslims. Allowing secular politics to influence the religious aspect of the Kingdom of Israel is the factor that brings disrespect to the faith that Jews confess in God. The mixed public outlook is probably the most dangerous political factor in the conflict of Israel and its Arab neighbors. Israel's passion for foreign military support is an attitude that contradicts Jewish national spiritual importance.

The Jewish citizens of Israel are being increasingly secularized by the attitude of the state of Israel, which responsively embraces the friendliness of its gentile allies. Instead of helping Israel to regain the natural area of the Promised Land, the foreign military defense allies of Israel encourage Israel to further decrease its size. The concession being demanded by the United Nations on behalf of Arabs of Palestine is unwarranted, given the current size and position of the state of Israel in the Middle East.

Dozens of abstract political negotiations for peace twisted the importance of Israel regarding religious faith. Ambiguity in the foreign military coalition with regard to the state of Israel jeopardizes the role Jews should play in everyday discussions about having true faith in the living God. Some of the accounts about the national defense strategy of Israel are intended to convince, but in reality, the accounts further separate Israel from the grand work of the truth. The Bible is crucial in setting straight the role of Israel in the political affairs of the world.

The first task that exists for every nation is to embrace the truth and determine by experience if truth exists in our own historical experiment. Manmade documents and experimentation are constantly challenged by huge mistakes. Consider the generations that passed while humanity believed the earth was flat. What if other things of this life that people think they know or think they have the solution to are not what they think they are?

The practical outcome of resisting the sovereignty of God is the deterioration of humanity. The human experiment regarding peace and stability validates the Bible as the primary source of truth. The enemies of Israel are not in the political peace process to make good negotiating partners but rather to make Israel suffer the hard way during every step of its existence.

Jerusalem and the Abrahamic Religions:

Jews, Christians and Muhammadans recognized Jerusalem as an important site of pilgrimage. The mutual conclusion lies with the faith that Abraham confessed in God. The three groups of God's worshippers confess faith in God with great honor being given to the relationship between God and Abraham, and all three groups accept the tradition that God personally revealed Himself to Abraham. The story of the life of Abraham does not serve the same benefit in the Koran as it does in the Bible. In writing the Koran, the Islamic scholars slightly differentiated the purpose of Abraham. Nonetheless, the differentiated thought did not confuse the common origin of the three beliefs. Abraham was first in his family and the first in Israel to be directly addressed by God. People of God in all past and present generations copy the example of Abraham's faith. Beyond his faithfulness to God, Abraham was a bearer of divine blessing. He was a historical figure by whom the goodness of God is made available in the world. Examining each of the three Abrahamic religions is useful for this topic.

Judaism is the system of worship of the Hebrew worshippers of God, and it was the first direct community worship of the living God. Judaism demonstrates the first public step into the footprint of the covenant of God and Abraham. It is the oldest form of the three Abrahamic religions. The system of worship was directed upon the children of Israel by God Himself. The holy book of Judaism contains the Torah, the Psalms, and the books of the prophets; it is largely the Old Testament.

The practice of Judaism is carried out according to the rule of God's law. Moses established the religion in accordance with the Word of God. The Kingdom of Israel was a God-ruled nation. Theocracy was organized in Israel with fundamental concern regarding the covenant that God had with the Jewish patriarchs. The children of Israel commenced practicing Judaism near the foot of Mount Sinai, where they renewed the covenant of Abraham with the presence of God. The Israelites departed Egypt as a freed nation and journeyed across the Red Sea on desert land until they arrived at Mount Sinai. The people camped near the base of the mountain for eleven months and five days. They had worship ceremonies there, and it was there that they experienced their first direct worship encounter with the presence of God.

The Lord descended on Mount Sinai and stood Himself before the people like a pillar of cloud. The people rejoiced at His presence and honored Him with prayers of verbal admiration. They offered burnt offerings to the Lord at the end of the worship ceremony.[92] This occasion is the beginning of worshippers of God honoring Him together with both silent prayers and praises of verbal admiration. Moses formed the first stone altar that was used for public worship by the gathered crowd. Moses constructed the tabernacle of the Lord after he received the law of God on Mount Sinai. The received instructions pertained to the rule of God's law and the blueprint Moses used when he constructed the tent of meeting.

The presence of the Lord descended on the entrance of the tent on every seventh day, and like a pillar of cloud He visited the people that gathered outside of the tent. Other than on the Sabbath, everyone who sought the Lord would go near the tent of meeting. Moses erected the tent outside the camp and fully separated it from where the people were living. The seventh day is the Sabbath of the Lord, and the Lord's people must honor Him and do no personal work on the Sabbath. God commanded Moses to write in the book of law everything that the people must know about keeping the ordinance of His worship.

God created the heavens and the earth in six days, and He rested on the seventh day, so the Lord said to the people of Israel, "Remember the Sabbath day to keep it holy. Six days you shall labor and do all your work, but the seventh day is the Sabbath of the Lord your God. In it you shall do no work – you, nor your son, nor your daughter, nor your male servant, nor your cattle, nor your strangers who visited your house. For in six days the Lord made the heavens and the earth, the sea, and all that is in them, and rested the seventh day. Therefore, the Lord blessed the Sabbath day and sanctified it."[93]

The children of Israel were the first worship community of the living God. From Sinai onward, the worship of God was at the center of Jewish national life. Worship belonged to the Israelites as the most precious item in the parcel of blessing to their father Abraham. The tent of meeting was an immensely important representation of God's idea of a place of worship. The special meaning of the tent is the likeness of the heavenly ideal tabernacle to come. The later Jewish temples were built upon the

---

[92] Exodus 24: 5 - 6.
[93] Exodus 20: 8-11.

notion of the tent, and Christians copied the notion in building churches. Altars of the Lord in Christian churches can be seen as modified models of the inner sanctuary of the Lord's tabernacle.

The terms "Jew" and "Judaism" originated in the Hebrew word "Yehudah." The equivalent of "Yehudah" in English is Judah. "Yehudah" – or rather "Yeshua" – is also the name of Jesus by way of Greek transliteration. The Jewish identity formed the moral fiber of the Southern Kingdom of Israel beginning in 931 BC. The term "Jew" or "Jewish" applied to anyone belonging to the tribes of Judah and Benjamin when the nation of Israel was divided into two brotherly kingdoms.

God created the Southern and the Northern Kingdoms of Israel after King Solomon died. King Solomon and his foreign wives and concubines led the people of Israel to commit the sin of idolatry against the commandment of the Lord. The reign of King Solomon ended with his death, and God divided the country of Israel into the two commonwealths. God separated the people of Israel and punished them in His disapproval of the sin of worshipping foreign gods, which King Solomon had led them to commit.[94]

Jerusalem was the capital territory of the Southern Kingdom, the Kingdom of Judah. The Northern Kingdom had its capital territory in Samaria, which is the present-day West Bank. Recognizing any Israelite as a Jew began after the Babylonian exile. The term "Jew" was extended to all people of Hebrew origin. It was essential for the native people of Israel to recognize the Jewishness of all Israelites, wherever they were, because the Israelites of the Northern Kingdom were not returned from the Assyrian captivity. From Samaria, the people of the Northern Kingdom

---

[94] "Now it happened at that time, when Jeroboam went out of Jerusalem, that the Prophet Ahijah the shilonite met him on the way; and he had clothed himself with a new garment, and the two were alone in the field. Then Ahijah took hold of the new garment that was on him, and he tore it into twelve pieces. And he said to Jeroboam, 'Take for yourself ten pieces, for thus says the Lord, the God of Israel: "Behold I will tear the kingdom out of the hand of Solomon, and will give ten tribes to you (but he shall have one tribe for the sake of my servant David, and for the sake of Jerusalem, the city which I have chosen out of all the tribes of Israel.) because they have forsaken me, and have worshipped Ashtoreth, the goddess of the Sidonians, Chemosh, the god of the Moabites, and Milcom, the god of the people of Ammon, and have not walked in my ways to do what is right in my eyes and keep my status and my judgments, as did his father David'"" (1Kings 11:29-39).

of Israel were taken into exile in 722 BC by the Assyrian army. There was no official return of the Israelites of the Northern Kingdom. History refers to the ten northern tribes as the lost tribes of Israel.

All people of Hebrew origin throughout the world gradually came to be comprehended as Jews in the same way that all non-Jews were called Gentiles. The Star of David is a symbol of the in-gathering of Jews from around the world, especially after the two major world wars that occurred on the continent of Europe. "Hebrew" was the name that God selected for Abraham and his covenant descendants from Isaac and Jacob. The equivalent of "Hebrew" in modern language is "Israelite." Abraham was the first person of the Old Testament Bible to be referred to as Hebrew.[95] Except through Abraham, the origin of the name Hebrew is uncertain.

The Christian faith is at the center of the New Testament concept of the worship of God. The belief is inherited from Jesus Christ, the Son of God. Christians are to follow the example of the life of Jesus Christ in worshipping God the Father. Christian theology teaches the incarnation of God, the transcendent Father. He first came to the earth in the person of God the Son, and after the Son ascended into heaven, He replaced His presence with God the Holy Spirit. Jesus Christ said to His disciples before He ascended into heaven, "When the Advocate comes, whom I will send to you from the Father, the Spirit of truth who goes out from the Father, He will testify about me. And you also must testify, for you have been with me from the beginning."[96]

The death of Jesus Christ ended all burnt offerings to God. The Son of God concluded the offering for sin with His shed blood on the cross. Now the everyday worship of God the Father is incurred with the power of His Holy Spirit. The redemptive blood of the Son made the spirit's worship gracefully acceptable to the Father without Him altering the rule of law that was in place. Jesus Christ did not change the law of the Mosaic tradition. He fulfilled the demand of the law with His death on the cross. The atonement for sin gives freedom to spirit's worship. The law said, "The wages of sin is death....But now the gift of God is eternal life in

---

[95] Genesis 14:13.
[96] John 15:26-27.

Jesus Christ our Lord."[97] In Him you are set free from sin. You are a child of God through the indwelling presence of the Holy Spirit, who redeems you from the mistakes of this life.

The Lord Jesus Christ said, "Here I am! I stand at the door and knock. If anyone hears my voice and opens the door, I will come in and eat with that person, and they with me. To the one who is victorious, I will give the right to sit with me on the throne, just as I was victorious and sat down with my Father on His throne."[98] The Lord's invitation requires you to surrender your life wholly to Him. He will bring about in you the joy of His salvation and of living the eternal life of God the Father. The indwelling presence of the Holy Spirit of God is the essence of saying that those that received Him are spiritually alive. The Holy Spirit is the miracle of living everyday life in God.

God loves both humankind and everything He created in nature. He uses His presence to overshadow His transcendent nature. God is brought closer to us by the Spirit's presence. The Son broke the barrier of sin to draw humankind back to having a rich personal relationship with the Father. The Christian faith shows that God is part of us through the miracle of His transcendent love. Christians believe that the Lord Jesus Christ is both the begotten Son of God and their personal Savior. His Holy Spirit is responsible for the renewed spirit of worship, and He establishes the Lord's name among the generations of the earth.

The Old Testament progresses into the New Testament in two ways. God chose two men of faith and used their time on earth to set on track the program of our redemption. The first man was Abraham. Abraham was born in the year of 1813 BC and begot the covenant children that inherited the land where the Messiah was born. The second man was King David. The descendants of David are direct ancestors of the Christ. The call and the blessing of Abraham are the true source of Christian belief, but Christianity does not exist to prove that Jesus Christ is the Messiah, and it is not necessary that Christians engage in the argument.

---

[97] Ezekiel 18:4; Romans 6: 23.
[98] Revelation 3:20-21.

Jesus Christ said He is the Messiah of the whole world. He will prove Himself to the world when He comes again. The true purpose of the Christian Gospel reflects the final solution to the spiritual suffering that humanity endures. The concern of God in giving His Son to die is the freeing of humanity from the bondage of sin. The atonement for sin is given, and the spirit's revival is the means to regain the lost closeness to God. The struggle to revive to life the human spirit justified the presence of God in the person of the Christ and the Holy Spirit. With sin, humanity is a problem to God, to each other, and to the environment in which they live. People put both themselves and the environment at risk because they rejected the very means that should help them to exist as moral humanity.

The religion of Muhammadanism was first conveyed to people of the Arabian Desert as the true way to God. The Prophet Muhammad started the religion, but he did not teach people to accept the belief by his own name. Referring to the religion of Muhammad as Muhammadanism suggests both the time period of the belief's inception and how the belief came to exist through the mistakes that dominated the Christian worship of the second century AD. The Prophet Muhammad sought to destroy the unorthodox rituals of both the Christians and the Jews, and he proposed himself to have a different outlook on the traditional theology. He claimed that God spoke to him and started to proclaim his own doctrine of faith.

The earliest people that observed the Prophet Muhammad teach his new faith listened to him with doubt. On hearing him speak about the true way to God, the people nicknamed his teaching Muhammadanism. The Prophet Muhammad had followers that accepted his teaching of faith, and the people called them the Muhammadans. The name of the religion of Muhammad was gradually changed from Muhammadanism to Islam through daily use of the Arabic word "salaam." "Salaam" in the religious sense refers to obedience to the law of God; and in a welcoming sense, it refers to peace and safety. A Muhammadan – or simply Muslim – is someone who believes in God according to the teachings of the Prophet Muhammad.

The Koran is the holy book of Islam, and being Muslim means being submissive to the will of God (Allah), as stated in the Koran. Islam is last in the line of the Abrahamic religions. The Prophet Muhammad was born in Mecca in 570, and he founded the religion of Islam in 610. The people of Mecca were particularly concerned about the Prophet Muhammad at the beginning of his movement, and basically they rejected him as the self-proclaimed prophet of God. Muhammad was forced to flee for his life from Mecca in 622. He escaped to Medina and was received by the people of Medina. It was in Medina that Muhammad organized the revolutionary army, which propagated his new religion with the sword. From then on, the worship of God took a violent dimension in the hands of men who believed the Prophet Muhammad was truly the messenger of God.

The Prophet Muhammad engaged his followers with the principle of his new belief, which was that followers should fight and destroy the corrupt traditional faiths. With his army, the Prophet Muhammad embarked on fighting the war that he called the jihad. His goal with the holy war was to convert all people to follow the true way to God. On horseback, Muhammad and his men forced their way back to Mecca and captured Mecca in 630. Muhammad did not live long enough to witness the expansion of his movement. He died in 632, shortly after he was sixty-two years old. The Prophet Muhammad had eleven women who were his wives, as well as many concubines. Beginning in the Middle East, the death of the Prophet Muhammad was marked by his followers spreading the Islamic Empire of the second century AD by way of caliphates.

Caliphates were ruled by supreme military commanders of the jihad, who were known to their subjects as caliphs. The successor of the Prophet Muhammad was the Caliph Abu Bakr.

Neither the Jews nor the Christians of the Middle East were concerned with the claims of the Prophet Muhammad during the early stage of his movement. The Jews in particular did not look upon the teachings of the Prophet Muhammad as anything that would threaten their traditional beliefs. The Prophet Muhammad was considered one of the many who made false claims about the salvation of God. The attitude of ridiculing the teachings of the Prophet Muhammad in public places was the main reason his followers turned to using brutal force to create converts. The widespread acceptance of the Islamic belief in the Middle East, North Africa, Asia, and some part of Europe was caused by the brutal religious cleansing of the jihad movement. Adversaries would either accept what the Prophet Muhammad said was the right thing to do when praying to God or they would die by his sword.

Jerusalem has been the land of pilgrimage to the Muhammadans since 637, when the Muhammadan army advanced the jihad to southeast of the Arabian Peninsula and captured the Jewish holy city. The Muhammadan army was both eager and desperate in destroying both the old faiths of Jerusalem and the infidels of the new Islamic faith. The army of Muhammad was ready for the war that Islamized many Jewish and Christian territories and some parts of the pagan world.

There are two religious events that linked the Islamic pilgrims to the Promised Land. The birth of Ishmael in Canaan is the first event, and the second event is the alleged visit of the Prophet Muhammad to the throne of God in heaven. Muslims believed the story of Muhammad's visit to be true. According to the account, the Prophet Muhammad took off one night and visited heaven. His journey to heaven started from the place where the Dome of the Rock now stands.

Three factors are attributed to the rapid success of the Muhammadans' jihad. The first factor is the enormous fear of the tribal communities around the Middle East. The second factor is the frustration people felt regarding the unholy practices of the early Christian Church. The third factor is the attitude of the Jewish religious leadership, who interpreted the rule of God's law according to the desires of their own hearts.

The concept of Muhammadanism appeared in the Middle East when serious corrupt practices and leadership failure were part of the Christian Church. The liturgy of the Church Service was saturated with both ritual images and relics of superstition. Perhaps the Prophet Muhammad was so sickened by the horrors of the unholy practices that his determination was hooked on wiping out the corruption. Some Muslim scholars argue that the Prophet Muhammad started the religion of Islam as a puritan and that it was after his death that his followers engaged his mission with the alleged brutal force. The truth of the matter is that the Prophet Muhammad was a strong-minded jihadist.

After he died, his army intensely sustained his defined mission and invaded lands beyond the tribal community of the Arabian Peninsula, where he started his movement. The army of Muhammad captured Syria in 634, Egypt in 638, Persia (Iran) in 689, and the north of Africa and Spain in 711. The religion of Islam then became the main factor that united the various Arabian tribes into one cohesive group of people. The ethnic groups of the Arabian Desert were in constant political and economic conflict before the Prophet Muhammad started both the religion of Islam and the jihad movement.

With the coming of Islam, the Arabian gold mine business was turned into a joint venture of the people. The money raised in the gold mine business was used to sponsor the jihad movement throughout the Middle East. The gold mines paid for the development of Islamic culture in the Middle East and North Africa. Like a swift tsunami, the jihad movement swept through to the lands of North Africa, East Africa, Europe, and Asia. The army of Muhammad almost ended the practice of both Christianity and Judaism in many regions. This was the era when mosques were raised in the temple area of Jerusalem and around the strategic worship places of the holy land.

Charles Martel commanded the Frankish army that defeated the Muhammadans' jihad movement in 732 during the Battle of Tours in France. [99] After that, Constantinople of the Eastern Roman Empire fell to the army of the Ottoman Empire in 1453. The fall of Constantinople jarred Europe with a second threat of the Muhammadans' mass invasion. John Sobieski led the second and final defeated of the Muhammadan army in 1683 during the Battle of Vienna. The Battle of Vienna was the battle of the alliance of John Sobieski and Emperor Leopold of the Polish-Lithuanian Commonwealth. The forces of the allied countries formed the holy league that defeated the invading army of the Islamic

---

[99] Charles Martel was a Frankish statesman and military leader.

Ottoman Empire. Nonetheless, it was Charles Martel and his decisive Battle of Tours in France that saved the rest of Europe and Africa from conversion to Islam by the sword of a brutal force. Without that victory, the concept of Christianity would have been completely overturned by the Muhammadan army.

If the creation of Islam was a judgment passed on both the Jewish religious leadership and the heads of the Christian Church, it is to be hoped the point was well taken. However, the Islamic faith is a worst-case scenario, especially to nations that it conquered. Except for the broad usefulness of Islam in mentioning the name of God every day, many Muslims propagate the Islamic belief with serious bitterness toward any people of a different belief. The current conflict over Jerusalem is not about the right of pilgrimage to Muslims. The fight is about claiming significant victory for Islam by overturning the traditional land ownership rights of the generations of Jews that returned to the holy land after the Second World War.

Genesis chapter 14:18 offers the first mention of the city of Jerusalem in the Bible. The city was then called Salem, and it was under the rule of King Melchizedek, the priest of the Most High God. During the time of the Tell-el-Amarna letters of 1400 BC, the city was called U-ru-sa-lem, which translates to "the city of peace." Jerusalem was the inheritance of the tribe of Benjamin when the children of Israel entered the land of the Canaanites as a free nation. Joshua captured the city in 1450 BC after he defeated King Adonizedek and his allies in battlefield. On the day of the defeat, God listened to the voice of Joshua as He listened to no other man. Joshua prayed to God for the victory, and God stood the sun still over the plain of Gibeon, and the moon was in the valley of Aijalon until the fighting men of Israel defeated King Adonizedek and his allied enemies of God.[100]

Jerusalem was called Jebus when the Jebusites occupied the city. The period of the Jebusites overlapped the period when David was king in

---

[100] This miracle was the result of the sovereign power of God that responded to the prayer of Joshua. It is written, "There has been no day like that, before it or after it that the Lord heeded the voice of a man; the Lord fought for Israel" (Joshua 10:12-14).

Hebron. David and the fighting men of Israel defeated the last stronghold of the Jebusites in Jerusalem and fully returned the city to the Israelites.[101] Jerusalem attained its first civil and ecclesiastical importance as capital of Israel in 1050 BC with King David on the throne of Israel.

King Saul was the first political king of the Israelites. Saul was the king when the boy David killed Goliath, the Philistine army commander. On the day of the defeat, the women of Jerusalem orchestrated songs of praise with flute and tambourine, and danced when the severed head of Goliath was displayed on the streets of Jerusalem.[102] The people of Israel praised God for the courage He gave to David. The boy David killed the mighty Goliath with sling and a stone.

> "As the women danced; they sang,
> 'Saul has slain his thousands and David his tens of
> thousands.'"[103]

Solomon got the throne of Israel after his father, King David, died. Solomon built the magnificent temple of Jerusalem and dedicated the temple to serve all conventional worshippers of the living God. King Solomon prayed to God on the night before the temple was dedicated to His worship, and he asked God to accept the temple as a place of prayer for all nations. The King said in his prayer to God, "Concerning a foreigner, who is not of your people Israel, but has come from a far country for your name's sake - for they too will hear of your great name and your strong hand and outstretched arm - when he comes and prays toward this temple. Then hear from heaven, your dwelling place, and do whatever the foreigner asks of you, so that all the peoples of the earth may know your name and fear you."[104]

In 587 BC, King Nebuchadnezzar of Babylon destroyed the temple of Jerusalem that King Solomon built. Rome destroyed the rebuilt

---

[101] See Joshua 18:28; Judges 19:10 and 1Chronicles 11:4-5.
[102] See 1 Samuel 17:54.
[103] 1 Samuel 17; 1 Samuel 18:7.
[104] 1 Kings 8:41-42.

temple when the Romans army seized Jerusalem in AD 70. The western wall that protects the temple's courtyard is the main gathering point of the present-day Jews who comes to the Jerusalem temple site to pray for restoration of the Kingdom of Israel. The Jews will not move on the mount itself. They respect the holiness of the site and avoid the possible mistake of stepping into the area where the Holy of Holies (the inner sanctuary) stood.

Jerusalem was the seat of the great kings of Judah. The kings and the prophets of the Jewish nation had the seats of their offices in Jerusalem. The Jewish monarchs that lived and ruled over the people of Israel in Jerusalem were King Abijah, King Asa, King Jehoshaphat, King Jehoram, King Ahaziah, Queen Athaliah, King Joash, King Amaziah, King Azariah, King Uzziah, King Ahaz, King Hezekiah, King Josiah, King Manasseh, and King Rehoboam. The most prominent kings among the headship of Israel were King David and King Solomon.

Jerusalem is the center of the major Jewish festivities. Of all the references by both the Old Testament and New Testament writers, the religious usefulness of Jerusalem is recorded with the strongest terms of Jewish sentiment. The New Testament generations of God's worshippers were inaugurated in Jerusalem during the first century AD. The holy city was honored by both men and God throughout the later centuries.

Jesus Christ ate His last meal with His twelve disciples in Jerusalem before He was crucified on the cross. The Last Supper of the Lord Jesus Christ is the scriptural basis for the Christians to celebrate the Eucharist (Holy Communion) during Church Service. Jesus Christ died on the cross in Jerusalem, and He was buried in Jerusalem. He was resurrected from the grave the third day, and forty days later He ascended into heaven from Jerusalem.

The Holy Spirit of God descended upon the disciples of Jesus Christ on the day of Pentecost in Jerusalem. The Acts of the Apostles gives this account of the day of Pentecost: "There were staying in Jerusalem God-fearing Jews from every nation under heaven. When they heard this sound, a crowd came together in bewilderment because each one heard them speaking in his own language."[105]

The Christian Council of the Apostles of Jesus Christ was established in Jerusalem when the number of Christians increased beyond the region. The Apostles of Jesus Christ endorsed Jerusalem by its holy marks as the seat of major Church councils. The city has been one of the most important Christian sites ever since.

Only twice in the political history of Jerusalem has the city served as a national capital. The first time was during the first and the second temple periods of the Bible. In those days, Jerusalem was the capital of the Jewish commonwealth. The second time is the modern day. Jerusalem is the capital of the political state of Israel. Jerusalem has never served any Arabian state as its capital, and Jerusalem is not the center of any major Islamic festival.

In passing through many years of political reform, the world witnessed the First and the Second World Wars. The wars were fought from the years of 1914 to 1918 and 1939 to 1945, respectively. The British Army marched into the city of Jerusalem on the December 9 in 1917 after the combined forces of the European allied nations defeated the army of the Ottoman Empire. The march into the city of Jerusalem was the way the British Army showed respect to the holy land. A peace agreement was signed on October 31, 1918, between the leaders of the defeated Ottoman Empire and the leaders of the European allied forces. The agreement both ended the four hundred years of Ottoman occupation of the holy land and disbanded the Ottoman Empire. The collapse of the Ottoman Empire in the aftermath of the First World War led to the rise of new political regimes both in Turkey and in the newly created Balkan and Middle-Eastern states of Europe.

Transjordan: The Land of the Northern Kingdom of Israel:

The legitimacy of the land across the Jordan River lies in the Word of God. God called the area the eastern boundary of the new earth. Jordan

---

[105] Acts 2:5-6.

is a territory under the rule of God's law, but the physical boundaries of Jordan were violated when the area was politically severed from the rest of the Promised Land. The place of the great biblical events in Jordan is not welcoming to non-Muslim pilgrims. Christian pilgrims to Jordan are mystified about the sites because of the Islamic atmosphere of the land. The Bible often provides the general locations of sites it mentions, and sometimes it supplies specific information that helps to identify sites. People who study the covenant heritage of the children of Jacob can tell better than others that pilgrimage to the state of Israel alone is an incomplete trip to the Promised Land. Any visit to cover every part of the Promised Land must take the pilgrim beyond the state of Israel, to at least five more countries of the Middle East. Some towns and villages of Egypt, Syria, Saudi Arabia, and Lebanon were built on the Promised Land. The Emirate of Transjordan is completely settled on the Promised Land. The islands of Cyprus and Cilicia in southeastern Turkey are included in the Promised Land according to Ezekiel chapter 48.

The current political map of the Middle East confuses more than it helps to identify the true areas of the Promised Land. The geography of the biblical land and the current map of Israel are quite different because of political changes that happened on the ground. The nation of Israel lost both its twelve tribes and its cultural structure, which otherwise should be the pride of the Bible students.

It is sad that we live in a generation in which history is hardly checked. People of this generation do not necessarily regard history by its real value. This is the age of resentment, in which the importance of history is underrated owing to increased dependency on both sentiment and scientific proof. People easily believe their thoughts and count on their feelings to convince them of anything. On many of the occasions, people do not care about the convincing of truth. I fear for the future because many people will not realize in time where humanity is headed next.

Peace is unlikely to increase unless the real cause of the siege of the homeland of Israel is ascertained with regard to the true history of the Promised Land, which is written in the Bible. The illogical political changes made to the biblical land and the complicated identity crisis that follows the changes are both telling regarding how the shift can affect every nation. Many of the historic places where scriptural events happened were systematically separated from the mainland of Israel as if the events never happened on any Jewish territory. The intention for separating the land so extensively is to show the God of Israel from the Arab and Muslim perspectives and to determine the concept of a holy land in Muslims' domain. Rather, the operation served to neutralize the holiness of the place.

Critics of the Bible eagerly support denying the account of the Bible and frown at Jewish theology as though none of the episodes were ever correct. The current state of Israel is small, and apparently the Promised Land many pilgrims recognized. What is more worrying is why portions of the Promised Land and names of the places in the Bible were so disrupted by foreign rebellion. The Jews were violently forced to move out of their places on every occasion that the map of Canaan was redrawn in favor of the Arabs. Many parts of the biblical land were snatched out of Jewish hands through political charters and mandates, and the current struggle to snatch it all is continuing. The Islamic country of Transjordan is an epicenter in the land-snatching politics. The meaning of "Jordan" is "descending," – or rather – "flowing down." Lot and his descendants were the first people of Abraham to inhabit the land. Lot chose to live on the plain of Jordan when he separated himself from his brother Abraham.[106]

Series of Anglo-Transjordan treaties were signed to create the country of Transjordan from 1928 to 1946. The political negotiations were spearheaded by both British and French army high commissioners that presided over the region from the end of the First World War. The name Transjordan was a short form of describing the Jewish territory across the River Jordan. The Transjordan treaties stipulated that Transjordan, as an independent country of Arabs in Palestine, would bring peace between the two peoples and give rest to the entire region. The Jews were impassively

---

[106] "Lot looked around and saw that the whole plain of the Jordan toward Zoar was well watered, like the garden of the Lord, like the land of Egypt. (This is was before the Lord destroyed Sodom and Gomorrah). So Lot chose for himself the whole plain of the Jordan and set out toward the east" (Genesis 13:10-11).

removed from Transjordan, as in the Gaza evacuation that was carried out in 2004. The territory was called the Hashemite Kingdom of Transjordan beginning in the month of May in 1946. The first appointed Arab leader of the territory was Emir Abdullah Ibn al-Hussein. The resettled Arabs of Jordan were responsible for designating the Emir Abdullah as king of Jordan. Transjordan, as the first Arab Palestinian state, effectively severed the northern province of Israel, preventing the territory from providing any future Jewish homeland in the region.

The Jordan River is an important boundary in the history of the Bible. Jordan is a blessed land with rich spiritual heritage that belonged to those of biblical faith.

The territory of Transjordan was the inheritance of both the tribe of Reuben and the half-tribe of Manasseh. Joshua shared the territory between the two tribes when the Israelites that came out of Egypt reached the Promised Land. Women and children of the two tribes were the first Jews settled on the land. Joshua commanded all the fighting men of Israel across the Jordan River to fight the Canaanites of the mainland. The defeat of the Canaanites opened the rest of the land for the remaining ten Hebrew tribes of Israel.[107] The book of Joshua, chapter 3, tells the amazing story of the grace of God that ran high on the Jordan River. God miraculously ceased the flow of the Jordan River and created on the riverbed the dried pathway on which Joshua and the Israelites crossed over to the vicinity of Jericho.

Moses set aside three cities of eastern Jordan as Cities of Refuge. The cities of Bezer, Ramoth, and Golan were used to provide refuge according to the rule of God's law. Each of the cities protected Israelites who accidentally caused the death of a fellow Israelite. The accused person would flee to any of the three cities and would not die by the hand of avenger before the case was judged by the council of the elders.[108]

Moses gave his final address to the people of Israel in Jordan. Out of anger that formed his personal weakness, Moses failed to honor the Lord when he struck the rock of Meribah twice in the desert to give

---

[107] See Deuteronomy 3:12-20.
[108] See Deuteronomy 4:41-43 and Numbers 35:6-15.

water to the people. The Lord felt anger with the act of impatience and denied Moses the opportunity to lead the Israelites beyond the Jordan. Referring to the interior of the new land, the Lord said to Moses, "But your assistant, Joshua son of Nun will lead Israel to inherit it."[109] Moses died on Mount Nebo in Jordan. The exact location of his grave is unknown. God prevented any rite of idolatry on the grave of Moses by hiding the burial place.

Joshua set aside additional three cities of western Jordan as Cities of Refuge. The cities were Kedesh, Shechem, and Hebron. The Lord said to Joshua, "Tell the people of Israel to designate now the Cities of Refuge, as I instructed Moses. If any man is guilty of killing someone unintentionally, he can run to one of these cities and be protected from the relatives of the dead man, who may try to kill him in revenge. When the innocent killer reaches any of these cities, he will meet with the city council and explain what happened, and they must let him come in and must give him a place to live among them."[110] The six Cities of Refuge were included in the forty-eight Levitical Cities of Numbers chapter 35. The Lord blessed the Levitical Cities, and then He said to the people of Israel, "And you shall not defile the land where you reside, in which I dwell, for I am the Lord who dwells among the children of Israel."[111]

Jacob wrestled the angel of the Lord in Jordan, and there the Lord gave him the name Israel.

Job and his family lived in eastern Jordan, in the land of Uz. Satan tempted Job on the native land. Afterward, God rewarded Job for his competent faith. The blessing of God to Job followed him to his younger generations.

Elijah ascended to heaven in Jordan, in a place that the Bible says is across the Jordan River. The Prophet Elisha was the strong prophet of the Northern Kingdom of Israel. By the command of God, Elisha appointed Jehu and made him king of the Israelites of the Northern Kingdom. Jehu brought to an end the dynasty of King Ahab. God condemned the family

---

[109] Deuteronomy 1:38.
[110] Joshua 20:2-4.
[111] Numbers 35: 34.

of Ahab for their part in leading the Israelites to worship Baal. The names of the kings of Israel that ruled the people of the Northern Kingdom from Samaria are King Omri, King Joram, King Jehoahaz, King Jehoash, King Jeroboam, King Zachariah, King Shallum, King Menahem, King Pekahiah, King Pekah, King Elah, King Ahab, and King Jehu.

Jordan was an important political land of the Northern Kingdom of Israel. Jordan was near Samaria, and the city formed part of the capital territory of the Northern Kingdom. Samaria (the West Bank) was the second major Jewish center of festivity after Jerusalem. Naboth's vineyard, which he had inherited, was located in his hometown of Jezreel, near Samaria. Naboth refused even at the point of death to sell his inheritance to King Ahab and his wife, Queen Jezebel. The story of Naboth's vineyard is told in the book of 1 Kings, chapter 21. "Naboth a man from Jezreel owned a vineyard beside the palace of King Ahab of Samaria. One day the king said to Naboth, 'Since your vineyard is so convenient to my palace, I would like to buy it to use as a vegetable garden. I will give you a better vineyard in exchange or if you prefer I will pay you for it.' But Naboth replied, 'The Lord forbids that I should give you the inheritance that was passed down by my ancestors.'"[112]

John the Baptist started his ministry of baptism and repentance in the wilderness of Judea. John baptized the people of Israel in the Jordan River. The popular proclamation of John was that 'he baptized with water but greater is He that will baptize with the Holy Spirit.'[113] Saint Mark's Gospel says, "John came baptizing in the wilderness and preaching a baptism of repentance for the remission of sins. Then all the land of Judea (the West Bank) and those from Jerusalem went out to him and were all baptized by him in the Jordan River, confessing their sins."[114]

Jesus Christ was confirmed the Christ in Jordan when John the Baptist baptized Him in the Jordan River. "At that moment, Jesus came from Nazareth in Galilee and was baptized by John in the Jordan. As Jesus was coming up out of the water, He saw heaven being torn open

---

[112] 1 Kings 21:1-16.
[113] Mark 1:8.
[114] Mark 1:4-5.

and the Spirit descending on Him like a dove and lighting on Him. And a voice came from heaven, 'You are my Son whom I love; with Him I am well pleased.'"[115] The Gospel calls the site of His baptism 'Betharaba.' The literal translation of "Betharaba" is "place of crossing." On entering Jordan, the site of Betharaba is opposite Jericho. Both Christians and Jews believe that Betharaba is where the Israelites under the command of Joshua crossed over the Jordan River to reach the interior of the Promised Land.

Jesus Christ endured the forty days and forty nights of praying and fasting in the desert of Judea. Satan tempted Him in the same area after He finished the fast.

The Apostle Paul and the leading figures of the Gospel were part of the events of Jordan. The men performed key elements of their mission in the land of the Northern Kingdom of Israel. Jordan is the land where God repeatedly interacted with the Israelites in the righteousness of His mercy. The very name of the territory and its famous river of baptism belonged to the biblical faith. Aaron, the brother of Moses, died in Jordan. He was buried on Mount Hor, near the Jordan town of Petra. Today a fourteenth-century mosque is seated on Aaron's tomb. The white dome of the mosque is visible from most areas of Petra. The miraculous healing of Naaman the leper is part of the memory of the unique heritage of Jordan.[116] Naaman, the leprous Syrian army commander, was told about the wondrous work of the living God of Israel by his Jewish maidservant. Naaman traveled to Israel with his military escort, expecting to be healed of his disease. The king of Israel told Elisha about his fear of the journey, and Elisha directed Naaman to come to his house in Tel Rehov of Jezreel, which was east of the Jordan valley. When Elisha heard that Naaman had arrived at the gate of his house, he sent his messenger Gehazi to speak to the Syrian army commander. Gehazi went and gave the message of the Prophet to Naaman. The message commanded Naaman to go and wash his body seven times in the Jordan River. But Naaman was proud of his rank and nationality. He felt disrespected by Elisha because he had sent

---

[115] Mark 1:9-11.
[116] See 2 Kings 5.

his messenger to speak to him. Naaman replied to the messenger of the Prophet, "I thought that he would surely come to me and call on the name of the Lord his God, wave his hand over the spot and cure me of my leprosy. Are not Abana and Pharpar the rivers of Damascus better than any of the waters of Israel? Couldn't I wash in them and be cleansed? So he turned and went off in a rage."[117]

Naaman was cautiously regarded by his military escort, who advised him to reconsider the instruction of the man of God. The Syrian army commander went and put himself into the Jordan River as Elisha told him to do, and he was cured on the seventh washing of his body. The Abana River, which Naaman mentioned in his remark, is identifiable with what we know as the Barada River according to modern geography. The river rises in the Anti-Lebanon Mountains and flows through the city of Damascus. The Pharpar River flows eastward from the Mount of Hermon to the south of Damascus.

In making his remark, Naaman recognized that the Jordan River ran on the territory of Israel and that the river belonged to Israel. But it might not occur to people who support the vision of a new Arab Palestinian state in the West Bank and Gaza that Transjordan is now an Islamic Arab Emirate. Other parts of the Promised Land in Syria, Lebanon, Egypt, and Saudi Arabia have been engulfed by the wider Islamic havens.

Both Christians and Jewish pilgrims to Jordan have limited access to the sites of the great biblical events. In Jordan, the ability to experience excitement in following the native footprints of the biblical heroes is greatly restricted. Verbal admiration of God's power on and around the heritage sites would be more glorifying if the areas were retained under the territorial integrity of the Jewish homeland. The occupation of Transjordan by Arabs is perhaps a foregone political conclusion. Transjordan is now the right of the Jordanian citizens.

The Islamic state of Jordan represents a political battle won by the caliphate builders against the Jewish heritage. Arabs living on the soil of Jordan represents a huge political sacrifice by the Jews. Analysis of

---

[117] 2 Kings 5:11-12.

the Transjordan treaties reveals the goal of peace that surrendered the territory to the Arabs. The Jews made the choice to surrender the land outside the rule of God's law, and therefore the sacrifice did not give any peace to either Israel or the region. Serving and defending the land of God according to the rule of God's law are the only viable means by which any leadership in Israel could count its effort on peace as righteousness.

Jericho – City of the Moon gods:

The national phase of the Israelites started with the conquest of Jericho in 1250 BC. Jericho was the first major city of the Canaanites to fall into the hands of the Israelites. The name "Jericho" means "moon city" in Aramaic. The city fell to the command of Joshua in a resounding victory that was aided by direct help from God.[118] The invisible army of God hovered above Jericho when the Israelites arrived on the ground around the wall of Jericho.

"Now when Joshua was near Jericho, he looked up and saw a man standing in front of him with a drawn sword in his hand. Joshua went up to him and asked him, 'Are you for us or for our enemies?' "Neither," he replied, "But I have now come." Then Joshua fell face-down to the ground in reverence and asked him, "What message does my Lord have for his servant?" The commander of the Lord's army replied, "Take off your sandals, for the place where you are standing is holy ground."[119] "Now, Jericho was tightly shut up because of the Israelites. No one went out and no one came in. Then the Lord said to Joshua, 'See, I have delivered Jericho into your hands, along with its king and fighting men. March around the city once with all the armed men. Do this for six days.'"[120]

The fighting men of Israel marched round the city wall each day until the six full days ended. On the seventh day of the compass, the commander of the invisible army of the Lord commanded the wall of Jericho to collapse.[121] The Canaanites of Jericho were destroyed, and

---

[118] See Joshua 6.
[119] Joshua 5:13-15.
[120] Joshua 6:1-3.
[121] See Joshua 5:13-15 and Joshua 6:1-15.

Joshua gave Jericho to the tribe of Benjamin. The place is part of their inheritance from the Lord. "So, the lot of the tribe of the children of Benjamin came up according to their families and the territory of their lot came out between the children of Judah and the children of Joseph. Their border on the north side began at the Jordan and the border went up to the side of Jericho on the north and went up through the mountains westward. It ended at the wilderness of Beth Aven"[122]

God's unconditional strategy in giving Jericho to the people of Israel contained the process of worship and a divine military operation. The conquest of the entire land of Canaan, region after region, occurred through series of military operation. God directed the operation, and the children of Israel enforced His command on the battlefield. In Jericho the war was fought wholly by the invisible army of God. The Israelites were left with no military task to perform, except that they marched round the wall of Jericho with songs of praise and sounds of the trumpet. The seven-day ceremonial march was led by priests carrying the Ark of the Lord's Covenant. The Israelites soldiers followed behind the priests, singing songs of praise to the Lord.

The fall of Jericho demonstrates the power of worship. The songs of praise by the people, the leading of the Lord's Ark of Covenant, and the continual blowing of the trumpet by the priests were altogether the elements of the covenant of worship that inspired the Lord to fight the enemy of His people. The Hittites, the Amorites, the Perizzites, the Hivites and the Jebusites were the major tribes in the vicinity of Jericho, which included the hilly and lower areas of the land. Joshua defeated each of the tribes and their kings on the battlefield.[123]

Jericho was rebuilt by Hiel of Bethel in the later days of the reign of King Ahab. The reconstruction work on Jericho was commanded by the Lord Himself.[124] After the days of Joshua passed, more than two dozen cities were built and destroyed on the site of Jericho. The time span from the time of Joshua's conquest at Jericho to the current day of

---

[122] Joshua 18:11-12.
[123] See Joshua 12.
[124] 1 Kings 16:34.

the Arab Palestinians' struggle is approximately five thousand years. The New Testament site of Jericho is about two kilometers south of the Old Testament site of the city. The modern city of Jericho is located about the same distance southeast.

Jericho, Tell es-sultan, or the moon city was the worship center for the moon gods before Joshua and the men of Israel conquered the land. The heavenly army that conducted the mission of Jericho destroyed not only the Canaanites of the city but also the Canaanites' moon gods. Jericho was declared holy ground after the battle was done. Taking out the moon gods was perhaps the motive for the divine pattern of the operation. Trumpet blowing, praise, and worship were used in both military and spiritual contexts to announce the presence of the Lord. The commander of the invisible army of the Lord made himself visible to Joshua, that Joshua would recognize his presence and keep a record of the Lord's trend. The commander told Joshua that he supported neither the Israelites nor their enemy. His answer to Joshua is a warning to all leadership of Israel.

God is the ruler of both the land and His people. Every battle against any enemy of God's people must depend on whatever God decides to do to the enemy. Jewish leaders such as Gideon and Daniel encountered familiar faces of the Lord's holy angels. In each of the encounters, the angels made known to the people that they were captains of the Lord's army.[125] The book of Daniel reveals the angel Michael as the one who played the important roles of the protector of Israel and the one to lead the battle of the End Time for the Christian Church.

The book says, "And at that time Michael the great prince who protects your people, will arise. There will be a time of trouble, such as has not happened from the beginning of nations until then. But at that time your people shall be delivered, everyone whose name is found written in the book will be delivered. Multitudes that sleep in the dust of the earth will awake: some to everlasting life, others to shame and everlasting contempt. Those who are wise will shine like the brightness

---

[125] See Judges 6:11, Daniel 10:5 and Daniel 10:20.

of the heavens, and those who lead many to righteousness, like the stars for ever and ever."[126]

Bethlehem - The Birthplace of Jesus Christ:

The country of Israel is the embodiment of the Jewish continuity, and the town of Bethlehem is a major part of historical theology. Bethlehem, in the land of Judea, was in Old Testament times the center of theological association. The meaning of "Bethlehem" is "house of bread" in Aramaic, and it could possibly be translated from Hebrew as "house of flesh." Bethlehem is the birthplace of the Lord Jesus Christ. The original name of Bethlehem was Beit Lachama, named after the Canaanites' god Lachama. It was called Bethlehem Ephrata during the time of Jacob. About twenty kilometers toward the northwest of Bethlehem was Gibeon, where God stood the sun still until Joshua and the fighting men of Israel defeated King Adonizedek and his allied soldiers in the battle for the city of Jerusalem. In the west of Bethlehem was Socoh, where David killed the giant, Goliath, in the battle against the Philistines.

The tribe of Judah inherited Bethlehem-Ephrata and changed the name to Bethlehem-Judah. The change of name happened when the Israelites were already settled in most parts of the Promised Land. The people used the name of Bethlehem-Judah to differentiate the city from the Bethlehem of Zebulon. Bethlehem-Judah is where Rachel, the wife of Jacob, was buried.[127] Scripture indicates that the mound of earth on her grave was still visible when God appointed Saul to rule the Israelites. The writer of the first book of Samuel mentioned the grave of Rachel. Rachael was a loving mother of her two children, and her burial site was a valuable pilgrimage site to the Israelites. The Israelites preserved the burial site and honored Rachel on the site with prayers of love.

The Prophet Samuel anointed Saul with oil in the territory of Zuph, and there Samuel named Saul king of the Israelites. Then the Prophet said to King Saul of Israel, "When you have departed from me today, you will find two men near Rachel's tomb at Zelzah, on the territory

---

[126] Daniel 12:1-3.
[127] See Genesis 35:16-20.

of Benjamin."[128] Rachel died by the side of her husband on the way to Bethlehem. Jacob placed a pillar on the grave of Rachel, and so he marked the resting place of his beloved wife. The Bible calls the pillar the "pillar of Rachel's grave."[129] Rachel is a symbol of love for all women, especially for remembering the sacrifices of those who died while giving birth to a child.

King David was native of Bethlehem. All the families of David; his father, Jesse; and his ancestral parents were born and raised in Bethlehem.[130] The Prophet Samuel anointed David with oil in Bethlehem when David was fifteen years old. God ended the dynasty of King Saul the Benjamite for his disobedience.[131] He then directed the Prophet Samuel to appoint David to the throne of Israel. David did not take the throne until he was thirty years old. He first ruled the tribe of Judah for forty years in the city of Hebron.[132] Then David became king of all the Israelites in 947 BC. He moved the seat of his office out of Hebron and dwelled in Jerusalem for the rest of his days.[133] David ruled the Israelites for thirty-three years in Jerusalem. He was about ninety years old when he died in 960 BC. King David was buried on the Temple Mount. His burial place was a popular visitation site in Jerusalem beyond the first century AD. The Apostle Peter said in Acts 2:29, "Fellow Israelites, I can tell you confidently that the patriarch David died and was buried, and his tomb is here to this day."

Bethlehem was the scene of the ministry of the Prophets Nathan, Isaiah, and Jeremiah. The city is referred to in the Gospel as the City of David because Jesus Christ was a descendant of David. Saint Luke wrote the narrative about the birthplace of the Lord Jesus Christ. His Gospel narrates some aspects of the history of the Roman Empire, which validates both the time and the season in which Jesus Christ was born.

---

[128] 1 Samuel 10:2.

[129] Genesis 35: 20.

[130] See Ruth 4:18-22; Jesse was grandson of Ruth and Boaz.

[131] See 1 Samuel 16.

[132] See 2 Samuel 2:1- 4.

[133] "David was thirty-nine years old when he began to reign, and reigned forty years. In Hebron, he reigned over Judah seven years and six months, and in Jerusalem, he reigned thirty-three years over all Israel and Judah" (2 Samuel 5:4-5).

Luke wrote in his Gospel, "Joseph also went up from Galilee, out of the city of Nazareth, into Judea, to the city of David, which is called Bethlehem because he was of the lineage of David, to be registered with Mary his betrothed wife who was with a child."[134] Luke was referring to the decree of Emperor Caesar Augustus, which required all people under the command of Rome to travel to their homelands during the season.

The year was 30 BC, and Emperor Caesar Augustus ordered his officers to conduct a head count throughout the territory where Rome had command. Every family registered their name in their hometown. Mary and Joseph traveled to their native land of Bethlehem, and there, in their hometown, they were registered. The baby Jesus Christ was born in Bethlehem on the occasion of the registration. "And afterward, the king Herod, when he saw that he was mocked by the wise men that traveled through his territory to see the newborn baby Jesus, sent soldiers who murdered all the children that were born in Bethlehem and in the coast around it, from two years old and under."[135]

Mary and Joseph lived in Nazareth at the time of the head count. Nazareth was about 150 kilometers away from Bethlehem, and about 10 kilometers to the south of Jerusalem. Emperor Augustus literally did not realize what his actions would bring about when he authorized the headcount. The Prophet Micah had prophesied the birthplace of the Christ over one hundred years before.[136] Micah prophesied, "But you, Bethlehem Ephrata, though you are small among clans of Judah, yet out of you shall come forth to me the One to be Ruler in Israel, whose going forth is from old; from everlasting."[137]

The revolt by the Jews against the Romans occupation of the holy land moved Emperor Hadrian in the second century AD to destroy most parts of Bethlehem. Empress Helena promoted rebuilding both the city and the Christian heritage of the city during the reign of her

---

[134] Luke 2: 4-5.

[135] Matthew 2:16.

[136] See Luke 2:1-3; Caesar Augustus issued a decree of census in the entire Roman world. It was the first census that took place when Quirinius was governor of Syria. Everyone went to his hometown to register.

[137] Micah 5:2-5.

son, Emperor Constantine the Great. Even to this day, the old places of worship are maintained in Bethlehem by groups of Christians and church denominations following in the identified footsteps of the Lord Jesus Christ.

Church buildings and Christian study centers were well established in Bethlehem before the start of Islam. The remarkable and glorious Church of the Nativity in Bethlehem is one of the oldest operating churches in the world. The church building is located on the site Christians believe Jesus Christ was born. The Empress Helena commissioned the first basilica on the site. Helena is a saint of the Roman Catholic Church, perhaps for her role in rebuilding the Christian sites in Bethlehem. She sponsored building the Church of the Nativity in honor of the birthplace of the Lord Jesus Christ. Construction started on the church site in 327, and the work was done under the supervision of Bishop Makarios of Jerusalem. The building was completed in 313. The place of worship was dedicated to conduct public Services on the May 31, 339. The open portions of the floor mosaics are still intact to this day.

There is a separate cave beneath the church building where the Latin reverend father Saint Jerome spent over thirty years of his lifetime in translating the Hebrew Scripture into Latin. The cave then became the burial site of Saint Jerome when he died. The Latin scholar worked in Bethlehem from 384.

The Arab Palestinians on the ground of Bethlehem are politically cornering the churches of Bethlehem in the ongoing conflict. The idea that Bethlehem is to fall into the hands of any future Muslim state is emotionally disturbing. Bethlehem is the headquarters of the Christian Church. The conflict in Palestine is gradually moving toward implying that both the Jewish and the Christian pilgrims to Bethlehem are safer if they submit to the scrutiny of the Muslims presence in the city.

The idea of surrendering Bethlehem to Muslims is disrespectful to biblical theology. Bethlehem is the place of the Lord Jesus Christ. The true motive of Islam in Bethlehem is to uproot from reality every gateway to Jewish and Christians heritage. Bethlehem is at risk of losing the legacy of its holy sites, similar to the disastrous losses of religious heritage sites in

Iraq, Syria, and Afghanistan. The defenders of Islamic fanaticism are on the site with the intent to gain absolute authority over all strategic places of worship in Israel. If they should win in the conflict, the world must accept that jihad and extremism gives Islam the respect that it desperately wants from the world's best religions.

Secondly, both the Gospel and the concept of a holy land are hereby ridiculed. The Christians and the Jewish pilgrims to Israel are being restricted from visiting some areas of Bethlehem. The Arab Palestinian interim authority has devised a policy of sharp demographic shift in these parts of Bethlehem by keeping the pilgrims in check. The native populations of both Christians and Jews in Bethlehem have incapacitated legal rights. The restrictions on both the sociocultural and religious freedoms of Christians and Jews of Bethlehem have forced their numbers to steadily decline since 1990.

Also, in Gaza, Christians living in the area are looked down upon as second-class citizens of the enforced Islamic rule of law. Arab Palestinian Christians are constantly harassed in the West Bank and Gaza. The suffering they endure is comparable to, and sometimes more intense than, the suffering of Christians in Muslims strongholds, such as Afghanistan and Pakistan. In humiliating the Christian faith, top officials of the Arab Palestinian interim leadership hover around churches of Bethlehem on major Christian occasions. Be it either during the Christmas or Easter periods, the Arab Palestinian leadership comes, desiring to receive the salutes of pilgrims in Bethlehem. It is ironic, and it is sad to notice, that the Arab Palestinian interim leadership welcomes the occasions of the birth, the crucifixion, and the resurrection of the Lord Jesus Christ with smiling faces while they host a building on the Temple Mount that bears an inscription stating that God has no son.

Saint Luke's Gospel says, "The Kingdom of God is not something that can be observed. It shall be on the day the Son of man is revealed that many of the observers are disappointed."[138]

The land of Israel is the soul center of both the Jewish and the Christian

---

[138] Luke 17:20-22.

worshippers. Political mediators of the conflict in Palestine should know that there is no foreign religion that conflicts with Islam in the cities of Mecca and Medina. The kingdom of Saudi Arabia is strictly Islamic. Neither the Jews nor the Christians nor the Hindus in the kingdom of Saudi Arabia can have the mind of occupation and the spirit of violent attack that Arab Muslims developed in the holy territory of Israel. The means that verified the mind-set of the Arab Muslims in the fight to own Bethlehem were provided by the conflict. The insight gained from the conflict was what we believed the United Nations wanted the divinity of the Kingdom of Israel to become in the future. The book of Joshua says, "But when we perceived these things and the future that is coming toward us, our hearts melted and everyone's courage failed because of you."[139]

Nazareth - The Village of Mary and Joseph:

The ancient village of Nazareth was built on basin land in the northern part of Israel. The village was formed approximately 1,050 feet above sea level. The whole area is covered with a mountain range. Mount Carmel is the most prominent peak in the range, which stretched out to southeast Canaan from the coast of the Mediterranean Sea. The hilltop provided a view of Galilee, and toward the north of Nazareth was Gath-hepher, the hometown of the Prophet Jonah. Mount Tabor was in the South, and near the village of Nain, where Jesus Christ raised to life the dead son of a widow. Nain was about twenty-five kilometers to the southwest of Nazareth and about a day's journey to Capernaum, where Jesus Christ healed the servant of the Roman centurion.

About fifteen kilometers to the west of Nazareth was Mount Carmel, where Elijah defeated the prophets of Baal in a fierce spiritual contest.[140] The topography of the mountainous area was ideal for the spiritual confrontation, which determined in Israel that Jehovah is the supreme God. Elijah defeated Baal and his false prophets in the contest and shamed the supporters of Baal. The Israelites were obsessed with the devilish influence of idol worship, and many of them perished because

---

[139] Joshua 2:11.
[140] See1 king 18:20-40.

of that sin. The Canaanites made Mount Carmel a vital haven for their worship of Baal and Ashtoreth. They built sanctuaries to the gods on the mount and went there to worship the gods. The Israelites adopted worshipping Baal on the sanctuary when King Ahab and his wife, Queen Jezebel, fully adopted Baal worship into the Jewish community.

Looking further into the area, the village of Shunem was about twelve kilometers south of Nazareth. Shunem is the place where Elisha resurrected to life the dead son of a Shunammite woman. Near the village of Shunem is the spring of Herod. After drinking water from the pool, Gideon and three hundred fighting men of Israel destroyed the Midianites in a battle in which an angel of the Lord commanded them. We read in Judges, "Now the camp of Midian lay below him in the valley. During that night the Lord said to Gideon, 'Get up, and go down against the camp because I am going to give it into your hand.'"[141]

Near the old village of Nazareth was the town of Jezreel. Jezreel was the hometown of Naboth and the town where the Queen Jezebel died. To the east of Nazareth was the village of Endor, where the witch of Endor invoked the spirit of Samuel and he answered King Saul. Mount Gilboa is within the range, and it is where King Saul and his son Jonathan died in the battle in which they led the Israelites to fight against the Philistines. To the southwest of Nazareth is the plain of Armageddon.

The native town of Nazareth was developed from a small Jewish village known to have hosted about five hundred Jewish families during the time of Mary and Joseph. Nazareth is part of the holy ground. The Archangel Gabriel visited the place when he revealed that the family of Mary and Joseph would bear the blessed burden of the birth of the Lord Jesus Christ. Mary and Joseph returned to their home in Nazareth after Jesus Christ was born in Bethlehem. The boy Jesus Christ lived in Nazareth until God publicly proclaimed His ministry at the Jordan River. The Messiah was widely called Jesus Christ of Nazareth. As Jewish boy, Jesus Christ received instruction in Hebrew. It is possible that Jesus Christ

---

[141] Judges 7:8-9.

answered people that came to Him in Hebrew, Greek, and Aramaic. The three languages were commonly spoken during His time.

The modern city of Nazareth was expanded from the old area of the traditional town. Nazareth now constitutes the largest city in the northern district of Israel. The Arab Palestinians have made up the vast majority of the city's population since the war of 1948. Political control of Nazareth has frequently shifted. The old cities of Galilee, Nazareth, and Jerusalem were in 1099 the seat of the Christian Crusaders Tancred. Control of Nazareth was surrendered in 1187 to the Muslim lordship of Caliph Yusuf Sala ad-Din. From Cairo the Caliph Yusuf Sala ad-Din led the jihad that defeated the Christian Crusaders in the Battle of Hattin. This piece of history is connected to the Islamic military incursion of the second century AD, which extended its horn of attack to all parts of the holy land.

The jihad movement of the second century AD overran both the Jewish and the Christian territories in phases. In 1263, Al-Din Baibars, the Mumluk Sultan of Egypt, destroyed almost all the Christian sites in Nazareth and declared the sites off-limits to the Latin clergymen who managed Christian religious studies in Nazareth. Some of the Christian sites, especially church buildings, were recovered and renovated. But the renovated sites and the city itself were never seen again in the traditional glory of the early Gospel era. Christians maintains the heritage of conventional worship in Nazareth in spite of the large population of Arab Muslims in the city.

Major Christian churches in Nazareth are at the following sites:

- Mensa Christi Church of the Franciscan Religious Order: The Christians believed Jesus Christ ate with His disciples on this site after He was resurrected from the dead.

- Church of Annunciation: This building is the largest Christian church of the Roman Catholic Mission in the Middle East. It stands on the site where the Archangel Gabriel stood when He announced the relevance of the baby Jesus Christ to Mary.

- Church of Saint Gabriel of the Eastern Orthodox: The church building is on the alternative site of the annunciation of the birth of Jesus Christ to Mary and Joseph.

- Church of Saint Joseph's Carpentry: Joseph was the beloved husband of Mary. The site of this church building is where Joseph's carpentry workshop stood. Jesus Christ grew up in the family of Joseph and Mary, and He often helped Joseph in his carpentry workshop.

- The Melikite Greek Catholic Church or the Synagogue Church: The location of this church building is the traditional site of the synagogue where Jesus Christ often preached among His people.

Hebron – The Burial Place of the Hebrew Patriarchs:

Hebron is located in the West Bank. The statesman Caleb inherited the old area of Hebron when the Israelites fully entered the land of the Canaanites from Egypt. Caleb gained the land of Hebron with his faithfulness to the Lord. The book of Joshua explains that Caleb and his descendants received Hebron from Joshua. It is written, "Now the men of Judah approached Joshua at Gilgal, and Caleb son of Jephunneh the Kenizzite said to him, "You know what the Lord said to Moses the man of God at Kadesh Barnea about you and me. I was forty years old when Moses the servant of the Lord sent me from Kadesh Barnea to explore the land. And I brought him back a report according to my convictions, but my brothers who went up with me made the hearts of the people melt with fear. I, however, followed the Lord my God wholeheartedly. So on that day Moses swore to me, 'The land on which your feet have walked will be your inheritance and that of your children forever because you have followed the Lord my God wholeheartedly.' Now then, just as the Lord promised He has kept me alive for forty-five years since the time He said this to Moses, while Israel moved about in the desert. So here I am today, eighty-five years old! I am still strong today as the day that Moses sent me out; I'm just as vigorous to go out to battle now as I was then. Now give me this hill country that the Lord promised me that day. You yourself heard then that the Anakites were there and their cities were large and fortified, but, the Lord helping me, I will drive them out just as He said." Then Joshua blessed Caleb, son of Jephunneh and gave him Hebron as his inheritance. So Hebron has belonged to Caleb son of Jephunneh the kenizzite ever since because he followed the Lord, the God of Israel, wholeheartedly." [142]

The Canaanites called Hebron Kiriath Arba. Arba was the fore-father of the tribe of Anak. The descendants of Anak on the land were called the Anakites.[143] Arba was a great man of the Anakite community, and Kiriath Arba represented the town of Arba. The town and its fortress were maintained in the name of Arba until the Israelites renamed the place Hebron. The name of Hebron is from the Hebrew word "ha-ver," meaning "male friend." The Israelites used the name of Hebron to describe Abraham as friend of God. Hebron is the oldest Jewish community in the world. It was the first place Abraham and his family settled on the land.

On entering the land of the Canaanites, Joshua and the fighting men of Israel destroyed the three Anakites tribes – Sheshai, Ahiman, and Talmai – and ended the place of the Anakites on the land. Hebron was the property of the Hittites during the early period of the Bible.

Abraham and his family lived as strangers among the Canaanites of Hebron. Sarah died in Hebron, and Abraham buried her on the land. Ephron, the son of Zohar the Hittite, sold to Abraham his piece of the land, which had a burial cave on it. The story of the death and burial of Sarah is told in Genesis chapter 23. "Sarah lived to be a hundred and twenty-seven years old. She died at Kiriath Arba, (that is, Hebron) in the land of Canaan, and Abraham went to mourn for Sarah and to weep over her. Then Abraham rose from beside his dead wife and spoke to the Hittites. He said, "I am an alien and a stranger among you. Sell me some property for a burial site here so I can bury my dead." The Hittites replied to Abraham, "Sir, listen to us; you are a mighty prince among us. Bury your dead in the choicest of our tombs. None of us will refuse you

---

[142] Joshua 14:6-14.
[143] See Joshua 15:13-15.

his tomb for burying your dead." Then Abraham rose and bowed down before the people of the land, the Hittites. He said to them, "If you are willing to let me bury my dead, then listen to me and intercede with Ephron, son of Zohar on my behalf so he sell the cave of Machpelah, which belongs to him and is at the end of his field. Ask him to sell it to me for the full price as a burial site among you." Ephron, the Hittite was sitting among his people and he replied to Abraham in the hearing of all the Hittites who had come to the gate of his city. "No my lord," he said, "Listen to me; I give you the field, and I give you the cave in it. I give it to you in the presence of my people. Bury your dead." Again, Abraham bowed down before the people of the land and he said to Ephron in their hearing, "Listen to me, if you will. I will pay the price of the field. Accept it from me so I can bury my dead here." Ephron answered to Abraham, "Listen to me, my lord; the land is worth four hundred shekels of silver, but what is that between me and you? Bury your dead." Abraham agreed to Ephron's term and weighed out for him the price he had named in the hearing of the Hittites; four hundred shekels of silver, according to the weight current among the merchants. So Ephron's field in Machpelah near Mamre – both the field and the cave in it, and all the trees within the borders of the field – was deeded to Abraham as his property in the presence of all the Hittites who had come to the gate of the city. Afterward, Abraham buried his wife Sarah in the cave of the field."[144]

Ishmael and Isaac buried their father, Abraham, next to Sarah's grave in the cave of Machpelah.[145] Isaac and Jacob and their wives were buried in the cave when they died. The cave of Machpelah in Hebron is the second holiest site in Judaism, after the western wall of Jerusalem. Rachel is the only Jewish matriarch that was not buried in the cave of Machpelah. Rachel died after she gave birth to Benjamin. The beloved lady of the house of Jacob was traveling from Hebron to Bethlehem when she died.

---

[144] Genesis 23: 1-19.

[145] "Abraham lived a hundred and seventy-five years. Then he breathed his last and died at a good old age, an old man and full of years; and he was buried to his people. His sons Isaac and Ishmael buried him in the cave of Machpelah near Mamre, in the field of Ephron son of Zohar the Hittite; the field Abraham bought the Hittites. There Abraham buried his wife, Sarah" (Genesis 25:7-10).

The Bible says, "And Rachel died, and was buried on the way to Ephrath, (that is, Bethlehem). And Jacob set a pillar upon her grave, which is the Pillar of Rachel's grave to this day."[146]

Jacob died in Egypt when his son Joseph was prince in Egypt. The body of Jacob received the most dignified burial rite that the Israelites ever gave to a Hebrew patriarch of any biblical time. Before he died, Jacob gathered his sons around his sickbed and blessed them. Then he gave them these instructions: "I am about to be gathered to my people. Bury me with my fathers in the cave in the field of Ephron the Hittite, the cave in the field of Machpelah near Mamre in Canaan, which Abraham bought along with the field as a burial place from Ephron the Hittite. There Abraham and his wife Sarah were buried, there Isaac and his wife Rebekah were buried and there I buried Leah. The field and the cave in it were bought from the Hittites. When Jacob had finished giving instructions to his sons, he drew his feet up into the bed, breathed his last and was gathered to his people. Joseph threw himself on his father and wept over him and kissed him. Then Joseph directed the physicians in his service to embalm his father Israel. So the physicians embalmed him, taking a full forty days, for that was the time required for embalming. And the Egyptians mourned for him seventy days. When the days of mourning had passed, Joseph said to pharaoh's court, "If I have found favor in your eyes, speak to pharaoh for me. Tell him, 'my father made me swear an oath and said, "I am about to die; bury me in the tomb I dug for myself in the land of Canaan." Now let me go up and bury my father; then I will return." Pharaoh said, 'Go up and bury your father, as he made you swear to do.' So Joseph went up to bury his father. All the pharaoh's officials accompanied him – the dignitaries of his court and all the dignitaries of Egypt – besides all the members of Joseph's household and his brothers and those belonging to his father's household. Only their children and their flocks and herds were left in Goshen. Chariots and horsemen also went up with him. It was a very large company. When they reached the threshing-floor of Atad, near the Jordan, they lamented

---

[146] Genesis 35:19-20.

loudly and bitterly; and there Joseph observed a seven-day period of mourning for his father. When the Canaanites who lived there saw the mourning at the threshing-floor of Atad, they said, "The Egyptians are holding a solemn ceremony of mourning." That is why that place near the Jordan is called Abel Mizraim. So Jacob's sons did as he had commanded them: they carried him to the land of Canaan and buried him in the cave in the field of Machpelah near Mamre, which Abraham had bought along with the field as a burial place from Ephron the Hittite. After burying his father, Joseph returned to Egypt, together with his brothers and all the others who had gone with him to bury his father."[147]

King Herod the Great built the great wall that surrounds the cave of Machpelah in Hebron. The construction work on the wall lasted from 31-4 BC. Pilgrimage to the cave of Machpelah was popular among both the Christians and the Jews before Islamic interference in the region became a subject of concern to the two religious groups. The mosque south of the cave of Machpelah was the first church of the Christian Crusaders in Hebron. The church building was converted to a mosque in 1187 during the Mamluks' jihad. The Christian Crusaders lost control of the church building to Sultan Yusuf Sala ad-Din.

Abraham is the only credible link between the Arabs and the cave of Machpelah. Abraham was the father of Ishmael, and all Arab natives came from Ishmael. The covenant blessing of Abraham, Isaac, and Jacob did not provide any room for the burial of Ishmael in the cave of Machpelah. Ishmael was not buried in Hebron, and he was not buried anywhere in Canaan. Ishmael lived his life in the covenant of his father, Abraham, and accepted the decree of God, which gave him and his descendants the Arabian Desert as homeland. The last known visit of Ishmael to Hebron occurred when Abraham died.

The Kaaba in the middle of the al-Haram Mosque in Saudi Arabia was constructed by the early Muslims to shelter the place where Ishmael and his mother Hagar were buried. Hebron is the only city of the West Bank that was left out of the Oslo Accord of September 1993. The Oslo

---

[147] Genesis 49:29-33 and Genesis 50:1-14.

Accord temporarily conceded governance of the cities of the West Bank to the interim administration of the Arab Palestinians. The government of Israel maintains the security of Hebron with an armed military guard. The peacekeeping force of the United Nations is also present in the city. The United Nations is the chief guardian of peace in the region.

The Arab Palestinians found increasing success in persuading the United Nations toward achieving their goal, and they have used this to their advantage. Using the United Nations and its agencies to push for the Arab state of Palestine has so far been successful. In 2011, UNESCO[148] upgraded the nonmember observer state status of the Arab Palestinians' representation to full membership status.

The ambiguous support of the United Nations to the Arab Palestinians pertains to the vision of a sovereign state. The support does not distinguish the short-term excitement from the long-term political goal of the PLO. Real peace is hard to forecast in the region with political support unless the PLO recognizes that it cannot eradicate the Jewish nation. The PLO diplomatic wing will always lure the member states of the United Nations to feel the Arab Palestinians have been both wronged and cheated. The PLO generates huge public support through the disguised outcry for help. But ultimately, the path that the PLO chose to follow might result in their losing part of the land that is now available to them. There will not be peace in the zone as long as the prospect of the Arab Palestinian state includes inheriting all the traditional land of Israel.

Gaza and the Land Across:

The importance of Gaza and Sinai is clear in the Bible, beyond the claims made by fascist political factions in the Middle East. The book of Exodus states in chapter 14 that the Israelites encamped briefly on the desert of Egypt after they left Goshen. From the camp they saw the army of pharaoh on chariots, chasing after them. Moses and the people of Israel cried out to the Lord, and the Lord used His power to lead and protect the people. The Lord protected the Israelites by day on a pillar of light and by

---

[148] United Nations Educational, Scientific, and Cultural Organization.

night on a pillar of fire until they reached the bank of the Red Sea. He then parted the Red Sea for the Israelites with wild winds that created a dry pathway on the sea floor. Moses hurried the Israelites into the pathway and led them past the territory of Egypt. The Israelites fully departed the territory of the Egyptians after they crossed the Red Sea and stepped into the desert of Shur.[149]

The desert of Shur was in Midian, and it was a familiar territory to Moses. Forty years earlier, Moses escaped Egypt to Midian through the desert route after he helped fellow Hebrews kill an Egyptian over a dispute. From the territory of Shur, the Israelites moved into the desert of Sin. After crossing the area of Sin, they came to Sinai, the mountain of God. On Sinai, God renewed the covenant of Abraham with the Israelites. God would not do such a great thing in the land of the Egyptians, where four generations of His people had perished after severe suffering. Moses completed the assignment to lead the people of Israel out of Egypt when he led them cross over the Red Sea and into the desert of Shur.

From Sinai God commanded Moses and Joshua and the people. The Lord took His revenge on the Midianites in the desert. The war against the Midianites was the last assignment of Moses. "The Midianites were the ones who followed Balaam's advice and enticed the Israelites to be unfaithful to the Lord in the Peor incident, so that a plague struck the Lord's people."[150] Therefore the Lord commanded Joshua and the fighting men of Israel into the battle that destroyed the Midianites' strong men. God extended the boundary of the Promised Land to reach the territory where the Midianites lived.

Neither the Egyptians nor the Midianites were Arabs. The area of the Arabian Desert reached the southern part of Mount Sinai, but it was not joined to Egypt. Part of the Promised Land at Sinai is a vast section of land between Egypt and the Arabian Desert.

The Apostle Paul wrote the epistle to the Galatians after four hundred years that closed the canon of the Old Testament prophecy. Paul stated

---

[149] See Exodus 15:22.
[150] Numbers 31:16.

in the epistle that the vast Sinai Peninsula is owned by Israel and Saudi Arabia.[151]

Joshua shared the land of the Canaanites with the twelve tribes of Israel. The allotment of the tribe of Judah was extended to the territory of Midian. "The allotment for the tribe of Judah, clan by clan, extended down to the territory of Edom, to the Desert of Zin in the extreme south. Their southern boundary started from the bay at the Salt Sea, crossed south of Scorpion pass continued on to Zin and went over to the south of Kadesh Barnea. Then it ran past Hezron up to Addar and curved around to Karka. It then passed along to Azmon and joined the Wadi of Egypt River, ending at the sea."[152]

The tribes of Judah were the first Israelites of the West Bank and Jerusalem. Joshua assigned parts of the land to Caleb and Othniel. He then shared the rest of the area, region by region, with all the clans of Judah. The area called Gaza extended as far as Sinai in the time of Joshua. Several battles were fought over the region by the Israelites against the ranks of the Canaanite tribal warriors. Joshua destroyed many of the Canaanite tribes on the battlefield and kept the less troublesome tribes in subjection.

When Joshua was old and well advanced in years, the Lord said to him, "You are very old, and there are still very large areas of the land to take over. This is the land that remains: all the regions of the Philistines and Geshurites; from the Shihor River on the east of Egypt to the territory of Ekron on the north, all of it counted as Canaanites (the territory of the five Philistines rulers in Gaza, Ashdod, Ashkelon, Gath and Ekron – that of the Avvites); from the south, all the land of the Canaanites, from Arah of the Sidonians as far as Aphek, the region of the Amorites, the area of the Gebalites; and all Lebanon to the east, from Baal Gad below Mount Hermon to Lebo Hamah."[153]

After Joshua died, remnants of the Canaanites grew considerably stronger by their numbers. Their fighting men on iron chariots encroached

---

[151] See Galatians 4:25.
[152] Joshua 15:1-4.
[153] Joshua 13:1-5.

a great deal into the mainland of Israel. The Canaanites' trouble reached a crisis point when Deborah was Judge in Israel. The Prophetess Deborah, wife of Lappidoth, was a devoted leader of the people. She commanded the statesman Barak and the fighting men of Israel on the battlefield, and together they defeated the Canaanites. "On that day God subdued Jabin, the Canaanite king before the Israelites. And the hand of the Israelites grew stronger against Jabin, the Canaanite king until they destroyed him."[154]

The Amalekites were another tribal people that lived across Gaza and as far as the Sinai Peninsula. Both the tribes of Edom and Amalek were descendants of Esau. Amalek was grandson of Esau and half-brother to the Edomites. The Amalekites were nomads. The people of this tribe survived both by hunting wild animals and by grazing livestock. They lived in the desert and moved around it through northern and southern routes at Sinai. The Amalekites were the first tribal people to attack the Israelites on the desert of Rephidim. They wanted to frustrate the Israelites' travel and stop them from reaching the mainland of the Canaanites.

"The Amalekites came and attacked the Israelites at Rephidim. Moses said to Joshua, "Choose some of our men and go out to fight the Amalekites. Tomorrow I will stand on top of the hill with staff of God in my hands." So Joshua fought the Amalekites as Moses had ordered; and Moses, Aaron, and Hur went to the top of the hill. As long as Moses held up his hands, the Israelites were winning, but whenever he lowered his hands, the Amalekites were winning. When Moses hands grew tired, they took a stone and put it under him and he sat on it. Aaron and Hur held his hands up – one on one side, one on the other side – so that his hands remained steadily up till sunset. So Joshua overcame the Amalekites army with the sword. Then the Lord said to Moses, "Write this on a scroll as something to be remembered and make sure that Joshua hears it, because I will completely blot out the memory of Amalek from under the sun.""[155]

Years later, when the Israelites were settled on the land, the Amalekites

---

[154] Judges 4: 23.
[155] Exodus 17:8-14.

started another war against the people. The statesman Gideon led the fighting men of Israel into the battlefield, and they destroyed almost all the Amalekites. The battle took place when the Amalekites joined forces with remnants of the Midianites and the Ishmaelites to fight against the Israelites. David recorded the event of the war in Psalm 83.[156] The Midianites were descendants of Abraham from his second wife, Keturah. Abraham married Keturah after Sarah died. The Amalekites that survived the Gideon-led attack reorganized after a while, and their men led a number of guerrilla attacks on the Israelites.

The Amalekites intensified their attacks on the Israelites during the period when the Prophet Samuel appointed Saul, son of Kish, to rule the people of Israel. Saul was the first political king of the Israelites. God instructed Saul to destroy everything of the Amalekites. "So, Saul attacked the Amalekites all the way from Havilah to Shur, to the east of Egypt. He took Agag king of the Amalekites alive and all his people he totally destroyed with the sword."[157] The Prophet Samuel killed King Agag when the fighting men of Israel returned home from the battlefield. Samuel criticized Saul for sparing the life of King Agag against the command of God.

The Old Testament explains the rich heritage of Gaza and Sinai through the history of the Israelites. The Gospel drew the importance of Gaza and Sinai from the Ethiopian who paid homage to God in Jerusalem. The Ethiopian visited the temple of Jerusalem and was excited to read the Scripture on the way back to his home country. He studied on his chariot the book of Isaiah and understood nothing about the text. The Holy Spirit heard his heart groaning to know the living truth and appointed the Apostle Philip to go and help the man on his chariot. Philip went in the direction the Holy Spirit pointed, and he met the Ethiopian on his way. Philip joined the Ethiopian on his chariot, and there he explained the text of Isaiah to him. The part of the Scripture the Ethiopian read is as follows:

---

[156] See Judges 6, 7, 8; "For they have consulted together with one consent; they form a confederacy against you: the tents of Edom and the Ishmaelites; Moab and the Hagrites; Gebal, Ammon, and Amalek; Philistia with the inhabitants of Tyre; Assyria also has joined with them; they have helped the children of Lot" (Psalm 83:5-8).

[157] 1 Samuel 15:7-8.

"He was led like a sheep to the slaughter; and as a lamb before its shearer is silent, so He did not open His mouth.
In His humiliation He was deprived of justice.
And who will declare His generation? For His life is taken from the earth."[158]

On hearing through Philip that the text is about Jesus Christ the Messiah, the Ethiopian surrendered his life to the Lord. Philip baptized him on the spot and turned him to the Christian faith.

Gaza contains desert corridors to the north of Africa. The desert route of Rafah, Kerem Shalom, and the Erez Crossing are the main existing gateways into the north of Africa. The Mamluk Sultanate of Egypt captured the Sinai Peninsula and held it from 1260 to 1517. The Sultan held the territory as part of Egypt's control because of the rich spiritual heritage of the area. The Saint Catherine Monastery at the foot of Mount Sinai is the oldest Christian monastery in the world. The monastery is the most popular tourist site in that part of the Promised Land.

The 1993 Oslo Accord recognized Gaza as the Arab Palestinian interim territory. The Arab Palestinian interim authority in Ramallah hopes that Gaza will be part of any future Arab Palestinian state. But the plan to keep Gaza out of Jewish hands is not workable with peace. Gaza cannot peacefully belong to different people and countries, especially with the factions of Islamic militants clustered in the area. Access from Gaza to the outside world is possible by the mainland of Israel or by the Mediterranean Sea.

Prime Minister Ariel Sharon evacuated the Jewish population in Gaza in February 2004. He completed the exercise in August 2005. Now the elite members of the Arab Palestinian society claim that Jews have never lived in Gaza. Not knowing about the history of the place, the lower classes of the new generations of Arabs accept the propaganda as historical fact. Mr. Ariel Sharon removed all the Jewish families in Gaza

---

[158] Acts 8:32-33.

to calm the frequent rioting, kidnapping, and killing of the Jews by the Arab Palestinian militants in the area.

The current outlook of increased military activity in Gaza represents yet another failure of the peace plan. Thousands of Jewish families were evacuated from their homeland in Gaza to give peace a chance. But Gaza, in the hands of Hamas, is the Arab Palestinian center of weaponry. The Hamas turned the city of Gaza into the home of both rocket factories and military hardware. The Jewish antiterrorism squadron has on several occasions discovered in Gaza secret underground tunnels leading into Egypt and into the mainland of Israel. The tunnels allegedly belong to Hamas, whose targets of attack are both the Jews and Jewish cities. Ariel Sharon was the prime minister of Israel from 2001 to 2006. He died in January 2014 at the age of eighty-five after he spent seven years in a coma.

CHAPTER 8

THE DOME OF THE ROCK

Moses made the first tent of meeting for the Israelites to worship God. The tent is the origin of God's place of worship in Israel. The Israelites of Moses' generation worshipped God in the desert outside of His tent. The tent is called the sanctuary of the Lord, the tabernacle of the Lord, and the tent of meeting. These three names, including the tent of God, represented the private worship place of the Lord.

God appointed the tribe of Levi to serve Him as priests of the people. The Lord said to the Israelites, "Male Levites qualified from the age of twenty-five and above and may enter the tent to perform service in the work of the tabernacle of meeting."[159] God made Aaron high priest in the work of the tabernacle. The Levites offered sacrifices to the Lord on behalf of the people, and only Moses and Aaron entered the inner compartment of the tent of meeting. Joshua and the Levites pitched the tent of God in Shiloh when the whole assembly of the Israelites arrived in the Promised Land. Later on, the Israelites converted the tent into a real house of worship according to the blueprint the Lord gave to Moses.[160]

Further along in the history of the nation of Israel, God revealed His dwelling in the temple of Jerusalem. People of different cultures then became more receptive to gathering in the temple to worship God. The

---

[159] Numbers 8:24.
[160] See Joshua 18:1.

covenant temple of God should not exist outside the homeland of Israel. God did not approve the establishment of the covenant temple on foreign land, and the Israelites have never had two existing temples at a time.

The Jews have synagogues everywhere in Israel. They gather in synagogues whenever they want to, including times of worship. Synagogues are independent community organizations. They exist in all places of the world where the Jewish community exists. Synagogues do not replace the temple, and there is no set of blueprints required to start a synagogue. Both the architectural shape and the interior design of any synagogue can be different from that of any other. The Jews sees synagogues as less important than the covenant temple, or rather like a place of worship with a role separate from that of the temple. The ark of God in a synagogue is almost always positioned in such a way that those who face it are facing toward Jerusalem. Synagogues are the Jewish equivalent of Christian churches. Using the term "temple" to describe Christian churches could offend the Jews.

The gathering of worshippers of the living God was energized by the Gospel. From the first century AD, as the Gospel began to spread faster, people of all tribes and cultures built churches in different sizes and architectural designs, and in every nation and place. Going to a church Service on Sunday morning and gathering in church on various occasions became the practice among people in whom the Gospel lived.

Christians worship God through the influence of the Holy Spirit, and gatherings of believers usually start in people's homes, in open fields, and in public schools. The Holy Spirit is the convincing force of the Gospel. He encourages people to believe in the Gospel, and He unites the believers' faith in God the Father. The Spirit's influence on Christian worshippers demonstrates His unique presence in the gathering of His people. The faith that the gatherers show in the oneness of God is the miracle of His love.

Jerusalem unites heavens and earth with worship and with the spiritual creation in the covenant of Abraham. But human nature is a big problem in the gathering of worshippers. Many houses of worship are not peaceful places, as is expected of a place devoted to loving one another

THE DOME OF THE ROCK | 133

and praying together to God. The true spirit of love that should exist in houses of worship is sometimes almost buried under the rubble of endless interpersonal and group conflict. The conflict is not about the true benefit of coming together in any house of God, and it is not for the love of God. Trouble in houses of worship is part of the war waged by evil spiritual powers. The war comes with self-delusion that originates in some of the gatherers. People that perform holy activities in the house of God are distracted by the trouble. The righteous God for whom people gather in His name is patient. He does not persuade Himself with the provocation. The name of the Lord has enduring principle, and the Lord does not take pleasure in destroying the wicked.

The Islamic mosque is the third edition of the house of worship after the synagogue, and the Christians' church. Jerusalem holds a special place in the heart of the Islamic faith, particularly because of the meaning that Muslims derive from both the Dome of the Rock and the al-Aqsa Mosque. The large mosque in the city center of Medina, the al-Haram Mosque in Mecca, and the al-Aqsa Mosque in Jerusalem are the three holiest sites in Islam. The mosques were built after the Prophet Muhammad died. Muslims of the time of the Prophet Muhammad faced toward Jerusalem when they prayed. For obvious reasons, Mecca was not an established place of worship in the time of the Prophet Muhammad. The caliphs and the Islamic lords of the Ottoman Empire were the powers that upgraded the worship of Mecca and Medina with huge mosques and domes that exist on burial sites of the founding members of the Islamic faith.

In present-day Islam, the Muslims of the Shia and Sunni sects turn toward the city of Mecca when they pray. The main reason to turn toward Mecca is the Kaaba, a cuboid structure in the middle of the al-Haram Mosque. The Kaaba is the most sacred place in the mosque; Muslims that enter the mosque to pray regard the small stone structure as God's place in the house of prayer.

So far in the conflict between Arabs and the state of Israel, the Arab Palestinians have insisted on making East Jerusalem the capital of their desired new state. The goal of the Arab Palestinians is to maintain full control of the Islamic shrine and the mosques placed on Mount Zion. The whole area of the Dome of the Rock and the al Aqsa Mosque in Jerusalem is called the Noble Sanctuary in Islam. Unfortunately, the name Noble Sanctuary does not exist in the Koran. It is a showcase for Islamic architecture and design from the time of Caliph Umayyad Abd al-Malik to the time of the Ottoman Empire, and it continues as an important religious and educational center for Muslims of the present day.

The Temple Mount is called both Mount Moriah and Mount Zion in the Bible. The story of the place is of deep religious importance to the Jews from the ancient time of their history. The Islamic structures on the site were built by the successors of the Prophet Muhammad, mostly by the Caliph Umayyad Abd al-Malik. People should study the Bible to realize the large amount of attention the Hebrew prophets gave to the Temple Mount because of events connected to Abraham, King David, the ruined Jewish temple, and the prophecy regarding the resurrection of temple worship in Israel. As a matter of fact, the God who first called Abraham to the site of Mount Moriah is still busy, and He has more plans to offer for the place.

The Bible indicates a third temple will be built on the site of the ruined temple.[161] The prophecy might seem to present a problem, given the political obstacles that stand in the way of the third and final temple. The Jerusalem Islamic Waqf is in control of religious activity on the Temple Mount. Yet nothing can stop the sovereign plan of God from reaching its goal. The Muslim leaders who run the affairs of the Temple Mount are tasked with fulfilling the prophecy written in the Gospel by Saint Luke. The prophecy is confirmed in the book of Revelation 11:2. Jesus Christ said in the Gospel, "Jerusalem will be trampled on by the Gentiles until the times of the Gentiles are fulfilled."[162]

The future of Jerusalem is well articulated in the Bible. The Islamic creations on the Temple Mount will not be there much longer. The structures are signs of demolition that will be done when the Jews are fully prepared to naturalize the heritage of Jerusalem, as it has always been the city of Jehovah. The political conflict over who owns Mount

---

[161] See Daniel 9:27.
[162] Luke 21:24.

Zion is currently going according to the hopes of many Arab Muslims. They expect that the conflict will in the end make Jerusalem a great symbol of the Islamic conquerors.

Islam was founded 630 years after Jesus Christ ascended to heaven, and practitioners of Judaism had settled the land for thousands of years before the Lord Jesus Christ was born. Yet the Arab Muslims in the Kingdom of Israel have an uncompromising position on the issue of owning the site. Mecca and Medina are the birthplace and the burial place of the Prophet Muhammad. For the sake of the Prophet, the Islamic monopoly in the Arabic cities of Mecca and Medina is not in dispute. The Islam of Jerusalem is virtually keeping barbarism alive in fighting the peace of the world.

The Dome of the Rock is the most famous Islamic vision of East Jerusalem. The building is both impressive and beautiful, and it can be seen from everywhere in the city. The Dome of the Rock is intended to stay on the temple site as a great sign of the Islamic conquest. The shrine is at the moment the crowning glory of the Temple Mount. Both the Shia and the Sunni Muslims consider the place of the stone building to be where the Prophet Muhammad stood when he ascended above the cloud in his nighttime journey to heaven.

In case you missed the earlier point I made about the visit of the Prophet Muhammad to heaven, the journey was neither physically taken nor spiritually occurred when the Prophet Muhammad died. The Islamic history of the life of the Prophet Muhammad says that a flying horse took him on the night of the journey from Mecca to Jerusalem (at the place where the Dome of Rock stands) and from Jerusalem to heaven, where he spoke with the prophets of old. The story alleges that the flying horse brought the Prophet Muhammad back to Mecca on the same night after again passing through the Jerusalem site. The authenticity of the story is not verified, and no one knows what the Prophet Muhammad discussed in heaven. The alleged journey to heaven is presumed to have happened in 621. Muhammad died eleven years later, and he was buried in the al-Nabawi Mosque (the Mosque of the Prophet) in the city of Medina.

The burial place of the Prophet Muhammad lies within the territory where the house of his first wife Ayesha, was located. The Prophet felt mysteriously sick in the house of Ayesha, and there he died. The importance of the mosque predates the death of the Prophet Muhammad. His grave on the site is not the reason for the high sanctity of the mosque. The Prophet Muhammad adjoined the mosque to the house of his first wife, Ayesha, when he lived with her, and when he died, the mosque was expanded to include his grave.

The grave of the Prophet Muhammad is a point of attraction to millions of Muslim visitors to the city of Medina. The grave cannot be seen within the flat view of the interior of the mosque. The area of his grave is secured with both gold mesh and a black curtain. The grave of the Prophet Muhammad is not lavishly decorated, and it should not be, because of the Islamic tradition regarding burial. The grave mound is approximately two meters above floor level. Above the grave of the Prophet is the green wooden dome that was built in the time of the Ottoman Empire. The green color of the wooden dome is the favored color for the emblem of the Prophet Muhammad and his beloved city of Medina.

The Caliph Abu Bakr and Caliph Umar were buried next to each other on one side of the grave of the Prophet Muhammad. On the other side of the grave lies an empty grave. I am not sure when the empty grave was dug. It is by the witness of the Muslim scholars who report on the situation of the mosque that I realized the empty grave truly exists. According to the Muslim scholars, the grave has been prepared for Jesus Christ upon His faithful return. The report on the mosque of the Prophet confirms that Muslims look forward to burying the Lord Jesus Christ again, next to the Prophet Muhammad. They expect the arrangement will be the last sign to show that Islam conquered the world.

Other predictions by the Muslim scholars and the motive for digging the grave are outside the scope of this book. Whatever the belief is, Jesus Christ is not flesh, and His purpose in coming to the earth again is not to die, but to begin the rapture of His saints. The End Time Rapture is for those who died in Him, for the love of His righousness, and for the sake of spreading His Gospel.

Muslims believe that the Lord Jesus Christ is a prophet of God. He is known in the Koran as Isa. The Lord's name Isa in the Koran is well respected among the Muslim community. But the Muslims do not honor the Lord Jesus Christ like they honors the Prophet Muhammad. They prefer to believe that the Prophet Muhammad is both the last prophet that came to earth and the greatest among the sent prophets of God. It is not strange that the Koran mentions the name of Jesus Christ more than it mentions the name of the Prophet Muhammad. Jesus Christ is the central figure of both the Old Testament and the New Testament theology.

Both testaments of the Bible and the Church of Christ were well established before the start of Islam. The Islamic translators that copied parts of the Bible into the Koran reflected the awareness of the Gospel in the new book of faith, especially to show that the Koran was written when Christians were already the most popular audience of the living God. The Jewish unbelief gave the Islamic faith fulfillment in the Prophet Muhammad. The Islamic translators seem to have drawn sharp lines of contrast with the Prophet Muhammad against the Orthodox Jews that rejected the Lord Jesus Christ as the Messiah of the whole world.

Both the content of the Koran and the caliphates' jihad movement were particularly involved in the fight to overturn both the Jewish unbelief and the resolve of Christians proclaiming the Lord Jesus Christ is the Son of God.

The ancient rock on the ground of the Dome of the Rock was declared a holy place before the interference of the Islamic movement arrived in Jerusalem. The Jews believed that the place the rock stood was where Abraham prepared his son Isaac as an offering to God. Muslim scholars placed the event of the sacrifice in Mecca on behalf of Ishmael. The issue is to determine if it was the Prophet Muhammad who deceived his followers with the altered information. Otherwise, the misinterpreted facts in the Koran were made by none other than the Islamic copiers.

The Koran does not teach any fundamental morality that the Bible does not teach. The Koran has no independent verification of both the

Creation and the End Time except by the revelation in the Bible. The writers of the Koran seem to have particularly denied every link that the Jews inherited from the historical theology, given the fact that the Hebrew Scripture is the main source of the Jewish history. It is unnecessary if the argument is to show that the message of the Koran is morally more correct and therefore superior to any message of the Hebrew Scripture. The Islamic scholars that wrote the Koran might have questioned the authenticity of the Bible from a human intellectual viewpoint. But it is unjustifiable by any means to use either the content of the Koran or any form of human philosophy to argue against both the message and the faith that the Bible represents. The Dome of the Rock stands near the site of the Jewish temple that was destroyed twice during the siege of Jerusalem. In 637, the control of Jerusalem was surrendered to the Rashidun Caliphate army that conquered both the holy land and Syria. The Caliph Umayyad Abd al-Malik built the Dome of the Rock near the site of the Jewish temple from the years 688 to 691. Both theological scholars and archeological historians have found the purpose of building the Dome of the Rock on the temple site more complex than the claim made by the Muslims scholars, which suggests that the building reminds the Muslim community of the visit of the Prophet Muhammad to heaven. The Dome of the Rock, built by Caliph Abd al-Malik, is a symbol of defeat both to the Jewish temple in ruin and to Christians worshipping near the site.

Islam is considered by its followers as the superior new faith that must destroy the old faith of Jerusalem. According to the content of a book by Jerome Murphy O'Connor, the dome by Umayyad speaks to Jews by its location and to Christians by its interior decoration.[163] Dogan Kuban mentions the building in one of his books, saying, "Art historians have kept up an unceasing flow of studies of the Dome of the Rock. In the context of Islamic architecture the building is unique, but in that of Roman architecture, its form is directly in line with the late tradition in Syria. All of its important features from the interior's double

---

[163] Jerome Murphy-O'Connor, *The Holy Land: An Oxford Archaeological Guide*, 4th ed. (Oxford: Oxford University Press, 1998), 85-89.

colonnades to the great wooden dome have been shown as faithful reproduction of features of the Cathedral of Bosra in southern Syria. Its well-known mosaic decorations are Islamic with the sense that the vocabulary is syncretic and does not include representation of men and animal. The entire building might be viewed as the last blossoming of the Hellenistic tradition before the Islamic synthesis created its own formula."[164]

The Dome of the Rock was the church of Saint Augustinian's Roman Catholic Mission during the Christian Crusades of the early twelfth century. The crusaders temporarily defeated the Islamic jihad movement in Jerusalem and returned control of Jerusalem to both the Jews and the Christians. The crusade of the Christian Knights Templar[165] was particularly keen at the time in defending the city. The al-Aqsa Mosque near the Dome of the Rock was headquarters of the Knights Templar. Until the collapse of the Knights Templar Crusade in 1244, the church in the Dome of the Rock was called Templum Domini. The place did not return to Western control until 1917 when the European allied forces seized Jerusalem by defeating the Ottoman Empire in the First World War.

Today there is a new pattern of tricky negotiation concerning the temple site. The aim of the negotiation is to twist the hand of the Jewish state capital on the site. The United Nations adopted the negotiation and seek to transfer control of the temple site to the Arab Palestinians, whose claim represents the Islamic mind-set of the old caliphate regimes. The so-called Arab Palestinian evidence of land ownership rights in East Jerusalem and the West Bank is the most elaborate practical joke of our

---

[164] Dogan Kuban, *Muslim Religious Architecture* (Boston: Brill Academic Publishers: 1974.

[165] The caliphate of the period in which the Dome of the Rock was constructed tolerated Christianity and Judaism, allowing pilgrims of both beliefs to freely visit the holy city of Jerusalem. However, the era was quickly ended in the year of 969 when control of Jerusalem was passed on to the Fatimid caliphs of Egypt. The radicalized and intolerant Shiites systematically destroyed a majority of the synagogues and churches of Jerusalem. In 1071, the Seljuk Turks defeated the Byzantines, displaced the Egyptian masters of the holy city, and closed the long-established pilgrimage routes used by western European Christians. Christian pilgrimage to Jerusalem was prohibited by the Muslim rulers, and the action angered the Western Europeans, offering a cause for the Crusades, which followed. By the end of 1099, a series of invasions that culminated in the recapture of Jerusalem has been carried out by the Christian crusaders.

time. The ongoing negotiation to have the proposed Arab Palestinian state capital in East Jerusalem is not bound to any true history of the Dome of the Rock. The outcome of the negotiation, whatever it might be, will not bring peace in the region unless the nation of Israel either agrees to relocate or vanishes. The most disturbing aspect of the Arab Palestinians' struggle is making the site of the covenant temple in Jerusalem look as though it exists in a foreign land. The implication of the plan is huge for every nation that worships God. In the future, the radical Islamic groups in Arab Palestinian society could do whatever they wanted to the holiest place of God on earth if they gained control of the site, especially if they are a sovereign state.

The Arab Palestinians lose nothing in the political conflict. Every political step into the conflict is a gain for them. The Jewish overture to have a peaceful resolution of the conflict is unfortunate. The writer of Psalm 83 stated the mind of the enemies of Israel. The Psalm is patterned to show the reality of the trouble in Palestine. The Psalm states that nothing will satisfy the enemies of Israel unless the nation of Israel is wiped off the earth and the people of Israel cease being a nation. The Psalmist wrote, "See how your enemies are astir; and those who hate you have lifted up their heads. With cunning they conspire against your people, and consulted together against your sheltered ones. They have said, 'Come, and let us cut them off from being a nation, that the name of Israel may be remembered no more.' With one mind they plot together; they form an alliance against you: the tents of Edom and the Ishmaelite; Moab, and the Hagrites; Gebal, Ammon, and Amalek; Philistia with the inhabitants of Tyre. Even Assyria joined them, and they have helped the children of Lot."[166]

The power of God at work is the surviving secret of Israel. The message, which the Prophet Isaiah sent to King Ahaz of Judah, should ring like a bell amid the current political situation in Israel. The kingmakers of Israel must decide either to trust in the Lord and let Him protect the land and the people or rely on foreign military alliance that undermines the

---

[166] Psalm 83:2-8.

authority of God over the land and His people.[167] The nation of Israel can hardly be saved from its enemy's plot unless the people genuinely return to God. The Bible is not against the strong national defense system that Israel has, and the Bible is not against the diplomatic friendship that Israel shares with nations of the world. Israel is guilty of idolatry, as its hope to have a proper defense system is primarily sited outside of God. The people of Israel must recall on a daily basis the event of the death of King Josiah at Megiddo. King Josiah made an unwarranted alliance with the king of Assyria, and both the kings joined forces and fought against Pharaoh Necho of Egypt.[168] King Josiah died on the battlefield. His death came about not because God failed to protect His anointed one in time of danger. The death of King Josiah in 609 BC refers to his leadership of spiritual blindness.

On a separate occasion, King Hezekiah of Judah survived the threat of destruction that King Sennacherib of Assyria made against Jerusalem and its citizens in 701 BC. King Hezekiah was terrified by the threat, and he prayed to receive the help of God to fight the battle against the Assyrians' strong army. God fought the battle by Himself and saved Jerusalem and its citizens from suffering humiliation. It is unfortunate that these things are recorded in the Jewish Holy Scripture and the Jews themselves do not act on them. God is forever ready to protect any generation of the Israelites that trusts in Him.[169]

Saying that Israel must trust in God should not mean that Israel must disband its military defense force. Trusting in God does not require the people of Israel to reject the support of friendly nations. But the state of Israel must allow God to take His rightful place in the national life of His people. Nations friendly to Israel must follow behind and not in front of the Lord's leadership. Jehovah is the great warrior, and the Lord is His name.[170] His battle brings the assurance

---

[167] See Isaiah 7:3-9; "So Ahaz sent messengers to Tigiath-Pileser king of Assyria, saying, 'I am your servant and your son. Come up and save me from the hand of the king of Syria and from the hand of Israel who rise up against me'" (2 Kings 16:7).

[168] See 2 Kings 23:29-30 and 2 Chronicles 35:20-27.

[169] See 2 Kings 19:14-19 and 2 Chronicles 32.

[170] See Exodus 15:3.

of justice to the oppressed, and the weapons of His war are never returned empty.

The inhabitants of Canaan and their neighbors will hear Him and be afraid of His authority. Fear will fall on them by the greatness of His outstretched arm, which rises up only for justice. Jerusalem is called Zion in the book of Psalms. It is the known city of God and the place of His prophets. The Lord declares Jerusalem is His own city forever. "For the Lord has chosen Zion; He has desired it for His dwelling place. 'This is my resting place forever, declares the Lord, here I will dwell, for I have desired it. I will abundantly bless her provision; I will satisfy her poor with bread'"[171] Jesus Christ called Jerusalem the sacred city of the Great King. He commanded that no oath should be taken on its name.[172] Jerusalem is forever God's royal city and the capital of His kingdom on earth.[173] The vision of the Prophet Isaiah concerning the future glory of Jerusalem depicted the reality of peace that people should expect in the nearest end of days. Isaiah said, "Now it shall come to pass in the last days that the mountain of the Lord's house shall be established as the chief among the mountains, and it shall be exalted above the hills; and the nations shall flow to it. Many people shall come and say, 'Come, and let us go up to the mountain of the Lord, to the house of the God of Jacob. He will teach us His ways that we may walk in His paths. For out of Zion shall go forth the law, and the word of the Lord from Jerusalem, He shall judge between the nations and rebuke many people with righteousness.'"[174] The national dimmed light of Israel will shine bright again. The message of Isaiah is that followers should have the courage to attach sufficient importance to the promise of God. The restoration will come first to the Jewish nation of Israel and then to people that genuinely call upon His name. The spiritual downfall of Israel is not an accident of history but a factor in the redemptive plan of God. The desire of your prayer to restore the Kingdom of Israel is a necessary end to expect. The Apostle Paul

---

[171] Psalm 132:13-15.
[172] See Matthew 5:35.
[173] See Revelation 20:1-6.
[174] Isaiah 2:2- 4.

said, "Did they stumble so as to fall beyond recovery? Not at all! Rather, because of their transgression, salvation has come to the Gentiles to make Israel envious. But if their transgression means riches for the world, and their loss means riches for the Gentiles, how much greater riches will their fullness bring."[175] "Israel has experienced a hardening in part until the full number of the Gentiles has come in. And so all Israel will be saved as it is written: 'The deliverance will come from Zion; he will turn godlessness away from Jacob. And this is my covenant with them when I take away their sin and set them free forever.'"[176]

The return of God to Zion is obvious, and His salvation is near. He will return in wondrous glory, His presence will dwell in Jerusalem. People of all walks of life shall feel the presence of the Lord and fear Him. The Lord said, "For the sake of Zion I will not keep silent, and for the sake of Jerusalem, I will not remain quiet until her righteousness shines out like the brightness of dawn, and her salvation like a blazing torch. The gentiles shall see your glory, for you shall be called by a new name, which the mouth of the Lord will name."[177]

Israel is a nation of prayer, and the unbelieving Jews are not forever outcast. God shall remember His long, loving mercy even in the midst of His anger. The Jewish nation descended from holy parents. If the root is reckoned as holy, the branches will eventually be holy. Grace does not run in veins, but the external privileges can follow the genetic material for thousands of generations. "Concerning the Gospel they are enemies for your sake, but concerning the election they are beloved for the sake of the fathers. For the gifts and calling of God are irrevocable."[178]

---

[175] Romans 11:11-12.
[176] Romans 11:25-27.
[177] Isaiah 62:1-2.
[178] Romans 11:28.

CHAPTER 9

THE MAKING OF A STATE IN JORDAN

Jordan was part of the traditional territory of the Canaanites. The place is separated from the rest of the land by the Jordan River. The area gained the name of Transjordan when the children of Israel entered the Promised Land from Egypt. The tribe of Reuben and the half-tribe of Manasseh inherited the area. Both tribes were often called the Hebrew people of the other side of the Jordan River. The land of Tranjordan was a significant part of the Northern Kingdom of Israel. The biblical history of the territory started around 2000 BC. At the time, the Amorites, the Hittites, and the Edomites settled on the land. The Israelites that came out of the Egyptian bondage arrived on the land by the end of the century.

The later history of Transjordan is characterized by different military incursions by both foreign empires and tribal peoples. The Ammonites, the Moabites, the Assyrians, the Babylonians, the Persians, the Greeks, the Romans, the Muhammadan jihadists, the Christian Crusaders, the Islamic caliphates of Seljuk, the Eyyubids, the Mongols, the Mamluks, the Ottomans, and the Circassians were people and empires that once occupied Transjordan. The last foreign military occupier of Transjordan was the British Army.

The British and the French armies took control of the Middle East after the military forces of the European allied nations defeated the forces of the Ottoman Empire in the First World War. The Ottoman Empire joined forces with Germany, Austria, and Hungary and fought the world war against the other European countries. The huge Ottoman Empire was completely disjointed after the First World War was won. Britain gained full control of the Kingdom of Israel by signing the Sykes-Picot Agreement with France in May 1916.

The Sykes-Picot Agreement was formularized into the League of Nations' mandate system on the September 29, 1923. Under the Sykes-Picot Agreement, France colonized Syria, Lebanon, Alexandretta, and a portion of southeastern Turkey. Britain ruled both Mesopotamia and Jewish Palestine, the latter of which included Transjordan.[179]

The agreement that returned control of Palestine to the Jews was concluded with the Arthur James Balfour declaration in November 1917. The Balfour declaration was incorporated into the mandate for the independent Jewish Palestine after the League of Nations aborted the Sévres Peace Agreement, which was signed by the officers of both the allied European nations and the defeated Ottoman Empire. Implementing the content of the Balfour document was not easy politics for the British occupiers in Palestine. The process suffered complications due to political trouble, and the plan to handover Palestine to Jews was delayed until 1948.

Double standards were exercised as political tools by both the French and the British authorities in the Middle East. Britain wanted to govern its controlled territory without violating the religious rights of the non-Jews in the area, and thereby the British command yielded to the struggle of Arab politicians who used organized revolt and civil disobedience to demand that Arab autonomy exist in Transjordan. At the top of the struggle were Abdullah Ibn Al-Hussein of Saudi Arabia and his brother, Faisal Ibn Al-Hussein. Both men were successful in using organized public rebellion to establish their political goals.

---

[179] See the British Mandate for Mesopotamia.

In 1920, with the battle of Maysalun near Damascus, the French army defeated Faisal Ibn Al-Hussein and his Arab militia. The French soldiers deposed Faisal from his self-appointed kingship of Syria. Faisal Ibn Al-Hussein had been able to position himself as king of Syria because of complex Arab revolts and massive political problems that had resulted from the partitioning of the Ottoman Empire in the aftermath of the First World War.

A year later, in 1921, the British authority in Palestine carved out the country of Iraq from Mesopotamia and gave Faisal the privilege of governing the new state of Iraq. The British authority further agreed to create the Arab Emirate of Transjordan, of which Abdullah Ibn Al-Hussein was desperate to be the ruler. The League of Nations approved creating the Emirate of Transjordan to maintain the control of peace among Jews and Arab immigrants in the Kingdom of Israel. It was certain that the formation of the Emirate of Transjordan was to solve the political problems both the British and the French authorities encountered by portioning the whole of the Middle East. Partitioning the conquered Ottoman Empire into British and French colonies was a huge political event with regard to people and territories that were divided into several new countries. The mandate for both the Jewish Palestinian state and the Islamic Arab Emirate of Transjordan was signed by British authorities in 1920, and a year later, the Emirate of Transjordan was established as a country.

The twenty-one-year period that passed between the end of the First World War and the beginning of the Second World War was an opportunity the Arab politicians used to unite the Arab tribes in Palestine. The Arabs in Transjordan made themselves a stronger political force by creating larger populations of residents than the Jews had. They were systematic in taking charge of controlling Transjordan while the Jewish population dropped into being the minority. Emir Abdullah Ibn al-Hussein and his brother Faisal were the key political figures that rebuilt the political unity among Arabs in Syria, Iraq, Lebanon, and Transjordan. The shattered unity was a direct result of the defeat that the Ottoman Empire suffered in the region.

In 1921, Emir Abdullah chose Amman to be the seat of government in the newly created Emirate of Transjordan. It had previously been expected that the city of As-Salt, as it was almost wholly dominated by Arabs, would be the capital of Transjordan. As-Salt was a Jewish desert city containing a large population of Arabs from Saudi Arabia. Business and politics in As-Salt were influenced by the Arabs. The Ottoman Empire established regional administration in the city of As-Salt in the nineteenth century and encouraged Saudi businessmen and Muslims to settle in most parts of the area. Also, the Romans, the Byzantines, and the Mamluks contributed to the development of As-Salt.

But perhaps Emir Abdullah chose Amman to be the capital of Transjordan because of both the history and the strategic location of the city. The city of Amman was built on a hilly area in the northwest of Transjordan. Amman was one of the oldest continuously inhabited cities of the world and the area of the Promised Land that is referred to in the Bible as Rabbath-ammon. The ancient city was the capital territory of the Ammonites. Ammon was descendant of Lot, the nephew of Abraham. The descendants of Ammon lived on the land, and they were called the Ammonites. Both the Moabites and the Ammonites were children from the two daughters of Lot, and both tribes lived with the Canaanites of the region when the Israelites arrived in Canaan from the Egyptian bondage.

Until the month of May 1948, Abdullah and his brother Faisal made serious efforts to seize as much of the Jewish land as was possible for the independent Arab state of Transjordan. Emir Abdullah included the desperate Bedouin tribes in the cohesive group of Arabs in Transjordan and created the political willpower that allowed the Arabs to have a majority hold over the Jewish population.

The increased Western political encroachment into the Middle East after the collapse of the Ottoman Empire was a factor in the series of other political problems of the region. To stand against the Western influence, especially in the politics of securing Transjordan, Emir Abdullah established the Arab Legion of Jordan and formally transformed the legion into being the parliamentary body that is today the legislative council of Jordan.

The United Nations, which replaced the League of Nations in October 1945, facilitated the speedy conclusion of the agreement to hand over the rest of Palestine to the Jews. The task to grant formal independence to the Jews was accomplished in the month of May in 1948. The Jewish people's Council gathered at the Tel Aviv Museum and approved the proclamation, which declared the establishment of the state of Israel on the May 14. Thus, the fifth of Iyar in the Hebrew calendar is celebrated as Israel's day of independence. The state of Israel was recognized the same evening by the United States of America, and three days later, the USSR, Nicaragua, Czech Republic, Slovakia, Serbia, and Poland also recognized the state of Israel. [180]

Almost immediately, the Arab Transjordanians and five Arab nations of the Middle East invaded the Jewish state. The Arab population in the West Bank and East Jerusalem were particularly pleased when the invading forces of Transjordan captured the area. The success of the incursion encouraged the Transjordanian government to preserve Arab control in the captured territory. In a conference that was held in Jericho in December 1948, Emir Abdullah was encouraged by the Arabs to unite the West Bank and East Jerusalem under the single leadership of his Emirate of Transjordan.

The Emirate of Transjordan held its first parliamentary election in April 1950, and the Arabs in East Jerusalem and the West Bank fully represented themselves in the election as citizens of Tansjordan. Ten days after the election, the Transjordanian parliament passed a law that concluded the takeover of East Jerusalem and the West Bank. On April 24, 1950, the King Abdullah merged all the held territory of Israel into the Emirate of Transjordan and formally granted Transjordanian citizenship to the Arabs in East Jerusalem and the West Bank. King Abdullah Ibn al-Hussein renamed the Emirate of Transjordan to what the nation is called today, the Hashemite Kingdom of Jordan. Britain and Pakistan were the only countries of the League of Nations that formally recognized

---

[180] USSR was the Union of Soviet Socialist Republics, commonly referred to as Soviet Union or just Russia. USSR was a communist federation that lasted from 1924 to1991 and it comprised of twelve main republics, now called Former Soviet Union (SFU).

the annexed territory of East Jerusalem and the West Bank as the Arab Jordanians' territory.

King Abdullah Ibn al-Hussein was assassinated on the July 20, 1951, at the entrance gate of the al-Aqsa Mosque in Jerusalem. He attended Friday prayer in the mosque and was about to leave the mosque's compound when he was killed by an unknown shooter.

The Jordanian parliament immediately appointed Talal bin Abdullah, son of King Abdullah, to succeed his father on his self-created throne of Jordan. Mental illness soon incapacitated Talal from ruling the Arab people of Jordan, and instead of him on the throne, his son Prince Hussein was handed over the governance of Jordan at the age of seventeen. During July 1953, King Hussein of Jordan, grandson son of King Abdullah Ibn al-Hussein, made East Jerusalem the capital of the Hashemite Kingdom of Jordan. He later terminated the Anglo-Jordanian treaty.

The state of Israel recovered the territory of East Jerusalem and the West Bank during the war of 1967. Since then, the ex-Jordanian diasporas, the Arab Palestinians, have established themselves as an autonomous people and have fought to reclaim the sites. The political consequence of King Abdullah's territorial expansion law was the improper adjoining of the main territory of Israel to the outline of a new country that has neither natural boundaries nor a preexisting constitution. King Abdullah created no definite political identity for his subjects on the annexed territory of East Jerusalem and the West Bank, even though his government from Amman maintained political control of the annexed territory until the war of 1967.

The Arabs' political position concerning the existence of Israel was compromised after the war. Almost all the Arabs in East Jerusalem, the West Bank and Gaza became refugees as result of the war. They made safe havens in Jordan, Lebanon, Egypt, and Syria, and as far away as Iraq and Kuwait. Since then, new generations of Arab Palestinians have been born to the population in exile. King Abdullah Ibn al-Hussein and his allied political combatants, who were to conclude the destruction of Israel, were halted in the Six-Day War, despite the gains the Arabs achieved through other political advances. The growing population of

Arab Palestinians in Israel has come about both from remnants of the Arab Jordanian diasporas that reorganized after the war and from the new generation of Arabs born into the population since 1967.

The Arab Palestinians did not at first question their loyalty to the Jordanian kings. The people recognized that they belonged to the Jordanian countrymen and countrywomen. The proposed Arab Palestinian national flag is complementary to the national flag of the Emirate of Transjordan. The flags resemble one another, such as two people related by blood often have similar features.

The Arab Palestinians have so far resisted rejoining the Hashemite Kingdom of Jordan even though the current political situation between them and the Jews is bad – so much so that they may not prevail in reaching their goal.

Hardship has taken a toll on both the political and the economic lives of the Arab Palestinians. The reality of the existing bitterness of life that the Arab Palestinians endure is stronger than any sentiment of blood relationship that they might have for the people of their political homeland of Jordan. The Arab Palestinians presumed that they were left out of the agreement that prepared the Emirate of Transjordan, which should have concluded the struggle for the Arab takeover of the West Bank, Gaza and East Jerusalem. The choice to return either to Jordan as second-class citizens or as Muslims to live under Jewish authority is unacceptable to the Arab Palestinians, especially in light of the continuation of the bitter political and economic conditions they are living in.

The Arab Palestinians gained much political luck by achieving autonomy on the Jewish side of the divided Palestine. The struggle is head-on, and the goal is to fully create an Arab Palestinian state. The Arab Palestinians have a mind-set of determination that could make their goal happen either now or never.

It is unfortunate that the Arab Palestinians' struggle is adjoined to a domineering version of Islam. The violent Islam of the Arab world turned the Arab Palestinians' struggle for self-rule into a struggle to occupy the entire Jewish homeland. Their resolve to destroy the Jews and have their places divided among Egypt, Lebanon, Syria, Jordan, and Iraq is the major setback in the series of various political problems that have undermined any success for the freedom of administration the Arab Palestinians want.

In 1970s, the late Mr. Yasser Arafat formed the Fedayeen militias, wanting to use them to divide the Emirate of Jordan. The group tried and failed to establish the Islamic state of Palestine on the Arabian Transjordanians' side of Palestine. Since then, the political struggle to create an Arab Palestinian state has been concentrated against the state of Israel. The political principle the Arab Palestinians adopted in the struggle was to create the state of Palestine in Israel's territory, as there was nowhere else to go.

The Jewish state of Israel is a victim of both self-neglect and multiplying greed of the Arabs. No government in the seven Arab countries where the Arab Palestinian refugees lived since the 1967 war ever integrated any of the refugees into their societies. The best gift to the Arab Palestinians' political aspirations was the Oslo Accord. Without the Oslo Accord, no establishment of any Arab Palestinian state would be possible in the Kingdom of Israel.

In 1959, the Iraqi leader Abd al-Karim Qasim suggested promoting Arab Palestinian nationalism to the Arab League. The plan was to stir up a new spirit in an Islamic movement that would drive Jews out of Palestine. The Arab League carved out a new political entity by promoting liberation movements in the West Bank and Gaza. Mr. Qasim can be said to have publicly embarrassed the leadership of King Hussein of Jordan. The member states of the Arab League knew that the authority of King Hussein would decrease if a new political movement were organized among the militant Arab Muslims in the West Bank and Gaza.

At first the Arabs in the West Bank were reluctant to transform their Palestinian-Jordanian citizenship to that of a different political entity. The political consequence of the new situation was uncertain regarding what would become of them if they lost both their Jordanian passports and the fringe benefits that came from Jordan. Nonetheless, PLO was founded in 1964 by the Arab League against the political will of King

Hussein of Jordan. King Hussein would neither oppose the formation of the PLO nor stop its political activity from expanding beyond the West Bank. This was the starting point of decades of trouble over deciding the shape of the Arab Palestinians' representation.

The first chairman of the PLO was Ahmed al-Shuqayri. The Arab League supported him to help reorganize the Arab Palestinian quasi-militant groups in the West Bank. The quasi-militant groups were made stronger, and they were constantly motivated to oppose both the state of Israel and the Jordanian judicial authority, which from Amman extended its power of control over the region. The leadership of the Jordanian King Hussein was forced by the opposition to grant autonomy to the PLO in the West Bank at the price of antagonizing the states of Egypt and Iraq, who had initiated the PLO through the Arab League.

The problem of deciding the structure of the Arab Palestinians' representation both in the regional conference and in the gathering of the international community is the main cause of mistrust and deep-rooted political bitterness that exists among the member states of the Arab League. The defeat of the Arab allied forces by the state of Israel in the 1967 Six-Day War became the main political factor that prevented the Jordanian authority from having any official encounter with the PLO. The Arab Palestinians that were made refugees through the war of 1967 had their Jordanian citizenship revoked, and they were denied any future claim to the Jordanian mainland.

Except through the Oslo Accord, the Arab Palestinians have never existed as an autonomous people. There was never a land owned and governed by the Arab Palestinians. The Arab Palestinians' history started after the Second World War with the political reform of Israel's territory by the United Nations, and particularly with the Oslo Accord. The origin of the Jordanian royal family was Mecca.

King Abdullah Ibn al-Hussein was born in February 1882 in Mecca. He was the second of the three sons of Hussein bin Ali and his first wife, Abdiyya Bint Abdullah. The true history of the conflict in Palestine is crucial, be it either by the facts stated in this book or by the facts that are obtainable from other true sources.

Following are the major wars Israel fought against its Arab neighbors since gaining political independence in 1948.

- The 1948 – 1949 Arab war against the political independence of Israel: The army of Syria captured the Golan Heights in the war. Between 1948 and 1967, the government of Syria used the Golan Heights as a springboard to attack Jewish farmers and fishermen in the northern region of Israel. The Golan Heights is the area of the Promised Land that is repeatedly mentioned in the Bible as Bashan. The Golan Heights (Bashan) has been the property of the Israelites since the defeat of Og, the Canaanite king of Bashan.[181] The Lord gave the Canaanite king and its land into the hand of Moses. "Then Moses gave to the children of Gad, the children of Reuben and the half-tribe of Manasseh son of Joseph the Kingdom of Sihon, king of the Amorites and the Kingdom of Og, king of Bashan—the whole land with its cities and the territory around them."[182] The modern Jews maintained the ancient Jewish community in Bashan. The population of the native Jews in Bashan is almost equal in number to that of the Druze inhabitants of the area.

- The 1956 Sinai war against Egypt: This war is known as the Kadesh Operation. The military defense force of Israel launched the attack from the ancient Jewish city of Kadesh in northern Sinai. Egypt blocked the Suez Canal against the Jewish ships that sailed through from the Straits of Tiran. The narrow water passage linked the sea ports of Israel to the Red Sea and the Indian Ocean. Egypt finally made peace with Israel in 1979, and since then both countries have been at peace.

- The Six-Day War of 1967 against the Arab allied defense force.

---

[181] Numbers 21:33-35; "Sihon king of the Amorites and Og king of Bashan; He gave their land as an inheritance, an inheritance to His servant Israel. He remembered us in our low estate and freed us from our enemies - His love endures forever" (Psalm 36:19-24).
[182] Numbers 32:33.

- The Yom Kippur War of 1973: Syria and Egypt joined their military forces in the 1973 war and attacked Israel on the Yom Kippur holiday. The joint military attack was aimed at recapturing the Jewish territory the Arabs lost control of in 1967. The time of the attack was perhaps intended to take on the Jewish national defense force by surprise and defeat them during their holy holiday season.

- The invasion of Lebanon in 1982: The national military defense force of Israel invaded Lebanon in 1982, intending to expel the Arab Palestinian guerrilla factions that had been carrying out attacks against Israel on the land. In 1985, Israel withdrew its army from most of the occupied Lebanese territory, and it maintained a narrow buffer zone inside Lebanon until 2000.

CHAPTER 10

ISHMAEL, THE SON OF ABRAHAM

The Apostle Paul used the story of the two sons of Abraham – Ishmael and Isaac – to illustrate the benefits of both the Mosaic Covenant and the New Covenant of the Cross. English translation refers to these two covenants as the Old Testament and the New Testament. The Old Testament explains the progression of the covenant of Abraham through his children from Isaac and Jacob. God renewed the covenant of Abraham with the children of Jacob, and He used the occasion in Sinai to mark the nation of Israel as a people of God. The New Testament gives motive to the death of Jesus Christ. He died on the cross at Calvary. His shed blood on the cross is the ultimate seal on the redemptive grace of God that forgives the sins of humanity.

The New Testament clarifies the amazing transcendent and immanent nature of God. Paul explained the two supreme qualities of God in the letter that he wrote to the Galatians concerning the power of His saving grace. Paul wrote, "Tell me, you who want to be under the law, are you not aware of what the law says? For it is written that Abraham had two sons, one by the slave woman and the other by the free woman. His son by the slave woman was born in the ordinary way, but his son by the free woman was born as the result of a promise. These things may be taken figuratively, for the women represent two covenants. One covenant is from Mount Sinai and bears children who are to be slaves: This is Hagar. Now Hagar stands for Mount Sinai in Arabia and corresponds to the present City of Jerusalem because she is in slavery with her children. But the Jerusalem that is above is free, and she is our mother. For it is written, "Be glad, O barren woman, who bears no children; break forth and cry aloud, you who have no labour pains; because more are the children of the desolate woman than of her who has a husband.""[183]

Paul illustrated the unfailing grace of God with the events that happened between Hagar and Sarah. Sarah was glorified because God kept the promise that He made about Isaac. Hagar was also honoured because God wants humanity to progress in one direction with the unity of His purpose. The illustration that Paul gave to the Galatians about the spiritual standing of the son Ishmael does not necessarily show that both Ishmael and other Gentiles represent the people in bondage. Rather, the illustration conveys that salvation to all Gentiles is secured in the universal covenant of the Cross.

Paul emphasised the vision that God planned for the Gentiles as a vision that died first, and then the ashes were resurrected to the eternal glory. The Gospel is understood as Paul stated: those God called to His purpose will win in the race for eternal glory if they remain faithfully attached to God. The victory is already given, and it comes to every individual when God sees the need.

The concept that Paul used in the epistle is not a new narrative to theology. Paul's illustration has been imperative from the time of Adam and Noah. Adam and Eve sinned, and God promised to redeem the generation of humankind from the sin. He said that we will see the final defeat of Satan when the "Seed of woman" crushes the head of the Serpent.[184] He unfolded the process of saving humanity and saved Noah and his family from the flood. Through the family of Noah, God spared humanity from suffering total destruction.[185] He gave His promise to

---

[183] Galatians 4:21-27.
[184] Genesis 3:15.
[185] "Noah was a just man, perfect in his generation" (Genesis 6:9).

Noah that never again will He destroy the world by flood because of sin. He used the covenant of Abraham according to His promise and demonstrated His love to humanity. God linked humanity to the grace that we inherited in the death and resurrection of His Son, Jesus Christ. But first of all, God called Abraham to Him and separated him from among his people of the homeland of Ur.[186]

God's agenda with Abraham and his wife, Sarah, was foreshadowing of His gracious response to the fornications of the generation of Babel that, according to their groups, scattered across the face of the earth.[187] God established Abraham in Canaan, and He decided that the land of the Canaanites is the place of His covenant worshippers.[188] God endorsed His blessing on the land for Abraham and his covenant generations from Isaac and Jacob, and He tested the faith of Abraham on the account of the covenant. The Bible says, "And it came to pass that when God decided to test the faith of Abraham, He called Abraham and said to him, 'Take your son, your only son Isaac whom you love, and go to the region of Moriah (Temple Mount) and sacrifice him there as a burnt offering, on one of the mountains, which I will tell you about.'"[189]

Faith and hope work together, but slightly to a different end. An empty religion betrays its faith in God and frustrates its hope of receiving eternal glory with an outlook that shows the salvation of God as one might accept a creed. Abraham understood faith and hope were two different things. Faith is to trust in God and patiently walk with Him in whatever His purpose is. Hope is the strength of patience that can help you reach any future blessing of faith.

God's blessing does not always follow the desires of our hearts. The unrighteous desire in people hinders the hope that should keep faith

---

[186] Ur is in modern-day Iraq; see Genesis 11:31.

[187] Genesis 11:8-9; "So the Lord scattered them from there over all the earth, and they stopped building the city. The place was called Babel; there the Lord confused the language of the whole world and scattered the people over the face of the earth" (Genesis 10:4); from Babel, the maritime people spread out into their territories in their clans, within their new nations, each with its own language.

[188] "Now, the Lord said to Abram, 'get out of your country, from your family and from your father's house, to the land that I will show you'" (Genesis 12:1-3).

[189] Genesis 22:1-2.

alive. The effort to manage hope and faith diligently and patiently is righteousness. If you have faith in God, you must know as well that God causes everything to work together for the good of those that trust in Him.[190] Everyone who walks with God bears the two demands of faith, which are patience and obedience. When God tested the faith of Abraham, Abraham carefully controlled his hopes while he used his faith to obey God. Abraham obeyed the instruction to sacrifice his son Isaac, and he went to the place of the offering as the angel of the Lord guided him. At the place, Abraham prepared his son Isaac for the offering and set him on the firewood. Abraham took the knife to cut his son. Then the angel of the Lord called to him and said, "Do not lay a hand on the boy, and do not harm him. Now I know that you fear God, because you have not withheld from me your son, your only son!"[191] Ishmael was a member of the household of Abraham, and he was an adult when the sacrifice occurred. Ishmael was thirteen years old when the boy Isaac was born. The Bible gave the signal of the future blessing of the sacrifice by pointing at the angel of the Lord, who took notice of the boy Isaac as the only son of Abraham. Ishmael was the firstborn son of Abraham.

The concept of Isaac as the only son of Abraham did not neglect the presence of Ishmael in the family. God used Isaac to preserve the future of the covenant. The Bible did not make known the manner of God's command to sacrifice Isaac; it was either by voice or by vision that God talked to Abraham. But we are familiar with the outcome of an honest faith on which Abraham demonstrated his love of God to whatever God's plan was. Abraham did not doubt the source of the instruction. He would not set out to perform a task like killing his own son without being certain that God had commanded him to do it. Whatever the manner was, the idea of sacrificing Isaac originated with God.

God prepared the minds of Abraham and his son Isaac, and He set both the father and the son to the journey. "So early the next morning Abraham got up and loaded his donkey. He took with him two of his servants and his son Isaac. When he had cut enough wood for the burnt

---

[190] See Romans 8:28.
[191] Genesis 22:12.

offering, he set out for the place God had told him about. On the third day, Abraham looked up and saw the place in the distance. He said to his servants, "Stay here with the donkey while I and the boy go over there. We will worship and then we will come back to you." Abraham took the wood for the burnt offering and placed it on his son Isaac and he himself carried the fire and the knife. As the two of them went on together, Isaac spoke up and said to his father Abraham, "Father, the fire and wood are here but where is the lamb for the burnt offering?" Abraham answered, "God himself will provide the lamb for the burnt offering, my son." And the two of them went on together to reach the place God appointed to Abraham.""[192]

There is, however, some disagreement about the object of the sacrifice. The Koran disputes the Bible's account in which of the sons of Abraham were to be sacrificed and who the true heir of Abraham's blessing was. Christians and Jews accepted the traditional narrative of the two sons of Abraham as it had existed in the Bible for thousands of years. The Koran was compiled after the religion of Islam started, by the merits of the Islamic scholars that did the compilation. The Koran was written to bring different meaning to the account of the Bible, and it is in fact achieving that aim. The debate about the two sons of Abraham is fundamental to the disagreements that have existed since the beginning of the written Koran. The issue that perpetuates the debate about the attempted sacrifice of Abraham's son is that of which of the two books contains the infallible revelation of God. Is it the Bible or is it the Koran that is reliable?

The two books claim to have divine inspiration as their source, but both books cannot be divinely inspired if they contradict each other, unless there is a human element in some aspect of the writings. The argument that the name of Ishmael brought into the covenant of Abraham is just one among many other differences that exist between the Bible and the Koran. Some other differences are the nature of God, the deity of Jesus Christ, and the salvation of God.

---

[192] Genesis 22:3-8.

The Islamic festival of Eid al-Adha is known to Muslims as the Sacrifice Festival. Muslims pay tribute to Abraham during the festival for his act of obedience to God. The Sacrifice Festival is celebrated every year, with the starting date of the festival being slightly different in each year. The season of the festival is determined from the tenth day of the last month on the Muslim calendar. During the three days of the holiday, Muslims celebrate the willingness of Abraham to sacrifice his son Ishmael on the altar. The Bible mentions the name of Isaac four times as the sacrificial lamb and provides detailed references to the event along with the name of Isaac.

Isaac was alive in the story of the sacrifice. On the way to the place of the sacrifice, he started the open conversation with his father, Abraham, about the missing item of the sacrifice. The Koran rephrases the story of the sacrifice and does not mention the name of the son Abraham wanted to sacrifice; nor does it mention the name of the son's mother. The unlikely story in the Koran is about Abraham and a strange dream he had at night about him slaughtering his son Ishmael. The next morning, he told the dream to Ishmael. The story of the dream does not exist in the Bible. The dream, as it is told to Ishmael in the Koran, does not represent in any way the burnt offering that the Lord commanded Abraham to perform with his only son. The Islamic scholars that adopted the event of the sacrifice from the Bible are the human influence that qualified Ishmael both as the son offered in sacrifice and as heir to the covenant of Abraham.

The mother of Ishmael was Egyptian, and for decades Egypt was both the cultural center of Islamic civilization and the seat of major Islamic caliphates. The Koran was probably compiled in Egypt. Ishmael spent his youth with his mother in Egypt, and he was married to an Egyptian girl. On the contrary, Isaac was Hebrew, and he represented the opposite of everything that the Islamic scholars want to see as the true story of faith. The thought that Ishmael was the sacrificial son is based on the vision the Islamic scholars held in writing the Koran.

Besides using the Koran to argue this case, the Islamic scholars continued to say that the position of Ishmael in the family of Abraham was traditional, as the firstborn son of any legitimate family was heir to the family's heritage.

Perhaps this second argument is the most likely reason the Islamic scribes overruled both the theme of the story and the divine setting when they copied this part of the Bible into the Koran. This is obvious; the writers of the Koran agreed to the known earthly standards of life that exist in the Bible but not to divine appointment if the appointment contradicts the natural standards.

It is theologically correct to say that Ishmael was the firstborn son of Abraham. The Bible confirms this aspect of the family life of Abraham. Ishmael is regarded in Islam more highly than both Isaac and the Lord Jesus Christ. The followers of the Islamic faith accepted that the Prophet Muhammad was a direct descendant of Ishmael, and therefore the name of Ishmael is more honored in their faith. There was nothing special about the lives and the positions of Ishmael and his mother, Hagar, when they lived in the house of Abraham. The Bible explains the great deal that should be learned from the life of Ishmael and his mother, Hagar. We are familiar with the trouble that Ishmael and his mother brought to the family of Abraham in Canaan, and we share in the loving grace of God, which followed Ishmael and all Gentiles to the future generations.

The deity of Jesus Christ is another covenant relationship where the Koran seriously deviates from the Bible. The Islamic scholars presumed the natural plausible things in every case where they exercised doubt about divine appointment. They founded no practical rationale to admit that the Virgin Mary conceived the baby Jesus Christ by the power of the Holy Spirit. Hence their reaction to His birth is that God has no son. The Koran admits that Jesus Christ was miraculously conceived by the decree of God to aid His ministry to the Jewish community. But the holy book falls short of admitting that Jesus Christ is God incarnate. The Koran emphasizes nothing about the divine power of the Holy Spirit, and the obvious reason for skipping Him is that the copiers did not encounter the indwelling power of His presence during the writing process.

The Koran states that Jesus Christ is both a prophet of God and the messiah that God sent to guide the children of Israel with new scripture (the Gospel). The Islamic scholars were outraged to read in the Gospel that the practice of childbearing is associated with the holy almighty God. Their narrow-minded outlook on spiritual ordination was that childbearing is natural and is the outcome of sexual intercourse by male and female creatures. Also, the Pharisees narrowly accepted the Lord Jesus Christ as a prophet. The Pharisees knew that the Messiah would be a descendant of David, but they did not understand that He would be God Himself.[193] Nonetheless, nothing from these two groups of unbelievers disqualifies the evidence of God's power at work. More often than the Prophet Muhammad, the Koran mentions the name of Jesus Christ twenty-five times. The Koran teaches that Jesus Christ ascended to heaven and that He will restore justice on earth. The Koran admits that Jesus Christ will defeat the false messiah figure who is the Antichrist, eliminate the work of wickedness, and give room to the elite. But the Islamic scholars teach their public to ignore these fundamental facts and accept the Prophet Muhammad is the most appropriate messenger of God. The teaching of the Islamic scholars rejects the resurrection of the dead. It denies the importance of Jesus' death to salvation and describes Him as a Muslim – that is, as a person that submitted himself to do the will of God. Muslims are allowed by their scholars to read only the Koran and Islamic journals. The terrifying attitudes of the Muslims who use both the religion of Islam and the content of the Koran to incite trouble are not helping the curiosity of other Muslims, which is what should be helping them discover the truth of the Gospel. Muslims respect the viewpoints of the Islamic scholars with great fear of facing charges of blasphemy. They must not read the Bible or any other religious text; otherwise, the punishment for blaspheming against Islam and the Koran is a painful death. The instructors of the law of Islam do not necessarily take the love of God into the heart of their message to the people.

Both the scholars of Islam and the local imams are highly regarded as the true guides to the knowledge of God, and whatever they decide to

---

[193] Hebrew 1:13 uses Psalm 110:1 to show that the Messiah is greater than David.

teach to their worship community is, in any sense, the correct knowledge from God.

The highlight of the disagreement between the Bible and the Koran is about Christians proclaiming Jesus Christ is God. Critics of the Christian faith dispute His deity by pointing at the Gospel, where Jesus Christ illustrates His teachings with His faith in God the Father. The unbelieving Jews rejected the Holy Trinity and condemned Christians proclaiming the three persons of the one true God. The Jews did not accept that Jesus Christ is God and supernatural.

The evidence in the Gospel shows that Jesus Christ partly lived a natural human experience and that He exhibited some human characteristics. He once died, although He was resurrected in three days. He wept to show His emotion, and He cried because He was afflicted with pain. He thirsted and asked for water to drink. He felt anger and hunger. He enjoyed parties and drank some wine. He had compassion for people that were afflicted with disease and pain. He slept when He felt tired. Jesus Christ prayed to God the Father, and He is constantly quoted in the Gospel as saying He came to do the will of His Father. Jesus Christ encouraged His followers to believe in Him and also in the Father who sent Him. Before He ascended to heaven, Jesus Christ told His disciples to wait here until He prepared a place for them in His Father's house in heaven.

The Gospel is not abused by critics citing both the human examples of the life of Jesus Christ and the statements He made in the Bible about believing in God the Father. But Christianity is the religion of the Holy Spirit. It is difficult to discern the true meaning of the Christian Gospel without the indwelling experience of the Holy Spirit. He is the essence of believers who are spiritually alive. The Bible is a spiritual book, and the content is best understood with the spiritual mind. To understand the Bible, you must do more than merely read it. Reading the Bible is meaningful, but reading alone often fails to bring about the true meaning. As a matter of fact, there are two ways in which people can read the Bible. You may read the Bible to be inspired by whatever teaching the Holy Spirit gives you, or you may read the Bible to discover where the Bible is wrong and perhaps expose the errors the Bible is hiding. Nonbelievers of the Holy Spirit argue against the Bible from the nonspiritual aspect of reading the book, and they show with the literal understanding that the Bible contradicts itself with its own stated facts. The fundamental problem in understanding the true message of the Bible is discerning spiritual thought. The difficulty is not the problem of personality, and it is not about culture and race; but rather, it is about unwillingness in people.

- Isaac was the promised child of Abraham. The Koran agrees that Ishmael was not the promised child. Isaac was miraculously conceived by his overage mother Sarah. The Koran agrees that Sarah was overage when Isaac was born. The Bible says, "Abraham and Sarah were already old and well advanced in years; and Sarah was past the age of childbearing. So she thought, 'After I am worn out and my master is old, will I now have this pleasure?'"[194]

- Hagar conceived the child Ishmael in the traditional way, and the Koran agrees that this was true.

- God confirmed to Abraham that only his descendants from Isaac would inherit the land of His promise. Abraham sent Ishmael and his mother, Hagar, out of the land of Canaan. Hagar and Ishmael were settled in the desert of Paran, which in present-day geography is mainly the Kingdom of Saudi Arabia. The Koran acknowledges that Abraham dismissed Hagar and her son Ishmael from the bosom of Isaac in Canaan. In each year of pilgrimage to Mecca, the pilgrims say prayers that reflect Hagar's distress before the angel of the Lord comforted her and Ishmael in the desert of Paran. The Sa'i, the main rite of the pilgrimage, is about finding help from God as Hagar did after she repeatedly searched for water around the Arabian hills. Pilgrims to Mecca walk seven times between the hills of Safa and Marwa in memory of the account. In the Koran, the pool of water that Hagar found in the desert was miraculously provided to her by

---

[194] Genesis 18:11-12.

the Archangel Gabriel. This account of her finding water in the desert was copied from the Bible. The Bible states in Genesis chapter 21:19, "God opened her eyes and she saw a well of water. So she went and filled the skin with water and gave the boy a drink." To complete the rite of the pilgrimage to Mecca, pilgrims drink from the well of Zamzam and often take home some of the sacred water to give the blessing to their family.

Abraham held his fear regarding who the seed of the covenant was even after Ishmael was born to his family. In Genesis chapter 17, Abraham pleads to God on behalf of Ishmael that the boy Ishmael might inherit the covenant blessing. Sarah was aged, and Abraham doubted her ability to produce the child that God promised to give to his family. But God replied to Abraham, "As for Sarai your wife, you are no longer to call her Sarai; her name will be Sarah. I will bless her and will surely give you a son by her. I will bless her so that she will be the mother of nations, kings of people will come from her." Abraham fell face-down; he laughed and said to himself, 'Will a son be born to a man of a hundred years old? Will Sarah bear a child at the age of ninety?' And Abraham said to God, "If only Ishmael might live under your blessing!" Then God said, "Yes, but your wife Sarah will bear you a son, and you will call him Isaac. I will establish my covenant with him as an everlasting covenant for his descendants after him. As for Ishmael, I have heard you: I will surely bless him; I will make him fruitful and will greatly increase his numbers. He will be the father of twelve rulers; and I will make him into a great nation. But my covenant I will establish with Isaac, whom Sarah will bear to you by this time next year."[195]

The Archangel Gabriel visited Hagar in the desert after she ran out of the house of Abraham. There in the desert of Paran the Archangel comforted Hagar. He told Hagar that her homeland would be separated and her descendants of various generations of nations would come from her son. God made Ishmael the father of twelve tribes of nations according to the promise that He made to Hagar. The Bible says, "This

---

[195] Genesis 17:15:22.

is the account of Abraham's son Ishmael, whom Sarah's maidservant Hagar the Egyptian bore to Abraham. These are the names of the sons of Ishmael listed in order of their birth: Nebaioth, the firstborn of Ishmael, Kedar, Adbeel, Mibsam, Mishma, Dumah, Massa, Hadad, Tema, Jetur, Naphish, and Kedemah. These were the sons of Ishmael, and these are the names of the twelve tribal rulers according to their settlements and camps.

Altogether, Ishmael lived a hundred and thirty-seven years when he died."[196]

The descendants of Ishmael were the Ishmaelites. The generations of the Ishmaelite tribes are predominantly the present-day Arabs. Paran (Mecca) originated in the Arabian Desert, and it was sparsely inhabited by the nomadic Ishmaelite tribes during the days of Jacob. The Arabian Desert was a vast land with scattered oases. The history of Saudi Arabia as a sovereign state begins in 1930, when Abdul-Aziz Al Saud united the various tribes of the Arabian Desert into one cohesive communal group. The country was named after the Al Saud royal family. Al Saud died in 1953, and he was survived by his five sons who, with their children, have led the country ever since. God gave His blessing to all the children of Abraham, but the blessing of Isaac had a unique purpose.

Abraham was compelled to separate the rest of his children from Isaac. The Koran agrees that except, Isaac the rest of Abraham's children went out of Canaan, each going on his separate way.[197] The Apostle Paul cited Isaac in his letter to the Romans as proof of God's sovereign right to choose and save by the rule of His grace. The election of Isaac was not intended to imply that God had failed anyone. Paul said, "Not all who are descended from Israel are Israel. Nor because they are his descendants are they all Abraham's children. On the contrary, it is through Isaac that your offspring will be reckoned. In other words, it is not the natural children who are God's children, but it is the children of the promise who are regarded as Abraham's offspring. For this was how the promise was stated, 'At the appointed time, I will return and Sarah will have a son.' Not

---

[196] Genesis 25:12-16.
[197] See Genesis 17 and Genesis 25.

only that, but Rebekah's children had one and the same father, our father Isaac. Yet before the twins were born or had done anything good or bad – in order that God's purpose in election might stand: not by work, but by Him who calls – she was told, "The older will serve the younger," and just as it is written, "Jacob I loved but Esau I hate." What then shall we say? Is God unjust? Not at all; for He says to Moses, "I will have mercy on whom I have mercy, and I will have compassion on whom I have compassion.""[198] Paul gave this clarification to show that any good system of belief must be worthy of its source. The clarification is fundamental and useful to the true teaching of faith.

Believers of the biblical God have the true faith if the Bible is inspired from heaven and teaches the divine mindset. If the Koran is both true and believable, Islam is the genuine system of worshipping God. The revelation in the Koran relies heavily on the Old Testament and slightly on the New Testament teaching about the life of Jesus Christ. The actual writing of the Koran began in 632, when the Prophet Muhammad died. The task of compiling the Koran was completed in 634 by Caliph Abu Bakr as-Siddiq. The Torah in the Holy Writ served as the basis for the Koran writers. The Torah in the Koran is the edited version of the five books of Moses. The word "Torah" is not an Arabic origin. "Torah" is a Hebrew word that explains the comprehensive meaning of the Mosaic Law. The Torah provided the impression that led to the five books of Moses being referred to as the Pentateuch. There was no Islamic doctrine or culture when the human authors of the Bible wrote the volumes.

The Islamic faith recognizes the biblical forefathers as prophets of God. The Koran defines Noah, Abraham, Moses, and David as discoverers of monotheism. It is implied that they were taught not by men but only by God. Ishmael, the Prophet Muhammad, and Isa (Jesus Christ) received the title of "prophet" in the Koran by the same thought and definition. The opinion that the Bible is unreliable cannot be verified with the content of the Koran. The portions of the Psalms of David in the Koran are examples

---

[198] Romans 9:6-15.

of the biased work of the Koran writers. The bad news is not the Koran per se but the negative thoughts that people glean from reading the Koran. The thoughts of some classical and Islamic scholars regarding the origin of the Bible are also part of the problem.

No part of the Bible was originally written in the Arabic language. The Arabic language evolved much later in history, from the ancient language of Syria, and it belongs to the 6th century AD Semitic family of languages. The Old Testament texts were completed in Hebrew except a few passages, such as some parts of the book of Daniel that were written in Aramaic. All sections of the Gospel – especially the epistles – were written in Koine Greek. The holy Bible was recorded by approximately forty human writers over 1,500 years. Both the content and the doctrine of the Bible shows an amazing unity of purpose. The Bible contains prophecies of detailed predictions that were perfectly fulfilled.

Contrary to the well-known skepticism of both classical and Islamic scholars, the Bible is free of error and has countless times vindicated itself of any error with evidence of God's power at work. The Koran was written when mixed thoughts about the revelations of God were already widespread. Paper-work was well-established in Hebrew, Greek, and Syrian-Arabic writings in the years 632 to 634, when the Koran was completed. Heresy was the number-one problem of the time, and certified content of the Koran was canonized from 653 to 656 by the Caliph Uthman Ibn Affan.

There are some other disagreements among Muslim scholars and non-Muslim scholars concerning when the Koran was actually compiled. A good number of Muslim scholars believe that the Prophet Muhammad compiled the Koran before he died. Others say that the Koran was collected by either the Arabic translator Ali Ibn Abu Talib or by the Caliph Abu Bakr as-Siddiq, or by both men. The Koran was revealed in disjointed verses and chapters. The heresy of the time made it important to bind together what were considered to be the authentic verses and chapters of the Koran. The trusted verses and chapters were gathered into a coherent whole text. Upon canonizing the Koran, the Caliph Uthman ordered all personal copies of the disjointed chapters and verses of the Koran to be destroyed as a measure against further spreading of heresy.

On the other hand, the non-Muslim scholars believe that the inspiration for the Koran was the passion of the Prophet Muhammad to restore in people the true way to worship God. Nonetheless, many Muslims accepted that the Koranic revelation started one night during the month of Ramadan in 610. The story alleges that the Prophet Muhammad was forty years old when he received the revelation from the Archangel Gabriel. The story goes on to say that the angel Gabriel gave the Prophet Muhammad the responsibility to inscribe the message from God and then to give the message to humankind.

False pride is the root of many evils and the cause of human suffering. But it is unlikely that pride motivated the Jewish scribes to record the Bible. There is nothing in the story of Abraham that suggests foul play against the son Ishmael. Ishmael was not responsible for Islam, and his belief was not in any way connected to the teaching of Islam. Ishmael worshipped God in the covenant of his father, Abraham, and he accepted his fate according the decree of God.

Isaac is the only scriptural patriarch whose name was not changed, and he is the only patriarch that spent his entire lifetime in Canaan. The story of Isaac in the Bible relates few incidents of his life. He was unlike Abram, who became Abraham; Sarai, who became Sarah; and Jacob, who became Israel. Isaac died at the age of 180 years. He was the longest-lived Hebrew patriarch.

The sequence of the scriptural prophecy points in one direction of purpose, which is the mission of the salvation of God. The Scripture essentially fulfill the mission with the birth, the death, and the resurrection of the Lord Jesus Christ, all of which happened before the start of Islam. The only outstanding prophecy of the Bible is the apocalypse, which will come when the Lord Jesus Christ returns.

Ishmael was born in the eleventh year of Abraham's stay in Canaan. His birth mother, Hagar, joined the camp of Abraham during Abraham's brief stay in Egypt. The Bible states that Abraham was eighty-six years old when Ishmael was born into his family, and he was one hundred years old when Isaac was born to him.[199] The dispute over the birth of Ishmael stems from a more fundamental dispute about the birth of Abraham.

Ishmael was thirteen years old when he was circumcised. The circumcision was not particular to Ishmael but was performed on all male persons in the house of Abraham. "On that very day, Abraham took his son Ishmael and all those born in his household or bought with his money, every male in his household, and circumcised them as God told him. Abraham was ninety-nine years old when he was circumcised, and his son Ishmael was thirteen. Abraham and his son Ishmael were both circumcised on that same day. And every male in Abraham's household, including those born in his household or bought from a foreigner, was circumcised with him."[200]

The Arab families that recognize themselves as direct descendants of Ishmael circumcise their male children at the age of thirteen, which is according to the age when Ishmael was circumcised. To them, circumcision is a rite of transition from childhood to manhood. The rite of circumcision brings the circumcised into full participation in the community. Circumcision in the Bible is the sign of God's covenant with Abraham. The ceremony is performed when a newborn male child is eight days old, which was the age of Isaac when his father, Abraham, circumcised him.[201] Sarah did not conceive the child Isaac when both Ishmael and Abraham were circumcised. Isaac was born a year later.

The position of Ishmael in the family of Abraham changed when the Lord gave to Sarah the favor that He had promised to her. Doing humanly impossible things is the everyday business of God, especially in the lives of those that believe in Him to bring His purpose to an end.

Abraham was one hundred years old when Isaac was born, and Abraham lived until he raised the child to adulthood. The feast Abraham and his wife, Sarah, celebrated on the day Isaac was circumcised was

---

[199] "So Hagar bore Abram a son, and Abram gave the name Ishmael to the son she had born; and Abram was eighty-six years when Hagar bore him Ishmael" (Genesis 16:15-16).

[200] Genesis 17:23-27.

[201] "When his son Isaac was eight days old, Abraham circumcised him, as God commanded him" (Genesis 21:4).

responsible for the jealousy that came up in both Ishmael and his mother, Hagar. Sarah noticed what transpired when Ishmael and his mother mocked Isaac for experiencing the pain of circumcision. Then Sarah decided that "the slave woman and her son must be sent away."[202]

Perhaps Sarah knew that the Archangel Gabriel had predicted Ishmael would terrorize both his brothers and his neighbors. The Archangel Gabriel spoke to Hagar in the desert when Hagar was pregnant with the baby Ishmael. He said to her, "You are now with child and you will have a son. You shall name him Ishmael, for the Lord has heard your misery. He will be a wild donkey of a man; his hand will be against everyone and everyone's hand against him, and he will live in hostility toward all his brothers."[203]

Abraham was troubled by Sarah, who decided to send Ishmael and his mother out of the land. Out of Sarah's limited view of God's plan came the problem of Abraham's family. Abraham feared what would happen to them if Sarah again took over for God. Already Sarah blamed Abraham for her predicament, and as a faithful husband, Abraham was concerned about her fears. Then the Lord intervened in the situation and said to Abraham, "Do not be so distressed about the boy and your maidservant. Listen to whatever Sarah tells you, because it is through Isaac that your offspring will be reckoned. I will make the son of the maidservant into a nation also, because he is your offspring."[204]

No one would conclude that God did not love Ishmael and his mother, Hagar, and that He liked the attitude of Sarah toward the mother and the son. God acted to bring order out of a disorderly situation that was the result of the sin of impatience. God acted in a manner that protected His plan for our salvation. God's mercy was divided between Isaac and Ishmael. The covenant blessing was reckoned with Isaac, and Ishmael was made the father of a large tribe of nations. We read in the Bible, "And God was with the boy Ishmael as he grew up. He lived in the desert and

---

[202] Genesis 21:10.
[203] Genesis 16:11-12.
[204] Genesis 21:11-14.

become naughty. While he was living in the desert of Paran, his mother got a wife for him among Egypt."[205]

Sarah had the attitude of impatience, which was founded by her failure of faith. Such an attitude of impatience exists in people of every generation. Many worshippers of God live on a daily overdose of stress because of impatience. There is probably nothing that is more difficult than waiting. The damage that is done by being impatient is common to every major experience of life. The obvious thing that people conclude regarding long times of waiting is that expectations are duped.

Sarah was biologically too old to hope for children. She waited to have children in her adult age and was ninety years old at the time. She accepted Hagar into her family and did with her something that is natural. Sarah approached her family situation with the common practice of the time. More family problems erupted after Isaac was born, and the struggle between Sarah and Hagar triggered in Sarah the frustration that is witnessed in her attitude toward Hagar and Ishmael. The mother and her son had names, but Sarah avoided using the names. Instead, Sarah commanded both the mother and the son as "that slave woman and her son."[206]

Sarah must have regretted the day she pushed God's time ahead of the schedule. She was destroyed by the agony of her own faithlessness. The sin of impatience is often related to jealousy. Because of impatience, people instinctively make decisions that often derail the course of true goodness. Impatient decisions have often produced results that continue to create harm even after the people responsible for making the decisions are long gone. But God often works through the suffering of people, and He prospers the work of His salvation.

Consider God's unlimited ability when you pray to put into action your desire to serve His purpose. You will discover that He is willing to use you more than you desire. We often think of our actions as things that should end with their immediate consequences. But reality suggests that the immediate consequences are short lived compared to the conclusion

---

[205] Genesis 21:20.
[206] Genesis 21:10.

of whatever harm or good is done. The Bible says, "Ishmael lived a hundred and thirty-seven years. He breathed his last and died, and he was gathered to his people. His descendants settled in the area from Havilah to Shur, near the border of Egypt, as you go toward Asshur. And they lived in hostility toward all their brothers."[207]

Ishmael was not the only male child that Abraham had outside his covenant marriage with Sarah. "Abraham took another wife, Keturah after Sarah died and she bore him Zimran, Jokshan, Medan, Midian, Ishbak, and Shuah. Jokshan was the father of Sheba and Deban. The descendants of Dedan were the Asshurites, the Letushites and the Leummites. The sons of Midian were Ephah, Epher, Hanoch, Abida, and Eldaah. All these were descendants of Keturah. Abraham left everything he owned to Isaac. But while he was still living, he gave gifts to the sons of his concubines and sent them away from his son Isaac, to the land of the east."[208]

Many of the children from Keturah formed the tribal people of East and North Africa, and perhaps some parts of West Africa. The prominent tribes among the children from Keturah were the descendants of Sheba and Deban. The queen of Sheba visited King Solomon during his reign in Jerusalem. Both the descendants of Hagar and the descendants of Keturah shared similar fates regarding the land of Canaan because of the covenant promise to the son Isaac. To some degree owing to marriage traditions, Keturah would claim some of the natural inheritance of Abraham. Sarah and Keturah were legally married to Abraham, but Hagar was not. Abraham had love relationships with Sarah, his covenant wife, and with Keturah, his second wife. He made love to Hagar, the family's maidservant.

The children from the three women pointed at Abraham as the father of many nations, but the result of the natural relationship did not result in mind of righteousness that God's word desired. The descendants of Hagar formed themselves into the true enemies of Israel.

The current issues regarding the state of Israel were introduced with

[207] Genesis 25:13-18.
[208] Genesis 25:1-6.

the religion of Islam. The birth of Islam in the region greatly worsened any opportunity to bring reconciliation closer to all the natural descendants of Abraham.

Ibrahim Suleiman said, "The Prophet Muhammad was a true descendant of Ishmael and so far there should be no real point of controversy between the descendants of Ishmael and the people of Israel. The blessing and the birthright is about material possessions and power, and the dispute over which of the two people possessed the wealth and the power would be settled as it has always been settled by the sword. The accomplished fact is that Arabs occupies greater part of the Promised Land. But there is a new point of dispute between the two people since the start of the religion of Islam. The dispute is about the Messiah and the Prophet Muhammad. The Jews do not recognize the fullness of the Messianic prophecy in both the Lord Jesus Christ and the Prophet Muhammad, but he has to be the Prophet Muhammad."[209]

Perhaps you would agree with the insight that is obvious in the new level of the conflict. Both the hatred and the jealousy that existed between the early descendants of Ishmael and Isaac were shifted to the arena of religion after the start of Islam – and not necessarily by continuing the domestic quarrel that happened between Sarah and Hagar. If the concept of Islam can be removed from the picture of the conflict in Canaan, there will be no other problem in the setting except human nature. The Islamic fanatics are in the fight to wipe out the Jewish state of Israel and accomplish a total takeover of Jewish heritage before the Messianic Kingdom comes to stay in Jerusalem.

---

[209] Religious analyst and Islamic instructor.

CHAPTER 11

THE BLESSING OF FIRSTBORN CHILDREN

God did not shift His position to a point where His grace cannot reach the descendants of Hagar and Keturah. The almighty God is merciful to all stages of human development. There is conflict in the world because of people that do not appreciate the blessing of God and the limit that He set in all things. The writer of the epistle to the Hebrews said, "It was by faith that Abraham obeyed God when he was called to go out to the place, which he would receive as an inheritance, and he went, but not knowing where he was going. By faith he lived in the land of promise as in a foreign country; he lived in tents as did Isaac and Jacob, the heirs with him of the same promise. For, he waited for the city, which has foundation, whose architect and builder is God." [210]

The election of Isaac, son of Abraham, was not an isolated incident in the Bible. The names of Isaac and his son Jacob are consistent with the pattern of salvation that God developed regarding the latter. God is consistent in choosing the people that advance His program. The blessing of Abraham embraced the entire human race according to the promise that God gave in Genesis 3:15. The call of Abraham gave a special motive to the upbringing of the children of Jacob. The covenant blessing of the

---

[210] Hebrew 11:8-10.

children of Jacob is the basic point of the Scripture. The blessing is the subject of faith that involves everybody else.

To understand the account, you must understand its purpose. The history of the salvation of God began in the Garden of Eden, and it expanded to reach the present age of the Gospel. The Bible shows God being God. He promised salvation to Noah and delivered him. He gave His covenant to Abraham and maintained His part of the agreement.[211] The father of Abraham and his family members were idolaters when God called Abraham. Joshua attributed Abraham's faith in the living God to His work of grace. Joshua said to the people of Israel, "This is what the Lord, the God of Israel says, 'Long time ago your forefathers, including Terah the father of Abraham and Nahor, lived beyond the River and worshipped other gods. But I took your father Abraham from the land beyond the River and led him throughout Canaan, and gave him many descendants. I gave him Isaac, and to Isaac I gave Jacob and Esau. I assigned the hill country of Seir to Esau but Jacob and his sons went down to Egypt.'"[212]

The anointing of God is not the human type of honor that discriminates between people. God looks at the inner person of all human beings and determines whether a person has the commitment to fulfill His purpose. The Bible does not talk about the blessing of Abraham from the point of Abraham's birthright. Perhaps Abraham was the firstborn male child, and perhaps he was among the last born sons of his father, Terah. All that we know is that God called Abraham out of his father's children and relatives according to the person that He perceived in him. The Scripture do not mince words when saying that Abraham was chosen by grace and that he responded to God by faith. The grace of God was evident in the life of Abraham from the beginning of his journey with God and in the outcome of his lifetime, which served the goal of our redemptive history.

Sin multiplied with the generations of Adam because of wickedness. God singled out Noah and his family, and through the family He gave

---

[211] See Genesis 22:15-16 and Heb. 6:13; God swears to Himself. There is no one and nothing greater than God by which He could swear.
[212] Joshua 24:2-4.

humanity a new opportunity to live forever. By blessing the family of Noah, God continued to love both humanity and nature.

The generation after Noah turned away from following God and lived adulterous lives. God said to the people, "Go, be fruitful and multiply, fill the earth and subdue it."[213] And the people said to themselves, "Come let us build for ourselves a city and a tower whose top is in the heavens, let us make a name for ourselves, otherwise we will be scattered over the face of the whole earth."[214] God checked the rebellion of the people by confusing the language. Then He appointed Abraham from the post-Babel people. What God did to the generation of Babel was to remind us that He is God and we humans are of a different order.

Sarah and Abraham failed in their faith in God, and yet at the appointed time, God fulfilled the promise He made concerning the son Isaac. God intervened twice in the life of Hagar and Ishmael. He protected the child and his mother in the desert and fulfilled the promise He made to Abraham about the future of Ishmael.

With Isaac came the story of his twin sons, Esau and Jacob. Esau and Jacob were the only children of Isaac. God chose the younger son, Jacob, and continued through him the heritage of the blessing of Abraham. Rebekah, the wife of Isaac, endured many years of barrenness like Sarah, her mother-in-law. When Rebekah finally conceived babies, they jostled each other in her womb. Rebekah was worried, and she appealed to the Lord concerning the situation. The Lord answered her appeal with the following revelation: "Two nations are in your womb, and two peoples from within you will be separated; one people will be stronger than the other and the older will serve the younger."[215]

The revelation of God was predetermined according to the personalities God perceived in the twin brothers. God predicted the future of the two sons of Rebekah, and that future was dependent on their choices.

The call and the anointing of God is not a matter for either the

---

[213] Genesis 1:28.
[214] Genesis 11:4.
[215] Genesis 25:23.

firstborn male child or the firstborn female child of a family. Our firstborn children are special. This instinct exists because firstborn children are the first fruits of the womb. But divine calling comes about by His sovereign decree. It can be both personal and specific. The right to receive the special privilege of divine calling is not granted according to natural descent, and it is not passed on by any human arrangement. Rather, it is an election of people who were born of God. Except the Passover in Egypt, there is no biblical event that gives support to God having a special relationship with firstborn male children. Every firstborn male child of the Israelites' families was dedicated to God in Egypt, and the occasion was as short-lived as the dedication – this was for a specific reason. God randomly selected people who came to higher positions of spiritual office even on occasions when human rationale disagreed with His judgment. The Apostle Paul said, "God's choice of people called to higher office is according to the plan of Him who works out everything in conformity with the purpose of His will."[216]

God gave to Abraham the covenant that separated Ishmael and Isaac. He allowed the blessing from Isaac to separate Esau and Jacob. Isaac inherited everything that his father had, which included the promise of a great covenant nation. As a boy, Isaac did not resist his father when his father wanted to sacrifice him on the altar. As a man, Isaac humbled himself to his father and allowed his father to choose a wife for him. Isaac was forty years old when Abraham sent Eliezer, the chief of his servants, into Mesopotamia to find a wife for him. "Abraham was old and well advanced in year; and the Lord has blessed him in every way. He said to the chief servant in his household, the one in charge of all that he had, 'Put your hand under my thigh. I want you to swear by the Lord, the God of heaven and the God of earth that you will not get a wife for my son from the daughters of the Canaanites among whom I am living, but will go to my country and my own relatives and get a wife for my son, Isaac.'"[217]

Mesopotamia included all native territories of modern-day Iraq, northern Syria, and southeastern Turkey. Isaac married his second cousin

---

[216] Ephesians 1:11.
[217] Genesis 24:1-4.

Rebekah, the daughter of Bethuel the Aramean of Padden Aram and sister of Laban the Aramean. The purpose that God intended by electing Isaac to the covenant position would have shifted if Isaac had married a Canaanite girl. Abraham took the wife of his covenant son among his own relatives, and thereby the covenant avoided making any blood contact with Abraham's pagan neighbors. Isaac and Rebekah provided the appropriate descendants to prepare the Promised Land for the coming of the Messiah. Abraham trusted in the Lord on the occasion of his son's marriage to Rebekah.

Abraham was convinced by the Lord's promise that the descendants of Isaac would prolong the experience of his blessing and bring it to serve the future of all nations. So Abraham said to his chief servant, Eliezer, "Make sure that you do not take my son back to my native land. The Lord, the God of heaven, who brought me out of my father's household and my native land and who spoke to me and promised me on oath, saying 'To your offspring I will give this land,' He will send His angel before you so that you can get a wife for my son from there.'"[218] Age eventually came to Isaac and Rebekah. But before then, their son Jacob was chosen to pass on the blessing of the covenant to the generations where the Lord Messiah was born.

Naturally, and according to the ancient law of primogeniture, the order of family birth should govern family succession. The law provided the natural incentive that placed the right of the eldest son above the rights of younger sons. The rule of the law of primogeniture did not approve of family succession by parental favor.

The tradition of primogeniture is perhaps what the Muslim scholars had in mind about Ishmael and the Promised Land. But God is not restricted in the natural tradition. His ways are not our ways. The Lord said, "My thoughts are not your thoughts, and your ways are not my ways; as the heavens are higher than the earth, so are my ways higher than your ways and my thoughts than your thoughts."[219] He chose Isaac instead of Ishmael and Jacob instead of Esau.

---

[218] Genesis 24:6-7.
[219] Isaiah 55:8-9.

Divine calling is the product of His sovereign power. The elected people of God are not the product of any natural law but are rather the result of His sovereign intervention in humanity's affairs. The decisions of natural law are not always irrelevant to God's plan. Sometimes the rule of natural law is set aside by His highest authority. Natural law is accepted into the plan of God whenever the law agrees with the divine mindset. Divine election is not intended to resolve humanity's disapproval of loyalty to God. His sovereign power will continue to dominate the affairs of humanity, despite objections to His plan.

God foresees all circumstances, and He does what is best for us. He has predicted the end of every plan from the beginning. God said, "I made known the end from the beginning; from the ancient time what is still to come and I say, my purpose will stand and I will do all that I please."[220] Our right to have tradition exists in what pleases us. The true tradition is inborn, and it demonstrates in us the rule of God's law. None of our traditions has priority over God's plan. We are responsible for whatever tradition we started, and the best way we can control any tradition is to examine its decision. So far we have failed in our relationship with God because we are unwilling to cancel the traditions that failed to demonstrate the principle of God's leadership.

Abraham, Isaac, and Jacob represented the new beginning that differed from the failed generations of Babel. With the calling of Abraham out of the post-Babel people, the story of God's way with humanity shifted its focus to a particular person and people. The many years that Sarah and Rebekah stayed barren emphasized that the elected people of God would not be the continuation of natural generations of the post-Babel people. Abraham, Isaac, and Jacob were placed in the history of the saving grace of God. At the appointed time, they produced the Seed, by whom the sin of humanity is not judged, as in the flood, or restrained as in Babel.

The unfolded plan of God is the central theme of the Bible, and it reaches to the end of time. The future of humanity is dependent on the salvation that Jesus Christ is the final outcome.[221] The 430-year period

---

[220] Isaiah 46:10.
[221] See Luke 3:31-33.

that developed the children of Israel to the size of a nation in Egypt was divinely intended. God's promise of a nation depended on the length of the time. Egypt served as a haven where the nation of God was incubated. The true blood of the covenant children of God would be hardly traceable if the children of Jacob had stayed in Canaan and multiplied by mixing genetic material with the Canaanites' pagan community. A direct link to the covenant children of Abraham would have disappeared in the living conditions the system of idol worship provided among the Canaanites.

On the other hand, the Egyptian pharaohs and their taskmasters left the legacy of autocratic rule on every generation of the Israelites they encountered in Goshen. But to this day, the loving grace of God to His people is not diminished by any effect of the long time of suffering.

The Lord said to Moses on the night of the Passover in Egypt, "Consecrate to me every firstborn male. The first offspring of every womb among the Israelites belongs to me, whether man or animal... After the Lord brings you into the land of the Canaanites and gives it to you, as He promised on oath to your fathers. You are to give over to the Lord the first offspring of every womb. All firstborn males of your livestock belong to the Lord. Redeem with a lamb every firstborn donkey, but if you do not redeem it, break its neck. Redeem every firstborn among your sons. In days to come, when your son asks you, 'What does this mean?' Say to him, 'With a mighty hand, the Lord brought us out of Egypt, out of the land of slavery. When pharaoh stubbornly refused to let us go, the Lord killed every firstborn in Egypt, both man and animal. That is why I sacrifice to the Lord the first male offspring of every womb and redeems each of my firstborn sons'"[222]

The unique occasion of the Passover was marked by the angel of death, who came to Egypt and killed the Egyptians' firstborn male children. God spared the lives of the Israelites' firstborn male children and owned them for His liking. Each of the Hebrew families coated their house's front doors with animal blood according to the instruction Moses received from God. The tradition of presenting firstborn male children

---

[222] Exodus 13:1-2 and Exodus 13:11-15.

to God in His temple was settled in Israel with the Passover. The baby Jesus Christ, Mary's firstborn son, was circumcised when He was eight days old. He was presented to the Lord in His temple on the fortieth day of His birth.

It is argued that the Passover explained the point of law of primogeniture with circumstances that showed Ishmael as being like every other firstborn son of the Israelites and therefore the likely heir to the inheritance of Abraham. In actual fact, the Passover took place approximately nine hundred years after the covenant blessing followed Isaac and his son Jacob. The Hebrews bought back every firstborn male child with an animal sacrifice. They did so in obedience, because the Lord's commandment concerning the Passover was about the importance of remembering the power of God's hand that delivered His people.

The Hebrew nation ate unleavened bread on the night of the Passover because they hurried to escape the land of the Egyptians. The annual feast of Passover reminds the Israelites of every generation about the haste of the night on which God delivered their forebears in Egypt. "For, the people took their dough before the yeast was added and carried it on their shoulders in kneading troughs wrapped in clothing."[223] The feast of Passover in Israel is celebrated beginning on every fifteenth day of the Hebrew month of Nisan. The English equivalent of Nisan is the months of March and April.

The damage that came to the Egyptians on the night of the Passover was as warning to nations whose gods demanded human sacrifice. People of earth are reminded through the event of the Passover night that God will punish the evil on earth. Nations whose systems incorporated slavery as a way of life were hereby warned.

The law of primogeniture allows the honor of family inheritance to be bestowed upon the firstborn son of a man and his legitimate wife. Some men have children other than the children of their legitimate marriage. Children born in such circumstances have no legal claim to their father's inheritance. The position of a firstborn son of any legitimate marriage

---

[223] Exodus 12:34.

connotes both physical and spiritual blessing, which includes a double portion of the family's inheritance and the honor of becoming a family leader one day. In the case of death, the next son in line will instantly assume the position.

In the family of Isaac, Esau sold his natural birthright to his younger brother, Jacob. By selling his birthright, Esau concluded what God had predicted about him when He said to his mother Rebekah, "Your elder son shall serve the younger son."[224] Esau presented himself as a man that did not reckon his own advantage.

The firstborn son of any legitimate family can lose both his leadership role and the benefits of the role if he neglects his responsibility. Esau rejected his birthright and chose to have his brother's meal. Blinded by his immediate need to get some food to eat, Esau was quick to say to his brother Jacob, "What good is the birthright to me while I die of hunger?"[225] Esau was absentminded in dealing with the situation, and he barely considered the consequence his impatience would bring to his future.

Isaac formally passed on the covenant blessing to Jacob when he realized what had happened between his two sons. Isaac called his son Jacob and said to him, "May God Almighty bless you and make you fruitful and increase your numbers until you become a community of peoples. May He give you and your descendants the blessings given to Abraham, so that you may take possession of the land where you now live as an alien; the land which God gave to Abraham."[226]

God confirmed that Jacob received the covenant blessing. Jacob was caught by nightfall on his way to Haran. He placed a stone under his head, lay under nearby bush, and fell asleep. The Lord came near Jacob in a dream and said to him, "I am the Lord, the God of your father Abraham and the God of Isaac. I will give you and your descendants the land on which you are lying. Your descendants will be like the dust of the earth, and you will spread out to the west and to the east, to the north and to

---

[224] Genesis 25:23.
[225] Genesis 25:32.
[226] Genesis 28:3-4.

the south. All persons on earth will be blessed through you and your offspring. I am with you and will watch over you wherever you go, and I will bring you back to this land."[227]

Esau joined himself to the family of Ishmael when he married the daughter of Ishmael in addition to the many Canaanite wives he had. It is written, "Esau then realized how displeasing the Canaanite women were to his father and mother, and so he went to Ishmael and married Mahalath, the sister of Nebaioth and daughter of Ishmael."[228]

The Bible contains another story that teaches us to accept the political favor that comes by divine election. The story about the kingship of Israel is included in the examples to help us understand the teaching. The first book of Samuel is about the fall of King Saul and the rise of David to the throne of Israel. God appointed David, and he took over the leadership of Israel from King Saul. Saul failed to honor God, and God displeased him with the throne of Israel.

King Saul lost his delightful attitude toward God in the later days of his reign. He placed his political pride above his anointing and worked by making decisions that did not honor the Lord. God did not judge Saul solely by the political mistakes that he made on the throne of Israel. God would strengthen Saul through correcting his mistakes if Saul truly recognized God as his remedy. "But because Saul rejected God with his actions, God rejected him from being king."[229]

The key problem that ended the dynasty of King Saul was the immunity he granted to King Agag of Amalek. The Amalekites were trouble to the children of Israel since the day they left Egypt to come to the Promised Land. The Amalekites' attack on the Israelites camp was both strategic and continuous. The attack intensified during the period when God made Saul king of the Israelites. God commanded the Prophet Samuel, and Samuel sent Saul to wage war against the Amalekites. Samuel said to Saul, "This is what the Almighty God of Israel says, 'I will punish the Amalekites for what they did to Israel when they waylaid them as they

---

[227] Genesis 28:13-15.
[228] Genesis 28:8-9.
[229] 1 Samuel 15:26.

came up from Egypt. Now go, attack the Amalekites and totally destroy everything that belongs to them. Do not spare them; put to death men and women, children and infants, cattle and sheep, camels and donkey.'"[230]

The Israelites called on the Lord to defend them against the Amalekites. God decided to use the Prophet Samuel to end the brutality of the Amalekites for good. But King Saul approached the situation with his own political desire rather than obeying the command of God. He spared the life of King Agag and brought him home to Israel with the good treasures of Amalek. God then dismissed Saul from the throne of Israel. The Lord said to Samuel, "I am grieved that I have made Saul king, because he has turned away from me and has not carried out my instructions."[231] He, the Lord, explored elsewhere in Bethlehem and found someone who had a better attitude to serve His sovereignty. In rejecting Saul, Samuel told Saul that having an adoring attitude toward His greatness is more rewarding than any sacrifice. [232]

After God appointed David to lead His people of Israel, Samuel said to Saul, "But now, your kingdom will not endure; the Lord has sought out a man after His own heart and appointed him leader of His people because you have not kept the Lord's command."[233]

Expressing his love to God was the key element of faith that got David to the throne of Israel. God called David a man after His own heart. Samuel repeated the expression to Saul when he described David to him. Perhaps with a different type of language, this expression by God is consistently reflected in the story of the divine calling. Jesus Christ used the same metaphor differently. He regarded those that show hearts full of love to God as His sheep.[234]

Before David was chosen as king of Israel, God commanded Samuel to go to the house of Jesse in Bethlehem and anoint Jesse's son with oil. Jesse had seven sons, and David was the youngest of the seven sons. When Samuel arrived at the house of Jesse in Bethlehem, he wanted to anoint

---

[230] 1 Samuel 15:2-3.
[231] 1 Samuel 15:11.
[232] See 1 Samuel 15:22.
[233] I Samuel 13:14.
[234] See John 10:25-28.

Eliab, the firstborn son of Jesse. Samuel set his eyes on him, deciding to fulfill the natural tradition. But the Lord said to Samuel, "Do not consider his appearance or his height, for I have not chosen him. The Lord sees not as men sees; men look at outward appearance, but the Lord looks at the inner heart."[235]

Judging by the experience of everyday life, everyone should notice the point that God made in this situation. The outward appearance of a person can be particularly deceitful, and it should not be trusted to tell everything about a person. Humankind is stigmatized by a lack of integrity. But God helps us. God chose David over his elder brothers and over the distinguished noblemen and noblewomen of Israel. David was not chosen by God because he had any birthright to govern the Kingdom of Israel, and certainly his righteousness was not the reason God loved him. God loved Saul, but Saul neglected His majesty and enriched his political pride by disobeying God on the throne of Israel. David showed to God a heart that provided the image of humility.

The first move David made when he became king of the Israelites was to make God's holy city of Jerusalem the seat of Israel's national worship. Remnants of the Jebusites, who had occupied Jerusalem since the time of Joshua, were swept out of the city soon after David became king. From the time of Joshua to the beginning of the reign of King David was four hundred years. It was through David that Solomon built the temple of the Lord in Jerusalem. Before then, the place of God was in Shiloh. David and the men of Israel brought the ark of the Lord's Covenant home to the City of David. There was joy throughout Israel when the ark of the Lord came to Jerusalem. "David was wearing a linen ephod and dancing before the Lord with all his might while he and all Israel were bringing up the Ark of the Lord with shouting and the sound of trumpets."[236]

King Solomon built the temple of Jerusalem for the Lord's worship. God did not approve David's plan to build His holy temple. David had much blood on his hands from the wars he led against the enemies of Israel. Nonetheless, David provided both material and logistical support,

---

[235] 1 Samuel 16:7.
[236] 2 Samuel 6:14-15.

which helped his son Solomon to complete the temple. The Psalms of David and the articulation in the first book of Chronicles are the most viable evidence of the way David conducted his love of God.[237] Psalm 125 describes the nearness of God to His people of Israel by comparing Him to mountains surrounding Jerusalem. The Psalm magnifies the glory of the Lord and cites His favor of the faithful land of Israel.

When sin prevailed in the life of David, he did not shy away from bearing the consequence. David recognized his crime with deep feelings of remorse. He accepted the punishment the Lord gave to him and concerned himself with having the required good spiritual standing.[238] He improved his relationship with God and accepted the divine authority of the Holy Spirit. David expressed his renewed attitude by saying that the Holy Spirit does not dwell in unclean hearts.[239] He spent the rest of his life creating national reconciliation among his people of Israel.

The rise of Solomon, son of Bathsheba, to the throne of Israel is one of the most unique examples of the elective power of God. The appointment of Solomon has merit regarding the allegation that the family right of the firstborn male son is equal to divine calling. Solomon was not the natural type of successor to the throne of David, yet God accepted him to rule His people of Israel after his father King David, died. Solomon showed his inner self to God when God asked him to pray for whatever he wanted, stating that it would be granted. Solomon honored the Lord with his prayer. He thanked God for His great kindness to his father, David, and for the great king that He made David over the distinguished people of Israel. Then he asked God to give him wisdom. Solomon asked God to give him a discerning spirit to help him lead His people into the path of righteousness.

The Lord answered Solomon, "Since you have asked for this and not for long life or wealth for yourself, nor have asked for the death of your enemies but for discernment in administering justice, I will do what you asked for – both riches and honor – so that in your lifetime you will

---

[237] See 1 Chronicles 29.
[238] See 1 Chronicles 21:13.
[239] Psalm 51:14.

have no equal among kings."[240] Solomon wanted to honor the Lord for whatever judgment he offered to His people. The request by Solomon moved God to elevate him to receive higher honors. God loves the heart that desires righteousness, and He is pleased with such a heart.

The mother of Solomon, Bathsheba, was not a likely link to the throne of Israel. Bathsheba was a lover of David, but she was not his concubine. David married Bathsheba after he orchestrated the death of her husband, Uriah the Hittite. The boy Solomon was born to David after Uriah was killed on the battlefield. Absalom was the natural heir to the throne of David. He was the firstborn son of David. Absalom motivated himself with greed, and he waged war to overthrow his father on the throne of Israel. Absalom wanted to inherit the throne of Israel by his own deed. He lost his life in the process of fighting his father's army.

Adonijah then became the heir to the throne of Israel. Adonijah followed the bad example of his brother Absalom and planned to seize the throne without the blessing of his father, David. King David was ill on his sickbed and almost near death when his son Adonijah proclaimed himself to be the king. The Prophet Nathan turned the luck against Adonijah for his lack of respect. Finally the crown of the throne was placed on Solomon's head. On his sickbed, David gave the order, and Solomon was immediately proclaimed king on his throne, and then he died. The lawful natural successors to the throne of David were his four elder sons: Absalom, Ammon, Chiliab, and Adonijah. Each of the four sons of King David died in the internal struggle for the power to rule.

The last Bible character in the storyline of divine election is Ruth, the Moabite woman. She is an outstanding example of reverence to God, who elects people that follow His own heart. People often think that the blessing of God can be received only by having material riches. They rarely consider having a good relationship with God as part of His blessing.

Ruth preferred the good relationship of God, and she was profited by her trust in the Lord. A poor but remarkable woman, Ruth was a genuine

---

[240] 1 Kings 3:11-13.

spiritual character. She was exceptionally rewarded for her trust in the God of Israel. The book of Ruth says, "It came to pass, in the days when the Judges ruled, that there was a famine in the land. A certain man of Bethlehem-Judah went to dwell in the country of Moab, he and his wife and his two sons. The name of the man was Elimelech, the name of his wife was Naomi, and the names of his two sons were Mahlon and Kilion – Ephrathites of Bethlehem-Judah."[241]

Kilion married Ruth in the land of Moab. The Moabites were descendants of Lot and distant relations of the Israelites.[242] But the Moabites worshipped idols. Their chief god was Chemosh, who was worshipped in the same way the Canaanites worshipped their gods. Mahlon and Kilion and their father, Elimelech, died in the land of Moab ten years after the family arrived. Naomi and her two daughters-in-law widowed, and together they mourned their dead husbands. Naomi decided to return to her home in Bethlehem-Judah after she survived the famine that forced her family to travel out of the land of Israel.

Naomi had a selfless attitude. She asked her two daughters-in-law to remain in Moab and remarry. Naomi said to her daughters-in-law, "Go back each of you, to your mother's home. May the Lord show His kindness to you as you shown your kindness to your dead husbands and to me; may the Lord grant that each of you will find rest in the home of another husband. Then she kissed them and they wept aloud."[243] But Ruth replied to her, "Don't urge me to leave you or to turn back from you. Where you go I will go, and where you stay I will stay. Your people will be my people and your God my God. Where you die I will die, and there I will be buried. May the Lord deal with me, be it ever so severely, if anything but death separates you and me?" When Naomi realized that Ruth was determined to go with her, she stopped urging her."[244] Ruth dedicated the rest of her life to serving in Naomi's misery. Ruth and

---

[241] Ruth 1:1-2.
[242] See Genesis 19:37, Deuteronomy 2:9 and Deuteronomy 2:19; Moab and Ammon were the sons of the two daughters of Lot. Their offspring were the generations of the Moabites and Ammonites.
[243] Ruth 1:8-9.
[244] Ruth 1:16-18.

Naomi had no prospect of any future happiness, except that both women placed their future lives in the hands of God.

Boaz fell in love with Ruth shortly after she arrived at the house of Naomi in Bethlehem. Boaz was a native of Bethlehem, and Ruth married him.[245] Naomi guided Ruth in the relationship and helped her to fulfill the custom that concerned her marriage to Boaz. The story of the amazing grace of God to Ruth is significant to faith and salvation. Boaz was a wealthy young farmer and a man that commanded the respect of his people. He joined Ruth to the linage of the ancestral parents of the Christ.

Obed was the firstborn son of Boaz and Ruth. The boy grew up and had a son that became the father of the King David. The Old Testament is about the coming of the Messiah, and Ruth is remembered for the sake of the Son of God, who was born into the world through the descendants of David. We read in the book of Ruth, "Perez was the father of Hezron, Hezron the father of Ram, Ram the father of Amminadab, Amminadab the father of Nahshon, Nahshon the father of Salmon, Salmon the father of Boaz, Boaz the father of Obed, Obed the father of Jesse, Jesse the father of David."[246]

---

[245] Ruth 2:4.
[246] Ruth 4:18-22.

CHAPTER 12

JESUS CHRIST: WAS HE BOTH JEWISH AND ARAB?

The strong desire in everybody regarding perfection is to return to the comfortable life that God provided in the beginning. People do not know how the world might again have total peace, surplus food, honest relationships, and sincerity in love. The opportunity to gain the ultimate life of comfort exists, but people celebrate conflict and enjoy being persuaded to ignore right ways of association. Individual reality rises up against the true nature of reality, and the path of having close friendships, is closed by people's wrong attitudes.

The worst thing about humanity is that everybody is suspicious about everybody else. People believe only the things they see and feel. Comfort in heaven and comfort on earth are not two parts to be balanced out. The equal status that people want to have with God in everything proves that they have the wrong foot on the rung. People want to have peace and comfort by focusing on only their personal desire for comfort, and therefore they fail to realize that peace can come only when they focus upon the nature of God that is in us.

Peace and comfort belong to God either on earth, for people to live the experience, or in heaven, for His faithful saints. The world failed to achieve peace and comfort in all the situations where it achieved political freedom and democracy. People of South Sudan finally gained self-rule after many years of suffering during war with people of (North) Sudan. Like everybody else, the people have neither peace nor comfort of life.

The European Union helped to provide a new country for the ethnic Albanians in the Serbian homeland of Kosovo. But the European Union has no mechanism of peace to deliver to the region. The living conditions in Kosovo do not provide any special comfort that might make the ethnic Albanians feel better than the rest of us.

The campaign for political reform by the black majority of South Africans was the tool that dismantled the white minority apartheid regime in the country. The impartial system of government the black people of South Africa fought for exists without any feeling of peace and comfort.

The point of my inclusion of these examples of political reform is that truth has no benefit if people can neither see it nor feel it. The outline for creating political reform on the Promised Land is the most complicated platform of all the reform systems. The outcome of the program is dangerously disintegrating the entire region with tensions of war rather than holding it together with the will of peace. The reform is a real test to humanity, which experiments with bringing peace to the region through both political deceit and religious armed rebellion. The United States of America and Europe are the most politically democratic regions on earth. Both regions have no peace to enjoy with the benefits of the democratic system in place, and both regions have no mechanism of peace to give to any people.

The new political system in both South Sudan and South Africa stands in favor of making a democratic system of government the principle for every nation. I agree that the people of both countries have stories to tell about their struggles for democracy, and now they have seen dignified outcomes of the struggles.

It is fairly reasonable to admit that the Kosovo Albanians gave up their original proper place in the struggle to gain self-rule in the land of Serbia. I have the same opinion as the people that say that the Kosovo Albanians are not a threat to Serbians nationalism. But what is the place of moral humanity to bring about peace in all of the arrangements?

There is neither peace nor the life of comfort to enjoy in the new conditions, because severing the border of a sovereign nation either by the rule of emotion or as a political symbol of defeat is unacceptable to peace. Things can be better when people do the right things for the right reasons and so achieve the right results.

The United Nations used its political influence in the conflict between Arabs and Jews by appointing members of the PLO to join the United Nations. The PLO has the courage to speak out loudly about the United Nations charters that defined the state of Israel as occupying Arab land. The PLO generates sympathy worldwide with the claim. But so far the sympathy has benefited the political elite more than it has addressed the suffering of the ordinary Arab Palestinians in refugee camps. The Arab Palestinians have a worldview that adjoins them to innocent victims of world political blunders. Their cry for help creates bad publicity for Israel's political effort to stop the struggle.

The land of Palestine suffers systematic destruction of its own historic artifacts, which should be accounted for in the conflict as evidence. Masters of antiquity and the American and European archaeological workforces that have investigated the Middle East deserve some compliments for the discoveries they have made so far about the cultural life of the early people of Canaan. Author Mark Smith stated, "Despite the long regnant model that Canaanites and Israelites were people of fundamentally different culture, archaeological data now casts doubt on this view. The material culture of the region exhibits numerous common points that existed between Israelites and Canaanites in the Iron I period of 1200–1000 BC. The record would suggest that Israelites culture largely overlapped with and derived from Canaanites culture. In short, Israelites culture was largely Canaanites in nature. Given the information available, one cannot maintain a radical cultural separation between Canaanites and Israelites from the Iron I period."[247]

Also, Jonathan Tubb argued that Israelites were themselves Canaanites. According to Mr. Tubb, historical Israel, as distinct from

---

[247] Mark Smith. *The Early History of God* (San Francisco: HarperSanFrancisco, 1990) 6-7.

literary or biblical Israel, was a subset of Canaanites culture. "Canaan" when used in this sense, refers to the entire Ancient Near Eastern Levant down to about AD 100, including the Kingdoms of Israel and Judah.[248]

Archeological discoveries made in Palestine are often related to the earliest Israelites, and sometimes to Canaanites. The archeological findings are not necessarily admitted as evidence for any solution to the ongoing conflict, even though the findings contain simple truth. It is not absurd to say in this situation that the ideology that radicalized both the Islamic mindset in the Middle East and the support from the Western states to the Arab Palestinians is passionately against any piece of evidence that supports the Jewish and Christian institutions.

On the other hand, many Jewish Diasporas are less enthusiastic about taking part in maintaining the root of their national theology than they are about living their lives in a secular free world. The Jewish Diasporas want to exist in secular democracy, and they support having secular democracy in Israel. Indulging secular democracy is not the reason Israel has a nation. One people of Yahweh should be the bond that unites all Israelites. Jews should live by the concept of the bond for the world to believe in them.

Moses charged the Hebrew nation to respond to any people in accordance with the Word of God. The Word of God is the hope that the Jews inherited with the land, and the Word of God is the hope that the Jews should give to nations of the world. The present-day Jewish state of Israel has more anti-God citizens than in any other time of its history.

When Jephthah was Judge of the people of Israel, the king of Ammon incited his army to wage war against the Israelites. His plan was to take back from the Israelites the Transjordan territory. The king of Ammon sent these words to Jephthah: "Israel took away my land when they came up out of Egypt, from the Arnon as far as the Jabbok, and to the Jordan. Now therefore, restore those lands peaceably."[249]

---

[248] Jonathan Tubb was on the team of British archaeologists that excavated the territories of Israel and Syria on behalf of the British Museum. He wrote books about historical Israel and the history of the biblical narratives.

[249] Judges 11:13.

Because Jephthah knew the Word of God, he was not concerned with the words of the king of Ammon. He replied to the king's sent messengers, "Israel did not take away the land of Moab and the land of the people of Ammon... Will you not possess whatever Chemosh your god gives you to possess? So whatever the Lord our God takes possession of before us, we will possess."[250]

Jephthah meant to tell the world of his age that the Word of God is the salvation of Israel. His Word must be kept among the people of Israel as the eternal law of the land. All Israelites have a responsibility to explain the purpose of God in the history of the nation. Explaining biblical history as it concerns the existence of Israel is a moral obligation to the Jews. When they explain the Word of God to the world, the Jewish people should include reconciling the world to God. The people of Israel should teach both the spiritual and the historical relevance of the Jewish nation to every generation of the earth.

Also, the Arameans, the people of northern Syria, are distant relations of Abraham. Israel should maintain peaceful theological association with the Syrians. Moses said, "My father was a wondering Aramean, and he went down to Egypt with a few people and lived there and become a great nation, powerful and numerous. But the Egyptians mistreated us and made us suffer, putting us to hard labor. Then we cried out to the Lord, the God of our fathers, and the Lord heard our voice and saw our misery, toil and oppression. So the Lord brought us out of Egypt with a mighty hand and an outstretched arm, with great terror and with miraculous signs and wonders. He brought us to this land and gave us this land, a land flowing with milk and honey"[251]

Islam is the reason the Arab Palestinian public information system is built on a false foundation. The system is determined to change every fact that pertains to historical Palestine. The Arab Palestinian information system is centered on promoting myths and martyrdom. It does not have the principle to engage its people in building a civilized society, and it does not forecast to its people the means to live in peace with the Jews.

---

[250] Judges 11:15 and Judges 11:24.
[251] Deuteronomy 26:5-10.

The organization for Arab Palestinian public information should at least provide to its younger generations the much-needed access to proper education. The Arab Palestinians are unlikely to run out of martyrs, thanks to Hamas, which uses the public information system to generate among the people a society of hate and frustration.

In the last few years before he died, Mr. Yasser Arafat publicly declared in Bethlehem that Jesus Christ was a member of the Arab Palestinian society. Mr. Arafat put the claim to his listeners on the eve of Easter Sunday of the year 2000, suggesting that Jesus Christ was the first martyr of the Arab Palestinians' struggle. Mr. Arafat seemed ridiculous to most in making the claim, but that was not the case among many Arabs. His motive resounded positively to his people and supporters. The young generations of the Arab Palestinians believe that every claim made by Mr. Arafat is legitimate. The Arab Palestinian youths create uprisings to harm the Jews, and they are being taught to believe that the Jews are wrong to be in any part of Palestine.

Also, the Palestine liberation movement does not hesitate to echo the claim that the Virgin Mary was an Arab Palestinian citizen. Mr. Yasser Arafat made the claim in a public statement, and he used the claim to portray both Nazareth and Bethlehem as Arab territory. Large numbers of Arab Palestinian Muslims live in both Bethlehem and Nazareth. The population of Arab Palestinians in Nazareth is so high that some visitors to Nazareth have referred to the city as the Arab capital of Israel. Nazareth was the home of the Blessed Virgin Mary. The holy family of Joseph and the Blessed Virgin Mary resettled in Nazareth after fleeing to Egypt from their home in Bethlehem. Nazareth is referred to in the Bible as the hometown of Jesus Christ. Since His birth, the city has been the center of the Christians' pilgrimage. But Mr. Yasser Arafat disputed the ancient traditions of the city with the allegations that he made in his public statement:

- We are proud of the holiness of our land and we are proud of ourselves in showing that the most important holy woman among nations was from the holy land. The Virgin Mary – the woman of love and peace was of the people of Arab Palestine.

- We are fascinated by the prophets of Islam, from Adam to Muhammad; those that represents the call of monotheism and the mission of Islam. The prophets were of the religion of Islam. Jesus Christ was born in the land of Bethlehem. He lived in Nazareth and traveled in and around Jerusalem.

- We respect Jesus Christ and we believe in Him as a prophet of Islam. Our struggle against 'the other side' is an eternal struggle. It started two thousand years ago and we demonstrate our struggle through the person of Jesus Christ. He came to this world with the message of justice and peace and 'the other side' did what they did to Him. This is the Palestinians' struggle from the beginning. Jerusalem is the city where the Jews murdered the first Palestinians' Nazareth son.

Mr. Yasser Arafat left for his people the legacy of making wild statements that should not be seen as meaningless bluffs. His information system has use with violence. The system makes dangerous allegations against Jewish and Christian institutions and provides nothing to support moral civilization. The expanding political tension in the Middle East is partly determined by the Arab Palestinian public propaganda system and partly by the problem of spiritual blindness that exists on the part of the United Nations. The United Nations assumes that the Palestine conflict will go away if the current generation of Arab immigrants in Israel receives a new independent state. There is no foreseeable end to the conflict if the nation of Israel and the Christian base on the land are not crushed.

The PLO delegates to the United Nations were thrilled in December 2012 when the Arab Palestinians' status within the organization was upgraded to that of a nonmember observer state, thanks to the member states and representatives in the United Nations that passed the motion. The observer state status on paperwork is yet another outlet for more attacks on Jewish cities and more kidnapping and killing of Jewish citizens. The momentum that elevates the Arab Palestinians' ultimate goal is derived from wider dynamics of states' arms sales –including the madness of both chemical and nuclear weapons, which extends deep into the region.

Beginning with Sweden on October 30, 2014, individual sovereign states have begun officially recognizing the non-existent Arab Palestinian state. This is happening because a majority of world leaders do not take truth seriously in dealing with conflict situations. Many world leaders accommodate the wickedness that motivates conflict, as if the wickedness is nothing that harms anyone. They restructure humanity according to their own political needs and standards. They neglect the real need that exists, which is to renovate degraded human integrity and wipe out the trend of hunger and conflict among people. A political worldview should not determine whether the process that God created is formless. We cannot measure divine truth with any form of human ideology and be correct in the result.

We read in the Bible about the pharaoh of Egypt who hardened his heart against the will of God. God hardened the pharaoh's heart as well and proved that the pharaoh was wrong to challenge His authority. On the other hand, a multitude of the Israelites was delivered from the bondage of Egypt, and only some of the people completed the journey to the Promised Land. The rebelliousness, which caused the majority of the Israelites to fall into desert dust and the pharaoh's army to perish beneath the Red Sea, is a pattern that constitutes the modern-day trouble. Nothing threatens the segment of humanity that disobeys God like the consequences of the humanity's action.

The Arab Palestinians' First Independent Bid in Transjordan:

The Arab League founded the PLO in 1964 to represent the political interest of the Arab Palestinians. The autonomous representation of the Arab Palestinians was therefore separate from the jurisdiction of the Arab Jordanians' leadership in Amman. The first attempt to establish an independent Arab Palestinian state was aimed at dividing Jordan with civil war. The civil war was fought between the Jordanian army and the Arab Palestinian armed militias.

In the 1960s, Mr. Yasser Arafat organized quasi-military power with the Arab Palestinian refugees in Lebanon, Syria, and Jordan. Each of the units was formed as armed militia and contained terrorist components. Most of the armed groups were concentrated in Jordan because in 1967 the Jordanians received a large population of Arab Palestinian refugees. The Arab Palestinian armed militias in Jordan were centrally part of the Fedayeen movement, which emerged from the 1967 war. These men carried live ammunition around the cities of Jordan. They functioned as armed gangs rather than as organized army units, and they frequently defied the control of the Jordanian authority. The Arab Palestinian armed men were increasingly bold in asserting their independence to the Jordanian national authority. Military conflict was foreseeable with the rising of the tension.

From 1968 to 1969, there were reports of at least a hundred cases of clashes by the Arab Palestinian gunmen rising up against the authority of the Jordanian King Hussein. The gunmen would go around in the cities of Jordan and attack government offices and officers, insult journalists, tear down the Jordanian flag, and kidnap Arab diplomats, and occasionally they raped Jordanian women. Civil war was imminent when King Hussein of Jordan declared martial law in all of Jordan. Fighting finally broke out in 1970 between the Jordanian national forces and the armed Arab Palestinian faction. The Jordanian forces prevailed in the conflict despite the Syrian government giving military support to the Arab Palestinian militias.

In September 1970, because of the conflict, the government of the United States of America moved one of its navy ships near the east coast of the Mediterranean Sea to monitor the civil war situation in Jordan. The state of Israel was quick to protect its main territory from the trouble in Jordan. Jewish soldiers were deployed in and around the West Bank and Gaza. The government of Iraq pulled out the state's army battalion, which had been stationed near Az Zarqa to prevent the forces from becoming involved in the civil war in Jordan.

Mr. Yasser Arafat's Fedayeen militias were on the defensive by the end of September 1970. They agreed to a ceasefire in a meeting held in Amman. The Arab Palestinian militias agreed in the meeting to recognize both the sovereignty of Jordan and the authority of King Hussein of Jordan. Mr. Yasser Arafat agreed to restrict his men from carrying arms outside their camps. The government of Jordan granted amnesty to Mr. Arafat and his Fedayeen gunmen in exchange for the ceasefire agreement. But guerrilla attacks continued to happen in the Jordanian capital, Amman, and in the cities of Irbid and Jerash, where the Arab Palestinian militias had bases. The Jordanian armed forces put pressure on the guerrilla groups to stop the attacks, and in April 1971, the Arab Palestinian gunmen were forced to withdraw from Jordan.

In exile, Mr. Yasser Arafat planned to introduce in Jordan a national rebellion that would overthrow the leadership of King Hussein, which he described as a separatist authority. The Jordanian government responded swiftly to the rumor and stopped Mr. Arafat's plan to form the Arab Palestine state while in exile. It destroyed the last stronghold of the Fedayeen movement in the cities of Irbid and Jerash and convicted the arrested members of the movement for committing treason against the Emirate of Transjordan.

In 1964 the Arab League called for the liberation of Palestine and formed the PLO, but conditions in the 1960s were not such that Arabs could be called to help create an independent Arab country in the West Bank and Gaza. The PLO charter of 1964 was drafted by Ahmad Shukeiri and his cabinet officers. The main intent of the charter was to dismantle the country of Israel with terrorism and share the country between Lebanon, Jordan, Syria, and Egypt. The charter did not have references to concepts like occupied territory and illegal settlement, which now feature in every discussion about the conflict. The concepts of occupied territory and illegal settlement came to be part of the conflict after the war of 1967. These concepts, if I may say so, are part of a propaganda plot created after the Arab allied nations were defeated in the Six-Day War.

A new charter of the PLO was drafted in 1968 as result of the defeat. The charter has been amended with seven new articles that were focused on achieving an independent political identity for the Arab Palestinians. In documenting the state of Israel, the League of Nations recognized the right to Jerusalem that Jews had enjoyed for thousands of years. The Palestine Mandate, which was drafted after the First World War, did not make any distinction between the right of Jews to Jerusalem and the right to establish the political state of Israel on the rest of the land.

The League of Nations was an intergovernmental organization with the legitimate goal of maintaining world peace. The organization was founded in the Paris Peace Conference, which ended the First World War in 1918. It was the first international organization with the mission to maintain world peace. The organization fell apart on the stage of the Second World War. The Second World War ended in 1945, and one year later a more formal organization, the United Nations, was created. The United Nations is not a continuation of the League of Nations, though the United Nations was founded by almost the same member states that formed the League of Nations. The goal of the League of Nations was discredited by its own ineffective respond to Germany and its allies after the First World War.

In June 1967 and soon after Israel recovered the occupied East Jerusalem and West Bank, the Prime Minister of Israel, Mr. Levi Eshkol, announced on the state's national television channel that the sacred places of different worshippers in Jerusalem were being safeguarded.[252] The Knesset – the Israeli legislature – supported the opinion of the prime minister and helped him to protect the rights of different worshippers in Jerusalem. Prime Minister Levi Eshkol signed into law an ordinance that he called the Protection of the Holy Places Law. The law allowed the Islamic Waqf (council) in Jerusalem to continue its administration on the Temple Mount. Freedom of access to all worshippers was included in the signed law.

Later on, the government of Israel enforced a ban on non-Muslims who came to pray on the Temple Mount. The ban was known by the Jews and the Arab Palestinians as the "status quo." Perhaps the ban was enacted for security reasons, but alternatively it portrays Islam as a religion worthy of staying on the Temple Mount.

---

[252] Levi Eshkol was the third prime minister of Israel (1963-1969).

Jerusalem's Islamic Waqf is an old Islamic trust that should have been excluded from the affairs of the Temple Mount. The trust originated in the caliphate regime, and it has managed Islamic associations in both the al-Aqsa Mosque and the Dome of the Rock since 1187, when the caliphs last conquered the old city of Jerusalem. The board members of the trust consisted of a director and an Islamic council.

Time that passes without history is no time at all. The Lord cried out in the book of Isaiah, "Hear, O heavens, and give ear, O earth! For the Lord has spoken: 'I have nourished and brought up children, and they have rebelled against me. The ox knows its owner and the donkey its master's crib; but Israel does not know, my people do not consider… Your country is desolate; your cities are burned with fire. Strangers devour your land in your presence; and it is desolate, as overthrown by strangers. So the daughter of Zion is left as a booth in a vineyard, as a hut in a garden of cucumbers, as a besieged city."[253]

The Arab Palestinian Muslims generally hold the ban on non-Muslims coming to pray on the Temple Mount as a law that came down from heaven. The Arab Palestinians regard any non-Muslim visit to the Temple Mount as haram. "Haram" is explained in the Koran as any act that is forbidden by God. Haram is a serious moral crime. The Arab Palestinian Muslims called the anger of haram upon Mr. Ariel Sharon on September 2000. The Likud party leader and few top Likud party politicians visited the Temple Mount on September 28. Mr. Sharon and his team were guided under heavy protection of an armed Jewish antiriot police force during the visit. Besides having the security precaution, Mr. Sharon and his men were greeted on the site with severe anger by the Arab Palestinian Muslims. The angry Arab Palestinian mob tried to block the team from entering the site by rioting.

There was severe condemnation of the visit by the foreign press because of the rioting. Nonetheless, the visit by Mr. Sharon demonstrated the strength of adverse voices of the enemies of Israel who deny the sovereignty of Jerusalem to Israel. The Jews can significantly nullify

---

[253] Isaiah 1:1-3 and Isaiah 1:7-8.

their enemies' voices. But first of all, the state of Israel must give the Temple Mount the pilgrimage status that it deserves and maintain complete jurisdiction over all worship locations in Jerusalem and throughout the land.

CHAPTER 13

AL-FATAH AND HAMAS

The name of al-Fatah marks the first political organization that gave the Arab Palestinian resistance movement a base in the West Bank. The word "Fatah" could mean both "conquest" and "victory," and the meaning drives home the enterprise of the organizers of the group.

The Arab Palestinian al-Fatah movement was founded in Kuwait in 1956 by a group of young Arab refugees from Gaza. The first meeting of the movement was held in the city of Kuwait by a number of Arab Palestinian refugees who wanted to see the Arabs' united front against the state of Israel extended to their place in Kuwait. Mr. Yasser Arafat and Mr. Khalil Ibrahim al-Wazir were both appointed at the meeting to lead the group. The men had strong political influence in the confederation of Arab nations, and from the beginning they won the support of Syria for the al-Fatah movement. The Syrian government allowed the headquarters of al-Fatah to be in Damascus.

The movement was energized by the self-determination of the founding members, whose ultimate goal was to establish a unified organization of diasporas to help coordinate Arab unity in the West Bank and Gaza. After the PLO was formed in 1964, the al-Fatah movement decided to help the PLO in the fight to eradicate the state of Israel. Self-rule was a key point of the Arab Palestinians. They had faith in Islamic jihad, which provided the much-needed makeover that enabled the people to develop the al-Fatah movement into a formal armed resistance group.

The political transition of al-Fatah from a small group of refugees to a strong resistance group was influenced by the aspiration that the Arab League demonstrated in 1964 through the formation of the PLO. Since then, different armed factions have been founded within al-Fatah, all of them serving the PLO as commando cells. The groups were fused together into what is known today as the Palestine National Liberation Movement (Harakat al-Tahrir al-Filastini). Each of the armed factions of the PLO has a separate identity of association, and each is intended to rally the Arab Palestinian diasporas in neighboring Arab states to launch commando raids on the state of Israel.

The defeat of the Arab allied forces in the Six-Day War of 1967 was foremost in the political factors that motivated al-Fatah to reform its goal in 1968. Mr. Arafat quickly took advantage of the power vacuum that was created in the West Bank and Gaza after the defeat and cultivated al-Fatah as the movement for Arab Palestinian autonomy. Mr. Arafat was successful with the plan, especially in raising money and collecting ammunition from Arab countries and philanthropists that supported his vision of fighting for Arab Palestinian nationalism in the West Bank. Mr. Arafat convinced all the armed factions of the Arab Palestinian resistance movement to accept the new plan. He amended the struggle that he had set against Jordan and concentrated the effort on recovering the territory of the West Bank, East Jerusalem, and Gaza, which the state of Israel recaptured from both the Jordanian and Egyptian authorities. This was the origin of the so-called occupied territory that the Arab Palestinians assume is central to their struggle.

Disagreement about new policy of the group emerged from a conference held in Kuwait. Mr. Arafat and his closest allies in the al-Fatah executive committee failed in the meeting to agree on a way to move the reformed al-Fatah forward. Syria had both recruited and trained guerrilla fighters for al-Fatah, and the problem was how to bring military expertise from other Arab countries to support the new and expanded goal of the movement. Pro-military figures – mainly from Iraq, Iran, and Saudi

Arabia – dominated control of the movement when the disagreement was resolved. Ever since, al-Fatah has been strong and has been the best-organized Arab Palestinian guerrilla faction.

Mr. Arafat ended Syrian control of al-Fatah after the Kuwait conference. He formally became chairman of the executive committee of the PLO in 1969. Chairman Yasser Arafat was the first official leader of the Arab Palestinians. He was the grand commander of the Arab Palestinians' aspiration and had control over the huge financial and military support al-Fatah received from Arab states and philanthropists. He attracted thousands of Arab Palestinian volunteer soldiers from the refugee camps in Syria, Lebanon, and Jordan, and he joined them to fight the security forces of Israel. Chairman Yasser Arafat is the only observer member of the United Nations to have held an AK-47 assault rifle when addressing the assembly.

The al-Fatah movement evolved into a full resistance group under the leadership of Mr. Yasser Arafat, and evidently the group dominated other factions of the PLO in fighting the Jewish state of Israel. From 1969 onward, there were serious incidents of terrorist attacks on the mainland of Israel, and al-Fatah claimed responsibility for the attacks. The Israel Defense Forces engaged the situation with counterterrorism tactics. They made several arrests among the guerrilla fighters and forced the leadership of al-Fatah to go into exile. Meanwhile, the Jordanian authority continued to eject members of the Black September faction of the PLO, and the group was eradicated from Jordan in 1972.

Mr. Arafat moved his power base from Jordan to Lebanon. In 1982, the Israel Defense Forces followed into Lebanon the al-Fatah guerrilla fighters who had attacked civilian positions in Israel. The leadership of al-Fatah moved to Tunisia after the Israel Defense Forces attacked its base in Lebanon.

The struggle in the West Bank and Gaza was not relaxed. Yasser Arafat's loyalist group, the al-Fatah Hawks, is known for the key role that it played in organizing the first Arab Palestinian uprising (the intifada) in 1987. Since his appointment in 1969, Chairman Yasser Arafat had been fully engaged with raising the armed factions of the PLO. He sufficiently engaged the groups to raid the state of Israel in such ways that the raids helped the organization toward its goal. He notably raised the bar for international terrorism with increased suicide missions in both Israeli and US locations.

The United States of America is a strong ally of the state of Israel. Yasser Arafat harassed American national support for the state of Israel through acts of terror, to his satisfaction. He tried to discourage Israel's foreign support system. His tactics included sending out both male and female suicide bombers to attack special targets, stabbing diplomats and taking them hostage, throwing stones at official cars and buildings, and hijacking passenger airplanes.

On the September 6, 1970, three guerrilla factions of the Popular Front for the Liberation of Palestine simultaneously hijacked in midair three passenger airplanes traveling from Europe to the United States of America. The hijackers demanded the release of members of the Arab Palestinian Liberation Front that were being held in both Jordanian and Jewish prisons. Two of the three hijackers' groups landed the hijacked airplanes at the Dawson's Field, an abandoned RAF airbase in Jordan, and asked to swap the passengers of the airplane with the PLF members in prison. On leaving the scene, the hijackers took the Jewish passengers from the airplanes and set the airplanes ablaze.

A third group of the gunmen hijacked Pan American flight 93, which took off from Amsterdam. The airplane was diverted to Cairo. In 1972, another group of gunmen from the Arab Palestinian Black September faction attacked the Olympic games in Munich, Germany. Eleven Jewish athletes, a Jewish coach, and a German police officer were killed in the attack. These events brought to light the capacity for terror of al-Fatah. Except recently, the European Union, the state of Israel, and the United States of America looked upon al-Fatah as a terror organization.

As al-Fatah entered into the 1980s, a lack of unity in the executive branch was discovered. Cases of internal struggles for power and charges of autocratic leadership were revealed among the top membership of the group. In fact, the administration of al-Fatah slowly degraded under the leadership of Mr. Yasser Arafat, especially after the Second Intifada. There were serious allegations of corrupt officials embezzling public funds and showing favoritism in appointing people into the top leadership forum of the party. The charges immensely contributed to lessening the influence of al-Fatah in the community, and thus came the rise of a more militant Islamic group, Hamas.

Mr. Yasser Arafat retained two powerful positions at the top level of the PLO. He was both leader of al-Fatah and the chairman of the Arab Palestinian interim government. Actually, Mr. Arafat strengthened his grip on power until November 2004, when he died in Percy hospital in Paris. Mr. Yasser Arafat could not prevent the split that was evident in al-Fatah. But he persuaded all factions of the Arab Palestinian Liberation Movement to accept the Oslo Accord.[254] According him, the accord was in the best interests of the Arab Palestinians.

The political effort of Mr. Yasser Arafat for the Arab Palestinians' ultimate goal was rewarded in various ways, especially by the international community. First, the PLO was permitted to appoint observer members to the United Nations as interim representatives of the Arab Palestinians' population. Second, the Arab Palestinian interim regime was formally established on the homeland of Israel in 1993 with the Oslo Accord.

After Mr. Yasser Arafat died, the Arab Palestinians held the first democratic election of their leadership in May 2005. The legitimate result of the election was rejected by the member states of the European Union, the state of Israel, and the government of the United States of America. Hamas won in the election. Both the countries and the union that rejected the result of the election claimed that the leadership of Hamas could not be trusted with promoting peace in the region.

The United Nations Security Council appointed Mr. Mahmoud

---

[254] The Oslo Accord is officially called the Declaration of Principles on Interim Self-Government Arrangements. The Declaration of Principles (DOP) was signed on behalf of peace between Jews and Arab Palestinians. The agreement represented a tiny fraction of major differences within the wider Arab conflict against the state of Israel. The Oslo Accord was the first direct, face-to-face agreement between the government of Israel and members of the Arab Palestinian Organization. The agreement provided a framework for future negotiations and relation building within which all outstanding issues between the people would be addressed and resolved. The Oslo Accord was undermined by Hamas. The group intensified attacks on Israel after the agreement was signed.

Abbas to the office of the interim leader of the Arab Palestinians rather than having the Hamas leaders form a new interim government. Mr. Abbas preferred himself to be president of the Arab Palestinians – unlike his predecessor, who accepted his office as chairman. President Abbas was, before his appointment, the leader of the PLO negotiations affairs department in Ramallah and a loyal cabinet officer of the late chairman Yasser Arafat. The Hamas movement easily won the hearts of the people during the 2004 campaign for the election. The campaign manifesto of Hamas was to create both the political and the economic reforms that the people desperately wanted. Moreover, the Arab Palestinians liked Hamas for its forceful resistance of Israel. The movement remains popular among the Arab Palestinians, especially in its power-base district of Gaza.

Hamas fully came to exist in 1987 during the first Arab Palestinian intifada.[255] The intifada was a violent uprising by unarmed Arab Palestinians. The people demanded that the state of Israel hand over the territory of the West Bank and Gaza to the PLO. The uprising started in the Jabaliya refugee camp in the north of Gaza on December 9 after an Israeli Defense Force truck accidentally collided with a civilian car. Four Arab Palestinians traveling inside the car were killed in the accident. The incident caused people in the camp to start rioting, and swiftly the riot spread as the news of the accident reached the West Bank and East Jerusalem.

More Arab Palestinians died in the uprising than the sum total of Jewish soldiers and Jewish civilians killed by the rioters. Before the intifada, Israel controlled all civil administration in Gaza and the West Bank. The angry Arab Palestinians staged civil disobedience during the intifada and stopped cooperating with the Jewish administration in the territory. In 1993, at Camp David, the president of the United States of America, Bill Clinton, helped the two parties negotiate the signing of the Oslo Accord. The accord was a platform for ending the civil

---

[255] "Intifada" is a word from Arabic that literally means "shaking off." Intifada is rebellion in the Arab Palestinian concept of resistance to Israel. The first Arab Palestinian intifada lasted from 1987 to1993. In September of 2000, a second and more organized intifada led to the military confrontation that happened between the Arab Palestinians and the state of Israel.

disobedience. The signed agreement gave birth to the Arab Palestinian interim government in the West Bank.

The Islamic militant group Hamas was formed by the Arab Palestinian youth movements that were not formally integrated into al-Fatah. The founding root of Hamas was the Muslim Brotherhood, which Hassan Al Banna created in Egypt in 1928. The name of Hamas is an acronym that means "Islamic resistance movement." Literally, the Arabic word "Hamas" means "zeal." Hamas is the second-largest movement of militants fighting for Arab Palestinian self-rule in the West Bank and Gaza. The formation of Hamas changed the political structure of both the West Bank and Gaza. The founding members of Hamas were mainly from the Mujama group. Prior to the intifada, the group had no military ambition, and it was encouraged by the government of Israel to counter the influence of the PLO.

Hamas posed itself in Palestine as an emerging new government. The movement exists via a two-way system of operation. The first way is by using the Izz ad-Din al-Qassam Brigade to commit terror acts against the nation of Israel. The second way is by the civil administration, which provides social and economic services to the population of Arab Palestinians in Gaza.

The Second Intifada saw a number of armed Arab Palestinian youth groups join Hamas. The most notable faction among the groups was the al-Aqsa Martyrs Brigade. In the beginning, the brigade was not formally recognized by al-Fatah even though the group offered political loyalty to the leadership of al-Fatah. Hamas has distanced itself from both the PLO and the Arab Palestinian interim government in Ramallah since 2009.

Mr. Mahmoud Abbas unilaterally extended his tenure of office in 2009 by one year, and he has been serving in the office ever since. There is not sufficient political will among the Arab Palestinian political factions to influence the organization of another election in the West Bank and Gaza. The underground politics of the government of al-Fatah do not please the leadership of Hamas. Thus, there is an ongoing political conflict between the two groups. It was only recently that the Arab League started to force the two groups to form a unity government in the West Bank. The leadership of Hamas maintains close ties with both the general population of the Arab Palestinians and the member states of the Arab League.

Hamas progresses with extremism and deeply opposes the soft diplomatic approach to Israel by the al-Fatah administration in Ramallah. The leadership of Hamas insists jihad is a viable solution to the problem of the Arab Palestinians. The group rejects all peace plans for the region and, notably, the Oslo Accord. Hamas regards making peace deals with Israel as a waste of time, and it looks upon the United Nations peace envoy to the region as infidel arbitrators of the affairs of the land of Islam. Hamas supports unending conflict in Palestine until the fall of Israel. The organization proclaims the land of Palestine is Islamic Waqf, consecrated for Muslim generations until the judgment day.

Egypt and Turkey are the only members of the Arab League that have good diplomatic relationships with the state of Israel. Hamas opposes both Egypt and Turkey on account of its disapproval of the state of Israel. Hamas bases its principle for fighting the Jews on the notion that the state of Israel has existed longer than it should.

Meanwhile, the Palestinian National Charter of 1964 was revised in July 1968. The amended charter includes a moderate addendum made by the Arab Palestinians. The revised charter was endorsed in Cairo by the Fourth Palestine National Assembly. The charter was drafted in a manner more oriented toward Arab Palestinian organization. It revised the first PLO charter, which called for the end of Israel. The focus was changed to the political means to achieve a sovereign Arab state of Palestine. Pan-Arabism, the dominant theme of the 1964 version of the charter, was replaced with the emerging Arab Palestinian nationalism.

THE WORLD OF WAR WITHOUT END

The nations that perceive their existence is under the threat of military attack are easy to spot, as they worry more than other nations about having strong national security. Nations like Israel and South Korea have tough military choices to make, especially during wartime and when organizing in advance effective counterattacks and reprisal plans that can handle their enemies' threats. But the everyday business of sinful humanity preparing and advancing heavy military mechanism is not a solution of peace.

Peace, as the cessation of hostility, is an enduring process that should persist in all nations and institutions. People of the Middle East have the nearest common ancestors. Arabs and Jews should learn to coexist and appreciate within their ranks both the life and the environment God gave to them. A lack of true democracy and a diverse approach to God's election are problems both people face – particularly in Jerusalem, where the religion of Islam is the enemy that does not speak of justice.

Beyond the Middle East, Islam is the great divider in many nations. But like everything of this life, the religion is useful even despite all its violent acts. The birth of Islam in the Middle East is not a coincidence of fate. Islam came about to judge the older beliefs, not as the true way to God. The only true way to worship God is to practice righteousness. Human nature is in many ways irreconcilable to righteousness. But because God is present in human nature, our bad actions are insufficient reason to conclude that humanity is useless to the love of God.

Likewise, the horrifying actions of radicalized Islamic groups do not sufficiently imply that holy and harmless Muslims are nonexistent. There are God-fearing Muslims that are as righteous as some Christian and Jewish saints. The horrifying life experiences that people endure because of Islamic extremism and because of corrupt influence and hypocrisy, which exist in other beliefs, is evidence that humanity's evil exists within humanity. Saint Matthew's Gospel says, "Blessed are those that are pure in heart; they shall see God. Blessed are the peacemakers; they are the true children of God, and blessed are those that hunger for righteousness; they shall be filled."[256]

Apart from national interests, defending the state of Israel is the reason the United States feels the need to maintain a military presence in the Middle East. The government of the United States of America is playing the hard part of mediation in the political conflict in the Middle East, and the national support of the United States of America to the state of Israel is decisive on many fronts. The US government carefully provides support to Israel to provide superior military and economic power in the region. The plan is efficiently engaged to calm the regional conflict under the influence of America's control.

In fact, both the military and the economic power are creating serious problems and abuses that extend to other parts of the world. The political impact of the power show is detrimental to the achievement of world peace. It only radicalizes the aspirations of nations and militant groups that want to acquire more dangerous weapons.

The importance of the United States of America to the Middle East peace problem cannot be underrated. The United States of America is the only nation among the so-called superpower regimes that has the foundation of evangelical revivalism and the potential to help achieve

---

[256] Matthew 5:6-9.

peace everywhere. The unfortunate thing in the outcome of the America's influence is that the power show is being largely frustrated. The US government assumed a worse political position in the world affairs than any other state or institution could have. The US government may exercise the right to act, according to international law, for peace in any conflict. But under international law, the US government has no right to pursue only the successful outcome of its own interest. This is the error that makes the US government act in many matters of public interest, like the eleventh-century AD Roman Catholic Church.

The Western Church gained the opportunity to play the role of moral leadership in the administration of the Roman Empire. The intention was to engage the Church in the political affairs of the Roman Empire as the chief moral policeman. The Church did not prosper morality in the Roman Empire even though it had the ability to do so. Instead, the Church was part of the worst crimes of the empire. The leadership of the Church engaged in corruption that ruled in the empire and gained absolute power of control over the earthly kingdom and its wealth. This historical viewpoint can be compared to the preventable abuses in foreign policy that the US government develops toward any conflict zone or unwanted government.

Regarding abuses on both war and human rights, the US government is widely viewed as corrupt. Many of its officers are charged with using double-standards, and many are shown as having moral deficiency. There should not be so many cases of extreme behavior associated with any leading country like the United States of America. The kingdom of God persuades the nations of the earth to act in righteousness, but the leading political figures of our world hassle the nations with moral deficiency.

John the Baptist proclaimed the kingdom of God is the rule of righteousness. Only those that show righteousness through the way they live can inherit the Kingdom of God. In a more personal dimension, every bit of help the state of Israel gets from the US government should support the nation in restoring to its citizens the moral pride of the Kingdom of Israel. The people of the state of Israel require evangelical revival, which should also affect its neighbors' strong negative worldviews. Israel could be more condemned than its enemies if no acts of the nation inspired the glory of God upon peoples of the earth.

There should be within Americans themselves a philosophical and ideological awakening of the principles that made the United States of America a great nation. The moral pride of American citizenship disappears within the illogical wars and terrorism that hold American prestige hostage. Fighting wars every day and in every situation is not part of the inspirational story of American success. I would agree with author David Philips, who said that democracy does not fight wars, it does not engage in terrorism, and it does not produce refugees. Rather than making allies, democracy makes more reliable friends for peace and reliable trade partners. True democracy is the best system of governance to realize the universal aspiration for peace and to support moral and intellectual development everywhere. According to Philips, "Decades of experience with democracy assistance has yielded some guiding principles, which proceeded from recognizing that America's role in democracy should always be to stand behind and not in front of democracy movement."[257]

There is, these days, the new concept of creating democracy with the machine gun. The concept of having democracy foisted upon them at gunpoint is more worrying to every society than any other conflict. Spreading democracy with artillery fire is a big problem, and big business to some modern civilization. The act of extending democracy by waging war in peaceful countries is a key element of repression that enables a few privileged nations to dictate their subjective meanings of democracy to the rest of the world. Many peaceful nations are destroyed by wars that imposed democracy on their people, and many nations lost the desire to belong to the United Nations after losing the right to exercise equal membership. There is a sense of emboldened dictatorship and a spirit of crime that are carefully blended into the democracy of the United Nations. The arrogant speech used in the United Nations' addresses regarding the affairs of weak and unpopular nations is one example.

---

[257] David L. Philips, *From Bullets to Ballots* (Piscataway, New Jersey: Transaction Publishers, 2008) 3.

On the subject of control,
Sanctions are placed on a whole nation on behalf of
members of the leadership.

Bacteria and disease are injected into foodstuffs and drinking waters of poor countries to have experiment to manufacture new drugs.

War is deliberately started in foreign lands to test both weapons and human skills and to exploit any available resources.

The refugee crisis is a massive issue, yet no offers of hope or security have come from major world powers. It is easier these days to create bombs and killing machines than it is to make a blanket.

Creating democracy at gunpoint lacks the touch of the Spirit. It violates both the principle of the Gospel and the very social freedom that a movement of true democracy can provide. The future is not likely to be a better place for anyone, especially given the diverse conflicts that violate human rights. The Bible predicts that human nature will show little moral improvement. The world likely faces more meltdowns of peace and the continuation of both political and economic instability. More street protests will do little to help calm the situation while enabling law enforcement agents to kill more innocent protesters.

Ideal democracy does not represent any governing system or policy that is forced on a people. Ideal democracy does not enforce conditions that could lead people to abandon their ethnic base of self-discipline. Freedom and democracy are social concepts from God. We have in us the moral instinct that should move us toward fostering peace in our environment with the ethnic fiber of our individual, social, and cultural free will. The present generation is being tormented by the clash of two extreme ideas that are the results of both secular and religious mindsets. These two notorious enemies of humanity converged in the Middle East, and the clash between them is being staged in both the political and the religious situations of the region.

The continent of Africa had its share of torment with the slave trade and colonization by European countries. Then the continent of Europe received its share of the torment with the First and the Second World

Wars. The United States of America and other places have experienced civil wars due to similar causes, with immense numbers of casualties. But the United States of America is the way it is today with regard to race-related problems, violent gangs, and individual abuse of firearms because the national political leadership shies away from correcting the negative history of the nation. The people of the United States of America should confront their negative history with sincere inspiration for change and equality. Both the fall of the Berlin wall and the raising of monuments for the Holocaust victims in Germany are signs that Germany is overcoming the past evils of the nation. There is nothing in the United States of America that represents a remedy for the social damages caused during its history.

The experience of Africa is a more sufficient reason in the analysis of past evils to distrust both the secular and the religious agenda in the Middle East. The history of humanity shows that people dubiously take advantage of other people at all times. The suffering that resulted from the slave trade in Africa and the identity crises that exist in the freed slave colonies around the world are not about the evils of the white race. The Roman, Russian, British, and the German Empires had slaves from the white race. As we speak, social and economic developments exist in countries like Thailand, Iran, Bhutan, Ethiopia, Korea, and China, and these developments spring up as proof to show that innovation a is natural phenomenon.

During the seventeenth and the eighteenth centuries, Western civilization was, because of its many pretenses, the reason that the European nations colonized the continent of Africa. The renowned Kingdoms of Africa and its useful natural economy were racially outsourced and looted by foreigners who came to Africa to help civilize the Africans. The tribal people of Africa suffered mass death, political defacement, and cultural disintegration as results of the colonial invasion.

Since then, the continent of Africa has come nowhere near to regaining the tranquility of its ethnic base. The cultural heritage of Africa was severely brainwashed through white colonial rule before African political activists managed to regain the independence of Africa in the manner that it was given. Both the political and economic conditions in Africa today are not the true worth of Africa. Many nations of Africa have no real economic or social freedom but continuing to struggle. If the black continent had not been so brutally disturbed, the Africans' homes and villages would be among the best places in the world.

There is an old saying in Africa that the Africans use to illustrate the misfortune that fell upon the black continent. The adage says,

"Then were when the moon lay slightly backward and the sun rays fell on half of its shoulders. The Africans saw the moon in half and called the season the season of the half moon. The shining moon was not the half of its original size and likewise is the shaded part of the moon, which was not visible to the people. The lump of illusion is like the Western civilization. The longtime that the moon was halfway visible on the sky is fully represented in the darkness of the age in which the continent of Africa was both humiliated and destabilized. Disrespect and torture gave new name to the Africa's tribespeople. It was discovered much later on, and as the shaded part of the moon is supposed to clear up, that the slave merchants were both religious men and women. They had the enslaved people of Africa secured on chain as merchandise and proclaimed on the gain the loving of a savior God who died to free all humanity?"

The well-organized kingdoms of Africa were banished to destruction through the slave mission the Western countries started in Africa. The places of Africa were divided according to the political whims of the colonial occupiers, who did not think of planning or reserving anything for the future geocultural development of the continent. Africa struggles to develop its children and suffers from the artificial setback. The indiscriminate partitioning of the continent of Africa against its ethnic and social bonds has over time been the cause of severe underdevelopment, such that the continent continues to suffer.

The difficulty of pan-Africanism relates to ethnicity-based colonial problems. The deep political corruption in Africa is one of the examples. Corruption in Africa is the result of tribal differences that emanated from groups having various languages, abstract cultural mentalities, and intruding ex-colonial masters that imposed various foreign policies on various aspects of Africa's development.

The exploitation boom in the European economy provided a motive for the major fallout that happened among the European nations. The continent of Europe faced fighting among themselves in the First and the Second World Wars. The end of the First and the Second World Wars gave rise to modern European nations that were born after the fall of the empires that engulfed the continents of Europe and Africa. The rising new nations appeared democratically motivated in the beginning. The new hope suggested to the world that the era of tyranny was over in Europe with the collapse of the Ottoman, British, French, German, and Russian Empires. The newly formed nations were believed to be the promising faces of real freedom and democracy in Europe. But then the leadership of the new nations gradually coaxed themselves to join the older nations' military alliance. Now the political situation in Europe has the aspect of the biblical time of Noah, when the human nature was left out while the flood wiped out a wicked generation.

The concept of democracy is oversimplified in almost all the nations of Europe. The right to freedom of everything is possible in Europe, and it is the illusion of tolerance that the secular democracy movement injects into the brains of the new generations of the Europeans. Belief in absolute truth is nonsense to many people of Europe. The secular outlook of European society makes the truth the subject of different kinds of negotiation. Every viewpoint has truth that it represents, and every viewpoint is considered to be equally truthful. Therefore, living the everyday traditional life in Europe is hardly sufficient. The problem is not the true concept of democracy but the philosophical concept of a secular system that damages the traditional Europeans' moral values.

The process of both the individual's and the family's democracy that exits in Europe and in the United States is about a secular agenda and nothing less. Any disruption to the democratic process in both regions is a disruption to the affairs of the secular movement. The idea of attaching secularity to everything is something that manifests through the stress that many Europeans live under.

Secular democracy is the wrong practice for Europe. It destroys whatever good is left in the Europeans' moral and spiritual fiber. True democracy is not exercised merely by majority opinion, and true democracy is not about the way anyone feels. To help democracy achieve value, we must make the process of the law to work with common sense. True democracy is able to preserve traditional humanity. The Dutch would say, "As wine is in a man, so is his brain in the wine's bottle."

A truth can be true in every way, but not every truth is useful to human lives. The book of Isaiah says, "Every head is sick and the whole heart faints. From the sole of the foot even to the head there is no soundness but wounds and bruises and rotting sores. They have not been closed or bound up or soothed with ointment."[258] His concern about us having a total breakdown compelled Jesus Christ to say, "Come to me all of you that labor and are heavy laden and I will give you rest. Take my yoke upon you and learn from me, for I am gentle and lowly in heart, and you will find rest for your soul."[259]

The clash of interests that exists in the Middle East between the secular mindset and the radicalized religious mindset is reflected in the problem of the ideological divide that exists in the Arab Palestinian leadership. There is serious animosity within the leadership forum of the Arab Palestinians, and the animosity makes the resolve to achieve self-rule in the West Bank morally impractical and perhaps politically biased.

The split among the Arab Palestinian leadership came to light in 2007. The nature of this split constitutes an ideological divide that has come to stay. The political platform on which the divide exists is not new per se. The problem is marked by the separation attempt that the world witnessed in Jordan. Both al-Fatah and Hamas claim the right to represent the legitimate leadership of Arab Palestinian nationalism, and each group casts an ideological spell on the people to gain their full support. Al-Fatah has the intent to create secular-tolerant nationalism in the West Bank, in contrast to the deep Islamic fundamentalism of Hamas. The ideological divide does not merely exist at the party leadership level. The problem

---

[258] Isaiah 1:5-6.
[259] Matthew 11:28-29.

runs deep into the grassroots level, where partisan appetites for politics shift in delicate balance.

The two main parties of the Arab Palestinian leadership are against each other in every way. They cannot together adopt political control of both the national and the religious symbol of their institution. Independent political analysts often state that the ideological gap is an insignificant setback to the Arab Palestinians' aspiration to gain self-rule. But if you take closer look at the gap, especially at the root cause, you might realize the danger that is ahead. The situation provides a complicated vision of an outcome no better than that the gap is likely to amend with time.

The only idea common to both al-Fatah and Hamas is that the state of Israel does not deserve to be a nation in the region. If you remove from the agenda the goal to destroy Israel, what is left will be the platform of serious political and religious problems that the members of al-Fatah and the members of Hamas will never agree to work out together. Both the political and the religious references to using jihad to settle problems will always constitute the reason for bloodshed in the Middle East. The Islamic concept of going to paradise by means of violent death is the ruler of the Arabs' hope. This is according to the Word of God that the Archangel Gabriel revealed to Hagar about Ishmael and his descendants. We have received the people that terrorize both their kind and the rest of the world. The Archangel Gabriel said to Hagar,

> "You are now with child and you will have a son.
> You shall name him Ishmael, for the Lord has heard your misery.
> He will be a wild donkey of a man; his hand will be against everyone and everyone's hand against him, and he will live in hostility toward all his brothers."[260]

This Ishmaelic character is genetic, and the religion of Islam has only made it worse in people that bear the gene. The state of Israel and the rest

---

[260] Genesis 16:11-12.

of the world are the unfortunate victims of false imagination of life in paradise. Hamas casts the dispute on religious differences against Israel, and it will continue do so even if an Arab Palestinian state is founded in the West Bank. Hamas will bring to reality the new political postscript of fighting for another Arab state in Palestine. The leadership of Hamas has the mindset to secure all the territory of Israel for future generations of Arab Muslims. The movement will finally launch a new concept of an Islamic state that will openly struggle to extend Arabs' grip on other parts of the Jewish land. The rising separatist government of Hamas in Gaza is a step moving quickly in that direction.

Hamas operates like a government and creates among its ranks ministerial posts that are only for sovereign states. The group has official state logo and flag. It raises money to make an annual budget and lists both local administration and a defense plan on the budget. It is only a matter of time before Hamas initiates a campaign to become an independent state.

The political footprint of Hamas is in the form of the old trick that prepared the Arabians who gained independence for Transjordan in the 1920s. The solution to the deep division between al-Fatah and Hamas is a three-state solution with Israel and the prospect of a final struggle for a non-Jewish state solution for the regional peace.

It was unthinkable to the political peacemakers of the 1920s that the Jews would again face this situation from Arabs after the emirate of Transjordan was carved out of the Kingdom of Israel. But here we are, dancing again to the same old music of hate. The Arab Palestinian leadership is complicated in delicate ways.

The population of the Arab Palestinians in the West Bank and Gaza lacks both the political structure and the intellectual incentive that could bridge the gap in their leadership ranks. The Islamic fundamentalists in both al-Fatah and Hamas reluctantly moved toward accepting their Christian brothers and sisters into the Arab Palestinian society as beloved fellow citizens. This act of clever politics fools even the Church of Rome into thinking of the Arab Palestinian leaderships as partners of peace. The shift is yet another political scam by the Arab Palestinians.

Both Hamas and al-Fatah need the support and the presence of Arab Palestinian Christians in order to gain full control of cities of the West Bank that are most essential to Christian pilgrims. Hamas in particular has the goal of Islamizing both the Arab Palestinians' law and public life.

It is only a matter of time before both Hamas and al-Fatah nullify any rights the Arab Palestinian Christians could claim in the controlled areas. The radical Islamic mindset of the breakaway Hamas movement is enough to foresee that creating an Arab Palestinian state any time soon will bring more problems into the world than if the conflict were settled by any other peaceful arrangement.

There could be other likely reasons that have perpetuated the internal struggle in the ranks of the Arab Palestinian leadership. Perhaps the two main leadership groups prefer the flow of financial support of the member states of the international community to the notion of having a meaningful Arab Palestinian state. If this is the case, the internal struggle for political power is comfortable pretense for the leadership to keep embezzling the public's funds. War gives any regime little room to account for its public expenses. If the Arab Palestinians found an independent state, the flow of donations to both al-Fatah and Hamas could significantly diminish. The state of Israel might decide to dismiss thousands of Arab Palestinian employees who come to work every day in its mainland.

Altogether, the created state of Jordan and the continuation of the terror campaign by all Islamic militant groups in Palestine are evidence to suggest that the current motive for fighting the Jewish state of Israel has the potential to prolong fighting in the region for all generations to come. As Jephthah, the Judge, said to the enemies of Israel, "Are you any better than Balak son of Zippor, king of Moab? Did he ever quarrel with Israel or fight with them? For three hundred years Israel occupied Heshbon, Aroer, the surrounding settlements, and all the towns along Arnon. Why didn't you retake them during that time? I have not wronged you, but you are doing me wrong by waging war against me."[261]

---

[261] Judges 11:25-27.

CHAPTER 15

THE EAST JERUSALEM GATE AND THE ENDING WORLD

Jesus Christ spent months traveling through towns and villages of ancient Palestine. He preached about the coming kingdom of God and healed sicknesses wherever He went with His disciples. During His last days on earth, Jesus Christ took His disciples to Jerusalem, knowing that the time was near for Him to fulfill His ultimate mission. Jesus had often been to Jerusalem, but this time, the journey was different. He said to His disciples on the way, "Behold we are going up to Jerusalem, and the Son of Man will be betrayed to the chief priests and to the scribes; and they will condemn Him to death, and deliver Him to the Gentiles to mock and to scourge and to crucify. And the third day He will rise again."[262]

When they came near Jerusalem, Jesus Christ told two of His disciples to go into a nearby village and bring a donkey whose owner would leave it waiting by the roadside. It was springtime and the season of the Passover festival. The two disciples of Jesus Christ returned from the village with the donkey. Jesus mounted the donkey and rode toward the entrance gate of Jerusalem. On seeing that it was Him coming inside the city, the crowd of people gathered in Jerusalem took off their coats and spread them on the ground in front of Him. Some of the people cut palm branches

---

[262] Matthew 20:18-19.

from nearby fields and waved them before Him. They shouted to Him, "Hosanna, hosanna to the son of David." According to the book of 2 kings 9:13, only kings were greeted in the way the crowd in Jerusalem received the Lord Jesus Christ when He arrived at the festival.

The great passion of the people did not particularly move the Lord Jesus Christ to celebrate openly at the honor He received. He knew everything about the people and understood how they felt inside them concerning His presence. They wanted Jesus Christ to be their great political king, and they called on Him with praises to accept their loyalty. Many of the Israelites understood neither the mission of the Lord nor the kingdom in which He is King. There was severe distress among the Israelites because of the tyranny of the Romans.

The people desperately wanted to regain their freedom, and they looked upon the Lord Messiah as the deliverer. But the kingdom of God is not about anything of this political world. The kingdom of God is both spiritual and the kingdom of righteousness. It grows in the hearts of people who put their trust in God's saving grace. The world remains vicious with its range of injustices. The cruelty in the world is daily reality to many lives. Patience is running out, and yet the Lord declares that it is not by military force and political rioting that He will free those in pain. "It is neither by power nor by might, but by my Spirit, says the Lord."[263]

On entering into Jerusalem, Jesus Christ fulfilled the prophecy that Zechariah made in 537 BC. The book of Zechariah says, "Rejoice greatly, O Daughter of Zion! Shout, Daughter of Jerusalem! See, your King comes to you, righteous and having salvation, gently and riding on a donkey, on a colt, the foal of a donkey. I will take away the chariots from Ephraim and the war horses from Jerusalem, and the battle bow will be broken. He will proclaim peace to the nations. His rule will extend from sea to sea and from the rivers to the ends of the earth."[264]

Saint Luke's Gospel recounts both the life and the mission of the Lord Jesus Christ. The Gospel points at the east gate of Jerusalem as the gate Jesus Christ passed through when He rode into the city on a donkey like

---

[263] Zechariah 4:6.
[264] Zechariah 9:9-10.

a king arriving in his kingdom. Christians remember the occasion with worship. On each year, they celebrate the Sunday before Easter as Palm Sunday. Jesus Christ drew near Jerusalem from the area of the Mount of Olives. He looked toward the city from the mountainside and stopped and wept when He saw the city. While He was in Jerusalem, He taught the people about the Kingdom of God and spoke to them every day both in the temple courtyard and on the streets. He spent nightfall with His disciples on the Mount of Olives and sometimes in the village of Bethany, which stood on the eastern slope of the Mount of Olives. Nightfall was a time of prayer for Jesus Christ and His disciples.

The Pharisees and the high priests sent their agents every day to monitor Jesus Christ and His disciples. Jesus Christ was popular because of His teaching and the miracles He performed among the people. The religious leadership of Israel made a plan to arrest and kill Him and so preserve the tradition of worship familiar to them. But in doing so, they did not realize anything else about the Scripture being fulfilled.

Before He came to Jerusalem, Jesus Christ predicted His death to His followers. He told them that He must suffer death to set free sinful humanity. While Jesus Christ was in Jerusalem with His disciples, He was troubled in His mind. He came to be sacrificed, and on seeing the sinfulness of the city, He cried out, "O Jerusalem, Jerusalem, you who kill the prophets and stone those sent to you, how often I have longed to gather your children together, as a hen gather her chicks under her wings, but you were not willing. Look, your house is left to you desolate. For I tell you, you will not see me again until you say 'Blessed is he who comes in the name of the Lord.'"[265]

Jesus Christ was arrested at nighttime when He was praying with His disciples on the Mount of Olives. The guards of the chief high priest and the Roman soldiers acted as they were ordered by bringing Jesus Christ before the assembly of the Sanhedrin.[266] The members of the Sanhedrin

---

[265] Matthew 23:37-39.

[266] The Sanhedrin was the supreme court of the Kingdom of Israel. The word "Sanhedrin" means sitting together. The assembly consisted of twenty-one to thirty-three men appointed from every city of the land of Israel. The court dealt only with religious matters.

gathered at nighttime in the courtyard of the chief high priest to hear Jesus Christ defend Himself. Standing before their presence, Jesus Christ was questioned by Caiaphas, the chief high priest, concerning His ministry. He was rejected by the assembly, and they delivered Him to the Roman officials in the early hours of the next morning. Both Pilate, the governor of Judea, and King Herod, the tetrarch, tried Him separately by the rule of the Roman law. The separate trials ended before noontime, and mainly owing to a lack of any evidence of His wrongdoing. It was the eve of the Passover festival; nonetheless, Pilate condemned Jesus Christ to die on the cross. Pilate satisfied the demand of the Jewish religious leadership, who shouted at him, "Crucify Him! Crucify Him!"[267]

The Roman soldiers carried out the order that Pilate gave to them to crucify the Lord Jesus Christ. They led Him out of the city through the same gateway by which He had entered. He was hanged on the cross at a hilly stone site, which the Gospel call Golgotha. Jesus Christ died on the cross before sunset on the eve of the Passover festival, and His followers laid Him to rest before nightfall. The meaning of "Golgotha" is "empty skull." "Calvary" is the Latin form of the transliteration. The place of Golgotha was near the city "and so near the outside wall that many Jews within the city and people passing by could read the inscription on the cross of Jesus Christ. Pilate had a notice prepared and fastened to the cross. It read: Jesus of Nazareth, the King of the Jews. The sign was written in Aramaic, Latin, and Greek."[268]

The Gospel describe the political era in which Jesus Christ was crucified. Neither the place of His death nor the location of His tomb is confused with the sixteenth-century reconstruction of the wall of Jerusalem by the Ottoman Empire.

The Jewish law did not permit people to carry out unholy acts, such as execution and burying dead bodies on the inside of the holy city. The crucifixion, the death, and the burial of the Lord Jesus Christ happened on outside of Jerusalem's wall. The way the Lord Jesus Christ was led out of the city fulfilled the prophecy that Ezekiel made about the Messiah's

---

[267] Luke 23:21.
[268] John 19:19-20.

exit. Ezekiel said, "The Prince would enter by the portico of the gateway and go out the same way."[269]

No religious power on earth is equal to the power of redemption in the death and resurrection of the Lord Jesus Christ, and no religious group proclaims a link to the Kingdom of God in heaven like Christians do with the power of His resurrection. Believers are, through Jesus Christ, the co-conquerors of sin and death. After natural death, believers shall be resurrected to the everlasting life of God the Father, in the same way that the master Jesus Christ was resurrected and lives forever.

Saint Luke's Gospel gives an eyewitness account of Jesus Christ ascending into heaven. The disciples of Jesus Christ watched Him ascend to heaven on the plain of the Mount of Olives. A cloud gradually hid Jesus Christ from view, and suddenly two men in white clothing stood by the disciples and said, "O men of Galilee, why do you stand here looking into the sky? This same Jesus, who is taken up from you into heaven, will come back in the same way you have seen Him go into heaven."[270] On hearing the two men speak to them, the disciples retired from the Mount of Olives and went into the city of Jerusalem. Jesus Christ said to His disciples before He ascended to heaven, "I am going to send you what my Father has promised, but stay here in the city until you have been clothed with power from heaven."[271]

Praying in the name of Jesus Christ started with the disciples. Thirty days passed after Jesus Christ ascended into heaven, and on the day of the feast of Pentecost, His disciples received the promised empowerment of the Holy Spirit. They gathered in the house of the mother of John Mark in Jerusalem and were praying in the upper room when suddenly they felt the empowerment. The disciples went outside the house immediately and started proclaiming on the streets that the resurrected Jesus Christ is Lord and Savior. They announced the Gospel that Jesus Christ will descend on the Mount of Olives and enter the city of Jerusalem again by the east gate through which He had been led out.

---

[269] Ezekiel 44:3.
[270] Acts 1:11.
[271] Luke 24:49.

On that day, the disciples performed miracles in the name of Jesus Christ and preached the Gospel in many different languages. Many people in Jerusalem believed the Gospel and turned their lives to the saving Lord. This occasion was the beginning of the Christian Church, and the many that believed in Jesus Christ were baptized into the faith by the disciples. From that day onward, the disciples of Jesus Christ proclaimed the Gospel everywhere they were guided to go by the Holy Spirit. They were first called Christians in the city of Antioch.[272]

More than two thousand years has passed since the day the Lord Jesus Christ ascended to heaven. The prophecy about His return is being proclaimed in everyday discussions of faith. The expectation of faith is that He will accomplish the final restoration of peace on earth. The Prophets Zechariah and Ezekiel gave the prophecy about the final return of the Messiah even before the Messiah was born. The Prophet Zechariah said, "On that day His feet will stand upon the Mount of Olives, east of Jerusalem, and the Mount of Olives will be split in two from east to west, forming a great valley; with half of the mountain moving north and half moving south."[273]

Christians are excited about the coming of the Lord Jesus Christ. The prophecy is being fulfilled, and the truth of God's word is firmly being established. But the people that oppose the Bible are worried about seeing the Bible while the prophecy is being fulfilled. The Ottoman Empire literally created a graveyard on the plain of the east gate of Jerusalem. The returning Lord is expected to travel through the gate to the temple site, and the graveyard was perhaps intended to prevent the fulfillment of the prophecy. The Sultan Suleiman first authorized the existing cemetery on the plain of the east gate of Jerusalem, and by his command the east gate was sealed in 1541. By reading the redacted version of the Torah in the Koran, the Sultan Suleiman and his men must have misinterpreted the true meaning of the prophetic law.[274] Besides, the study of Old Testament

---

[272] See Acts 11:26.
[273] Zechariah 14:4.
[274] Numbers 19:13; Leviticus 21:10-12.

theology indicates that the Jewish high priests avoided both touching dead bodies and stepping on the graves of dead people for fear of their priestly holiness being desecrated.

What the Sultan Suleiman would not know is that prophetic law is not significant setback to the Lord's power of sanctification. The cemetery at the east gate cannot prevent the returning Messiah from reaching the city temple if He follows the way the Prophet Zechariah described in the Bible. Holy people cannot defile their holiness either by touching a dead body or by stepping on graves. Only sin can defile holiness in a person. The sin of a person must give way to the spirit's life in the Lord Jesus Christ. The Old Testament structure of purification is the rule of law that Jesus Christ nullified when He raised from the dead, Lazarus, the daughter of Jairus, and the son of the widow of Nain.[275] The holiness in Jesus Christ would have been defiled when He touched the three dead bodies, but in each case He raised the dead person to live again.

He touched the lepers, and they were healed. He touched the cripples, and the cripples walked. The woman with the issue of blood touched His garment, and she was healed from her illness. Jesus Christ reconciled life and death with His power of God's love. He demonstrated with His Spirit of reconciliation that He is lord over the living and the dead and over sickness and disease. The Old Testament system of purification is mostly maintained for proper hygiene in the Jewish community. It is important to God that people pay proper respect to dead people even in their final resting place. Cremation is the abuse of a dead body. The Bible say the dead should rest in peace, not in pieces.

The Arab Palestinians consider the graveyard at the east gate of Jerusalem as part of their exclusive heritage from the Islamic Ottoman Empire. The sealing of the east gate fulfilled the second prophecy Ezekiel gave about the Messiah. The Prophet gave his vision of the site as the angel

---

[275] "Jesus, once more deeply moved, came to the tomb. It was a cave with a stone laid across the entrance. "Take away the stone," He said." (John 11:38-39); "Jesus took the dead child by the hand and said to her, *"Talitha koum,"* (which means "little girl get up.") Immediately the girl stood up and began to walk around." (Mark 5:41); "Then He went up and touched the bier they were carrying Him on, and the bearers stood still. He said, "Young man I say to you, get up!" The dead man sat up and began to talk, and Jesus gave him back to his mother" (Luke 7:14-15).

of the Lord guided him into the revelation. Ezekiel said, "Then the man brought me back to the outer gate of the sanctuary, the one facing east, and it was shut. The Lord said to me, 'This gate is to remain shut. It must not be opened; no one may enter through it. It is to remain shut because the Lord, the God of Israel, has entered through it.'"[276]

Perhaps the Islamic regime of the Sultan Suleiman that sealed the east gate never realized that God is not one of us. There is no plot in all of creation that can hinder the sovereignty of God's plan. His sovereign plan is so deep that we may never fully understand it. God transforms both the foolishness and the wrath of men into praise for Him. His enemies end up serving Him in spite of themselves. The fulfilling prophecies of the Bible are evidence of the work of God that must accomplish His mission at the appointed time, and although using the surface of the entrance gate in east of Jerusalem as graveyard is deliberate, it indicates that the enemies of God's word and work also understands what the future of His word and work imply. Jesus Christ said to His listeners, "I tell you the truth, I say to you that until heaven and earth disappear, not the smallest letter, not the least stroke of a pen, will by any means disappear from the law until everything is accomplished... Heaven and earth will pass away, but my words will by no means pass away."[277]

Some Bible scholars have suggested that the east gate will be reopened to the appointed Prince according to the word of the Prophet Ezekiel.[278] The scholarly approach to the divine revelation presumes that the east gate is sealed for good and that no one may enter by the gateway until the day the Lord returns. According to the vision of the Prophet Ezekiel, "Then the man brought me to the gate facing east, and I saw the glory of the God of Israel coming from the east... The glory of the Lord will enter the temple through the gate facing east. Then the Spirit lifted me up and brought me into the inner court, and the glory of the Lord filled the temple. While the man was standing beside me, I heard someone speaking to me from inside the temple. He said, 'Son of man, this is the

---

[276] Ezekiel 44:1-2.
[277] Matthew 5:18; Matthew 24:35.
[278] See Ezekiel 46:1-2 and Ezekiel 46:12.

place of my throne and the place for the soles of my feet. This is where I will live among Israelites forever.'"[279]

Children of God must be cautiously watchful as to how they predict the experience of unfulfilled prophecy of the Bible. The wisdom that inspired the Scripture is far beyond any human intelligence. It is perhaps the political development in Israel that demonstrates the most urgent reason for Bible scholars to be fearful about the present age. It is possible that the housing ministry of Israel may reopen the east gate in the near future to expand housing in Jerusalem. Caution is therefore necessary when reviewing the prophecy of Ezekiel if the housing ministry decides to reopen the gateway. If the prophecy of Ezekiel is indeed about the physical gate, the untimely reopening of the gate could indicate the full presence of the Antichrist.[280]

There is yet a man of sin to be revealed as the son of perdition before the Messiah comes. The Apostle Paul said, "Now brethren, concerning the coming of our Lord Jesus Christ and our gathering together to Him, we ask you not to be soon shaken in mind or troubled, either by spirit or by word or by letter, as if from us, as though the day of Christ had come. Let no one deceive you by any means; for that Day will not come unless the falling away comes first, and the man of sin is revealed, the son of perdition, who opposes and exalts himself above all that is called God or that is worshipped, so that he sits as God in the temple of God, showing himself that he is God."[281]

The Antichrist will come first, and then the Messiah. The Antichrist will impersonate the Christ, and he might attempt to enter Jerusalem at some future time through the east gate. The epistle of Paul explains that the Antichrist will exalt himself to the description of the Messiah. It is important that believers observe the point of the Apostle Paul, who said

---

[279] Ezekiel 43:1, Ezekiel 43: 4-7.

[280] Some Bible scholars argue that the main east gate lies beneath the ground and is not in the same location as the existing east gate. The Land of Israel Faithful Movement believes the real east gate should be about a hundred meters southward and that the temple's holy of holies should be directly beneath the Dome of the Rock. The group favored destroying the Dome of the Rock as a means to pave the way for rebuilding the temple on its original site.

[281] 2 Thessalonians 2:1-4.

that "the misery of lawlessness is already at work with unrighteousness and deception that exist in those that perish; because they did not receive the love of the truth that they might be saved."[282] It is not the returning of the Messiah that should worry this generation, but the sudden appearance of the Antichrist.

The Bible reveals that the Antichrist is a person who will imitate the Messiah with great signs and wonders.[283] The Antichrist will be identifiable when he comes to Jews with a precious peace proposal.[284] He will present himself to the world as the great king to be worshipped in the temple of Jerusalem.[285] The Antichrist could be Jewish, and he could possess any personality and nationality. He will give the world cause to believe in him by all manners of deception.[286]

The obvious casualty of the Antichrist is the people that will fall to his deception, of which many will be condemned by the pleasures of his unrighteousness.

At the moment, the member states of the United Nations Security Council are divided on when to divide Jerusalem and give the eastern part of the city, which includes the Temple Mount, to the Arab Palestinians fighting to have a separate state in Israel. This is yet an unfulfilled prophecy in the Bible. The prophecy awaits the action of the multinational force of the United Nations that will stand up and fight against the homage of Jewish nationalism. Zechariah said, "Behold, the day of the Lord is coming, and your spoil will be divided in your midst. For I will gather all the nations to battle against Jerusalem; the city shall be taken, the houses rifled and the women ravished. Half of the city shall go into captivity, but the remnant of the people shall not be cut off from the city."[287]

Jerusalem is a spoil waiting to be divided, and the city waits to be forcefully taken by the Gentiles. The prophecy is presumably what the Arab Palestinians expect will happen in the near future. The divide will

---

[282] 2 Thessalonians 2:7-12.
[283] See 2 Thessalonians 2:9.
[284] See Daniel 9:27.
[285] See Revelations 6:2, 2 Thessalonians 2:4 and Daniel 9:27.
[286] See Revelations 13:3, and Revelations 13:12.
[287] Zechariah 14:1-2.

give the Arabs control of the old city area that was under the Jordanians' occupation from 1948 to 1967. Altogether, the secular approach to peace and sovereignty on the private property of God will continue to produce war on earth. I have hope that the temple of God will be rebuilt on the Jerusalem site and the Antichrist will be the first person to approach the throne.

It is scary but true that Israel is not ready yet to meet God by way of His right person. I share the view of many Jews in suggesting that rebuilding the temple of Jerusalem will hasten the coming of the Messiah. My deep fear is that the false messiah figure will bring about the fates of people that will perish in the aftermath of his atrocity. The vision of the Antichrist's atrocity worries me like the vision of someone experiencing time in hellfire. Jesus Christ said to the Jewish community before He ascended to heaven, "I have come in my Father's name, and you do not receive me. If another comes in his own name, he you will receive. How can you believe who receive honor from one another, and do not seek the honor that comes from the only God?"[288]

Both the predictions of Zechariah and Ezekiel concluded that the one Israel is about to receive will enter the rebuilt temple with blasphemy. The so-called land settlement agreement is in the air, waiting to be fulfilled, as is the false messiah figure who will demand adoration for bringing about peace in Palestine. The dark moment of a spiritual nightmare that the present Sanhedrin and many faithful believers endeavor to prevent in Israel will not be realized in the present age. The good news for the Sanhedrin is that the present effort to safeguard the Kingdom of God on earth is righteousness, and God will reward the effort of those that rebuild His temple. This generation will soon see people of all religions surge into Jerusalem. They will commence worshipping the beast on the Temple Mount. The true Messiah will finally come, and His coming will not be according to the time of any of us.

I did not mean to scare you by ending this book with the coming of the Antichrist. The spiritual energy around us proves that creation is not

---

[288] John 5:43- 44.

scientific theory and experiment. Creation is a unique spiritual project of God, with clearly a defined objective and definite time of end. I have performed my duty to you as priest of the Most High God. I pray that His grace and mercy abide in you, especially to help you live through the upcoming difficult times. In Jesus Christ, even death is a friend, and in Him you are always blessed. Amen.

Printed in the United States
By Bookmasters